World Human Rights Guide

Originated and compiled by
Charles Humana

PICA PRESS
New York

Published in the United States of America in 1984
by PICA PRESS
Distributed by Universe Books
381 Park Avenue South, New York, N.Y. 10016

© Charles Humana 1983
Research assistance by Anne Carter

ISBN 0-87663-738-1

83 84 85 86 87/10 9 8 7 6 5 4 3 2 1

Printed in Great Britain

Contents

Acknowledgments

Help or support has been generously offered or gratefully received from many authorities, institutions and individuals. The following have been of particular assistance:

AMNESTY INTERNATIONAL

ANTI-SLAVERY SOCIETY

BBC EXTERNAL SERVICES

BRITISH INSTITUTE FOR HUMAN RIGHTS

FOREIGN AND COLONIAL OFFICE LIBRARY

NICHOLAS FRANGISCATOS

ANDREW GRAHAM-YOOLL

JON HALLIDAY

INDEX ON CENSORSHIP

INSTITUTE OF ADVANCED LEGAL STUDIES

INSTITUTE OF LATIN-AMERICAN STUDIES

INTERNATIONAL FEDERATION OF PLANNED PARENTHOOD

INTERNATIONAL INSTITUTE OF STRATEGIC STUDIES

INTERNATIONAL LABOUR ORGANISATION

LONDON SCHOOL OF ECONOMICS

DR ANTONIO OLINTO

POLICE REVIEW

RIGHTS AND JUSTICE

MICHAEL RUBINSTEIN

SCHOOL OF ORIENTAL AND AFRICAN STUDIES, LONDON

SCHOOL OF SLAVONIC AND EAST EUROPEAN STUDIES, LONDON

UNITED NATIONS ASSOCIATION

UNITED NATIONS INFORMATION CENTRE

US DEPT. OF STATE'S REPORTS ON HUMAN RIGHTS

UNIVERSITY OF BIRMINGHAM – FACULTY OF LAW

UNIVERSITY OF NIGERIA

UNIVERSITY OF SHEFFIELD

WORLD BANK PUBLICATIONS

WORLD HEALTH ORGANISATION

Preface

In 1966, during research on political prisoners, I needed a handy country-by-country guide to human rights. The discovery that such an elementary work had not been published anywhere in the world puzzled me. Were the difficulties so insuperable, was the subject so remote from our lives that publishers were justified in believing there was no market for it? These questions were followed by others directed at myself. What had I really been looking for – and what should constitute such a guide? I began to compile what I considered to be a list of important questions, assessing and rejecting a profusion of imagined 'freedoms' and 'rights' ranging from suicide and euthanasia to gambling and prostitution. As the years went by, the questions became more relevant and definitive, bringing them more into line with internationally accepted concepts. After a wait of sixteen years, during which period the required guide had still not appeared, it seemed time to compile one for myself.

Two knowledgeable friends were consulted, Professor W. H. Armytage and John Paxton, editor of Macmillan's *Statesman's Year-Book*, and their responses were encouraging. Generosity with advice and reference books and introductions to authorities and experts followed the encouragement, and the years of preparation and hesitation turned at last into the obligation to complete the project. To these two gentlemen, then, my sincerest thanks for their help.

From the beginning I was fortunate in finding experts and those with special knowledge who were willing and eager to assist, reassuring evidence that the work was both timely and important. I am particularly grateful to the following: Professor I. Lapenna and George Schöpflin of the London School of Economics, to Professor Neville Brown and Jeremy McBride of the Faculty of Law, Birmingham University, to Philip Baker of the School of Oriental and African Studies, to V. Swoboda of the School of Slavonic and East European Studies, to Peter Davies and Leah Levin of the Anti-Slavery Society, to George Theiner and Lek Hor Tan of *Index on Censorship*, to Philip Crookes of the BBC, to Penny Kane of the IPPS and to Judge K. C. Nadarajah.

Many Embassies and High Commissions were equally helpful and I am indebted to their legal, press or information attachés. Not all, however, were cooperative and it is to correspondents in countries intent on suppressing the truth that I must offer a special word of thanks. At great physical risk to themselves, these courageous, unnamed individuals have regularly supplied me with facts and information.

I affirm that those whose help and support I have acknowledged bear no responsibility for possible mistakes or errors of judgment that may be contained in this work.

An appreciative note should be added for the editorial guidance of Anthony Whittome. He has applied himself with great purpose during the pre-publication period.

Finally, I warmly record my gratitude, first, to my research assistant, Anne Carter, who complemented her legal training with an abundance of dedication and effort, gave encouragement when it was necessary and whose contribution to the completion of the questionnaires has been a major factor in the expeditious production of the Guide. And, secondly, to Ralph Estling for his labours on many of the countries in 'summary form' and for wise advice drawn from his years as a diplomat in the Middle East and the Far East.

Charles Humana
April, 1983

Introduction

'Man did not enter society to become *worse* than he was before, not to have fewer rights than he had before, but to have those rights better secured. His natural rights are the foundation of all his civil rights.'

From the *Rights of Man* by Thomas Paine, 1791

The usual guidebooks to a country cover almost every aspect of its society and history except the most meaningful one of all, that of human rights. Tourists find information readily available on hotels and restaurants, galleries and museums; researchers and students discover much about the politics, the economics and the laws of a state, but what has not before been devised is a concise 'everyman's' handbook on the rights and freedoms of the inhabitants of the different countries of the world.

The purpose of the *World Human Rights Guide* is to correct this omission. A number of groups and institutions, it is true, publish much on the subject, and newspapers are becoming increasingly aware of the worldwide concern for human rights, but what has been unobtainable by the ordinary reader up until now is a detailed picture on a country-by-country basis. How do states vary in such diverse areas as political opposition and women's rights, capital punishment and freedom of movement? How repressive are the authorities? Is the government honouring signatures put to international agreements and treaties?

This introduction should begin with a definition of human rights. What are they? In simplest terms they are the laws and practices that have evolved over the centuries to protect ordinary people, minorities, groups and races, from oppressive rulers and governments. It would be wrong, however, to imagine they are universally observed. Of a world population totalling more than four billion, only one-fifth, about eight hundred million, can be said to enjoy lives consistent with modern ideas of what constitutes human rights. The rest must wait their turn in an evolutionary process that is a succession of advances and retreats along the road towards the ultimate goal.

The division of rulers and ruled has, of course, been a feature of society from the moment that one group or individual sought power over others or believed that they were best able to order the affairs of the people or country. But at certain moments in history, the excesses of rulers have forced oppressed subjects to protect themselves and to seek the freedoms they were being denied. In later centuries, the most significant of these charters have been the *Magna Carta*, the American *Bill of Rights* and the French *Déclaration des Droits de l'Homme et du Citoyen*, and they form the basis not only of modern ideas on the matter but of the *Universal Declaration of Human Rights* which was adopted without a dissenting vote in 1948 by the General Assembly of the United Nations.

The progress towards human rights has been slow and faltering and their promotion and protection by the United Nations does not necessarily mean that member states practise them, as will be seen from the questionnaires which follow. However, despite constant violations by countries that have signed and ratified its binding Covenants, this international organization has gained enough importance and respect to be needed by even the most erring of governments. It is for this reason, the worldwide acceptance of its place in our lives, that the Guide has kept as closely as possible to the standard Articles of the *Universal Declaration* and of the later Covenants.

There are two major areas of human rights and these should be clarified to explain the method adopted for the questionnaires in this Guide. One may be regarded as the traditional Western approach to human rights, and is covered by the United Nations' *International Covenant on Civil and Political Rights*; the other, the *International Covenant on Economic, Social and Cultural Rights*, more contemporary in its purpose, was adopted also in 1976. The first of these two is intended to specify freedoms and rights which should be guaranteed to every individual, 'classic' or 'natural' rights related to movement, behaviour, thinking and choice. The second instrument, which reflects a greater social awareness, covers what the individual should receive from the state. This recent development, in essence, regards the state as being directly responsible for the material needs and welfare of its citizens, and it is expected to provide adequate employment, health and educational facilities, and various other social requirements.

The *World Human Rights Guide* is limited to the first instrument, the *International Covenant on Civil and Political Rights*. To cover, on a country-by-country basis, both 'classic' and 'collective' freedoms is beyond the scale and purpose of this work and this choice must in no way be seen as declaring one to be more important than the other. Criticisms of this limited purpose may, however, be anticipated. It will be said, in the simplest terms, that bread comes before freedom. Restrictions on human rights are always necessary when a whole nation is trying to create a better society – 'real needs' take precedence over 'ideal needs'. But the same denial of traditional freedoms in pursuit of a higher cause could be claimed on religious grounds as well as ideological ones. A clerical state, for example, may equally believe that *voluntary* obedience to a religious faith is a *voluntary* rejection of such alien ideas as 'human rights'. These, it may be claimed, suit 'Western liberal' countries but not a society of true believers.

A number of questions used in the Guide are not from the usual human rights categories. The acceptance of the *Universal Declaration* and the later Covenants was a major achievement by the United Nations because it brought together opposing ideologies and traditional enemies, but it was also a consensus approach that had to avoid certain contentious issues. This Guide is not similarly bound by what is acceptable to all and is therefore free to extend its inquiry with explicit questions about divorce and abortion, about compulsory military service and maximum sentences for standard offences. Is it not relevant to human rights if the punishment for a crime in one country is the death penalty while in another it is simply a modest prison sentence or a ten-dollar fine?

A second deviation from standard questions is in areas of everyday life which are not always recognized as controls over the individual. Part of the questionnaire, for example, deals with documents required by the state. The constitution may enshrine a citizen's right to travel abroad but how easy is it to acquire a passport? And is the citizen free to travel to the country of his choice? Similarly, there may be freedom for writers and painters to work on their creations but if there is official disapproval of subject or style their works may be denied to the public. How, then, can they live?

The accuracy and objectivity of the answers to the questionnaires have been considered of paramount importance. In most instances information has come from the most authoritative sources and is the latest available at the time of compilation. Many countries, however, are reluctant to make public facts or documents that are usually obtainable by the researcher, in some cases even their penal codes and constitutions. In these cases, where official documents or information has been withheld or should be regarded as dubious, the Guide has used facts from unofficial but authoritative sources. These have always been subject to further scrutiny.

Where the difficulties of gathering factual information have defeated the compiler, and the questionnaire would have contained too many 'informed estimates', countries have been assessed by summarized surveys and rated FAIR, POOR or BAD.

The questionnaires reveal extreme disparities between human rights in different countries. How liberal or oppressive is a state? To what extent is it honouring its pledges to the Charter and Covenants it may have signed and ratified? One of the purposes of this Guide is to make possible comparisons between countries. Such comparisons, by the distinctive nature of each society, *can only be approximations*, and objections to such an exercise can be predicted and understood. But from the evidence of fifty different questions across a broad spectrum, the Guide reveals enough about a state's policy towards human rights to place it within a universal context. In simple terms, how close is it to the spirit and principles of the *Universal Declaration*? The drawing up of a human rights rating, and using this as an approximate measurement, seems neither unrealistic nor unfair.

The method adopted to measure the *human rights rating* of a country is, first, to grade the answer to each question into four different categories. These appear in the vertical column of the questionnaire in descending order of freedom, and are as follows: *most free* = **YES**, *moderately free* = yes, *severe* = no, and *most severe* = **NO**. These categories are then visually defined in the last column of the questionnaire with indicators ranging from white to black, as in the example below:

YES (Most free/most liberal)   ○

yes (Moderately free/moderately liberal) ◑

no (Severe/restrictive)   ◐

NO (Most severe/most restrictive)   ●

The measurement of the human rights rating has therefore been calculated on the basis of awarding 3 points for **YES**, 2 for yes, 1 for no and 0 for **NO**. The individual countries' percentages can then be compared with others and with the world average.

An examination of human rights and relating them to a method of comparative evaluation must reveal certain unavoidable anomalies. Since nearly one-fifth of the countries assessed are either totally or partly Islamic, the questionnaires will be greatly influenced by Sharia (Islamic) law, and this is reflected in the rating. At the other extreme, of Western liberalism, such factors as legal abortion, legal homosexuality, equal rights for women and, in some instances, freedom from military conscription, will favourably influence the rating. If this seems to create a bias, it must then be conceded that the United Nations' *Universal Declaration* and Covenants are similarly biased in many areas.

There are more convincing arguments, however, against being too rigid in comparing countries, and these concern the tragedies and the hardships that seem in so many parts of the world to be the natural order of things. There are about 190 countries or nation states in the world. In 47 of these, people live below the 'absolute poverty line'. In 63 countries people are prevented from freely and peacefully protesting against or even disagreeing with their governments. Armed rebellions, civil wars and wars between nations are currently disturbing the state of societies and of people's lives and add a further complexity to a fair and consistent evaluation of human rights. Equally, the poor and undeveloped countries of Africa and Asia are at an unavoidable socio-economic disadvantage when compared with Western systems. Human rights are inevitably one of the privileges that flourish in societies abundant in wealth, confidence, social stability and a continuity of liberal traditions.

The human rights rating must therefore take account, and with understanding, of the great differences between rich and poor nations, advanced and undeveloped. These are distinctions, however, that do not apply to countries signing and ratifying international instruments such as those of the United Nations. If the deprived and the weaker nations of the world claim equal rights within such an international body, and agree to honour the responsibilities that go with this status of equality, then this Guide would be guilty of discrimination if the laws of human rights were less vigilantly applied. It could also be guilty of providing many oppressive regimes with an excuse for their conduct. This fact is succinctly stated in a Memorandum presented to the Netherlands parliament:

'The governments concerned often argue that certain restrictions of the classic freedoms are essential in order to cope with the problems that face their countries. However, violations of such fundamental human rights as the right to life, liberty and the integrity of the person cannot possibly be justified by pointing to the necessity of achieving economic progress.'

Human Rights and Foreign Policy, 1949

It may seem surprising, from the evidence of the questionnaires that follow, that the average human rights rating is as high as 64%. There are two reasons for this. One is the earlier reference to regional, religious or social distinctions which establish certain areas of tolerance in different groups of countries. For example, communist countries are among those with fewer restrictions on birth control and abortion, divorce and equal rights for women, while many Third World countries with oppressive governments have fewer resources available for large and modernized armed forces, so may not have compulsory military service or directed employment, and are possibly without a rigid political ideology to which the people must conform.

The second reason for the deceptive average rating of 64% is that the efficiency of a state usually falls short of controlling all aspects of life. It is enough, in some oppressive countries, to enforce most strictly only that which is necessary to maintain and perpetuate the power of the government. Further, if we add to the reckoning those countries dealt with in summary form, most of which have unsatisfactory human rights records and were therefore less open to inquiries, the average rating falls to approximately 58%.

A system of weighting each of the questions was considered. In human rights terms some are undoubtedly more important than others – but would there be general agreement on the exact order of the fifty questions? With so many questions of extreme importance, the different priorities of individuals could lead to endless disagreements. It was therefore decided that the overall picture offered by the range of fifty questions would be enough to inform the reader adequately, and would avoid the impression of an arbitrary selection on the part of the compiler.

The division of the Guide into two sections, countries dealt with in questionnaire form and those receiving only brief summaries, was partly decided by the impossibility of assembling accurate details on such confused areas as Afghanistan and Iran, Kampuchea and Uganda; in the case of Lebanon, not even a brief summary could have been written. Other countries to be omitted from full consideration are, in most instances, those with populations under two million. But the abbreviated form of these summaries is not always a reflection on the status of the countries or their record in the field of human rights.

A further major problem concerned a handful of countries with such complex social situations that they are really amalgams of totally different societies. How does one, for example, apply a single questionnaire to South Africa with its bewildering contradictions of human rights for its white citizens and a denial of most of those rights for the non-white two-thirds of the population who do not qualify, because of their colour, for citizenship? As the Guide accepts the premise that in the field of human rights mankind is one, the only honest treatment of South Africa is to apply the questionnaire to the least favoured of the population. And this approach has been followed.

A second complex situation is that of Israel. For a variety of reasons it has occupied much neighbouring land, frequently referred to as the Occupied

Territories. These are administered by a separate military government, and law enforcement and breaches of human rights are much more repressive than in the relatively liberal society of Israel itself. For the purposes of this Guide, Israel has been assessed without the Occupied Territories.

This introduction concludes with three quotations. Elsewhere in the Guide there are excerpts from both the UN *Universal Declaration* and the *International Covenant on Civil and Political Rights*, and it will be seen from the following quotations that mankind has constantly aspired to the freedoms and rights proclaimed by the world organization of today. The first two examples come from single countries, Holland and France, and the last shows how the revolutionary dreams of yesterday have become the universally recognized – though not always practised – values of our present society.

'. . . God did not create the subjects for the benefit of the Prince, to obey him in all things whether godly or ungodly, right or wrong, and to serve him as slaves, but the Prince for the benefit of the subjects, without which he is no Prince . . .'

The Netherlands Act of Abjuration, 1581

'Men are born, and always continue, free and equal in respect of their rights. Civil distinctions, therefore, can be founded only on public utility (*usefulness*).'

Déclaration des Droits de l'Homme et du Citoyen, 1789

'All human beings are born free and equal in dignity and rights. They are endowed with reason and conscience and should act towards one another in a spirit of brotherhood.'

Universal Declaration of Human Rights, 1948

Universal Declaration of Human Rights

Adopted by the UN General Assembly in 1948 without a dissenting vote

Article 1

All human beings are born free and equal in dignity and rights. They are endowed with reason and conscience and should act towards one another in a spirit of brotherhood.

Article 2

Everyone is entitled to all the rights and freedoms set forth in this Declaration, without distinction of any kind, such as race, colour, sex, language, religion, political or other opinion, national or social origin, property, birth or other status.

Furthermore, no distinction shall be made on the basis of the political, jurisdictional or international status of the country or territory to which a person belongs, whether it be independent, trust, non-self-governing or under any other limitation of sovereignty.

Article 3

Everyone has the right to life, liberty and security of person.

Article 4

No one shall be held in slavery or servitude; slavery and the slave trade shall be prohibited in all their forms.

Article 5

No one shall be subjected to torture or to cruel, inhuman or degrading treatment or punishment.

Article 6

Everyone has the right to recognition everywhere as a person before the law.

Article 7

All are equal before the law and are entitled without any discrimination to equal protection of the law. All are entitled to equal protection against any discrimination in violation of this Declaration and against any incitement to such discrimination.

Article 8

Everyone has the right to an effective remedy by the competent national tribunals for acts violating the fundamental rights granted him by the constitution or by law.

Article 9
No one shall be subjected to arbitrary arrest, detention or exile.

Article 10
Everyone is entitled in full equality to a fair and public hearing by an independent and impartial tribunal, in the determination of his rights and obligations and of any criminal charge against him.

Article 11
1. Everyone charged with a penal offence has the right to be presumed innocent until proved guilty according to law in a public trial at which he has had all the guarantees necessary for his defence.
2. No one shall be held guilty of any penal offence on account of any act or omission which did not constitute a penal offence, under national or international law, at the time when it was committed. Nor shall a heavier penalty be imposed than the one that was applicable at the time the penal offence was committed.

Article 12
No one shall be subjected to arbitrary interference with his privacy, family, home or correspondence, nor to attacks upon his honour and reputation. Everyone has the right to the protection of the law against such interference or attacks.

Article 13
1. Everyone has the right to freedom of movement and residence within the borders of each state.
2. Everyone has the right to leave any country, including his own, and to return to his country.

Article 14
1. Everyone has the right to seek and to enjoy in other countries asylum from persecution.
2. This right may not be invoked in the case of prosecutions genuinely arising from non-political crimes or from acts contrary to the purposes and principles of the United Nations.

Article 15
1. Everyone has the right to a nationality.
2. No one shall be arbitrarily deprived of his nationality nor denied the right to change his nationality.

Article 16
1. Men and women of full age, without any limitation due to race, nationality or religion, have the right to marry and to found a family. They are entitled to equal rights as to marriage, during marriage and at its dissolution.
2. Marriage shall be entered into only with the free and full consent of the

intending spouses.
3. The family is the natural and fundamental group unit of society and is entitled to protection by society and the State.

Article 17
1. Everyone has the right to own property alone as well as in association with others.
2. No one shall be arbitrarily deprived of his property.

Article 18
Everyone has the right to freedom of thought, conscience and religion; this right includes freedom to change his religion or belief, and freedom, either alone or in community with others and in public or private, to manifest his religion or belief in teaching, practice, worship and observance.

Article 19
Everyone has the right to freedom of opinion and expression; this right includes freedom to hold opinions without interference and to seek, receive and impart information and ideas through any media and regardless of frontiers.

Article 20
1. Everyone has the right to freedom of peaceful assembly and association.
2. No one may be compelled to belong to an association.

Article 21
1. Everyone has the right to take part in the government of his country, directly or through freely chosen representatives.
2. Everyone has the right of equal access to public service in his country.
3. The will of the people shall be the basis of the authority of government; this will shall be expressed in periodic and genuine elections which shall be by universal and equal suffrage and shall be held by secret vote or by equivalent free voting procedures.

Article 22
Everyone, as a member of society, has the right to social security and is entitled to realization, through national effort and international co-operation and in accordance with the organization and resources of each State, of the economic, social and cultural rights indispensable for his dignity and the free development of his personality.

Article 23
1. Everyone has the right to work, to free choice of employment, to just and favourable conditions of work and to protection against unemployment.
2. Everyone, without any discrimination, has the right to equal pay for equal work.
3. Everyone who works has the right to just and favourable remuneration

ensuring for himself and his family an existence worthy of human dignity, and supplemented, if necessary, by other means of social protection.
4. Everyone has the right to form and to join trade unions for the protection of his interests.

Article 24
Everyone has the right to rest and leisure, including reasonable limitation of working hours and periodic holidays with pay.

Article 25
1. Everyone has the right to a standard of living adequate for the health and well-being of himself and of his family, including food, clothing, housing and medical care and necessary social services, and the right to security in the event of unemployment, sickness, disability, widowhood, old age or other lack of livelihood in circumstances beyond his control.
2. Motherhood and childhood are entitled to special care and assistance. All children, whether born in or out of wedlock, shall enjoy the same social protection.

Article 26
1. Everyone has the right to education. Education shall be free, at least in the elementary and fundamental stages. Elementary education shall be compulsory. Technical and professional education shall be made generally available and higher education shall be equally accessible to all on the basis of merit.
2. Education shall be directed to the full development of the human personality and to the strengthening of respect for human rights and fundamental freedoms. It shall promote understanding, tolerance and friendship among all nations, racial or religious groups, and shall further the activities of the United Nations for the maintenance of peace.
3. Parents have a prior right to choose the kind of education that shall be given to their children.

Article 27
1. Everyone has the right freely to participate in the cultural life of the community, to enjoy the arts and to share in scientific advancement and its benefits.
2. Everyone has the right to the protection of the moral and material interests resulting from any scientific, literary or artistic production of which he is the author.

Article 28
Everyone is entitled to a social and international order in which the rights and freedoms set forth in this Declaration can be fully realized.

Article 29
1. Everyone has duties to the community in which alone the free and full

development of his personality is possible.

2. In the exercise of his rights and freedoms, everyone shall be subject only to such limitations as are determined by law solely for the purpose of securing due recognition and respect for the rights and freedoms of others and of meeting the just requirements of morality, public order and the general welfare in a democratic society.

3. These rights and freedoms may in no case be exercised contrary to the purposes and principles of the United Nations.

Article 30

Nothing in this Declaration may be interpreted as implying for any State, group or person any right to engage in any activity or to perform any act aimed at the destruction of any of the rights and freedoms set forth herein.

International Covenant on Civil and Political Rights

In 1948 the *Universal Declaration of Human Rights* was proclaimed by the General Assembly of the United Nations. It did not have the force of law, however, and in 1976 the Assembly adopted the *International Covenant on Civil and Political Rights* which transformed the original principles into treaty provisions. This established legal obligations on the part of each ratifying state. At the beginning of 1983 it had been signed or signed and ratified by seventy-seven individual members.

For a list of those included in this Guide, and a table of their human rights record, see pages 24–5. The Articles of the Covenant most relevant to this work are set out below.

PART I

Article 1
1. All peoples have the right of self-determination. By virtue of that right they freely determine their political status and freely pursue their economic, social and cultural development.
3. The States Parties to the present Covenant, including those having responsibility for the administration of Non-Self-Governing and Trust Territories, shall promote the realization of the right of self-determination, and shall respect that right, in conformity with the provisions of the Charter of the United Nations.

PART II

Article 2
1. Each State Party to the present Covenant undertakes to respect and to ensure to all individuals within its territory and subject to its jurisdiction the rights recognized in the present Covenant, without distinction of any kind, such as race, colour, sex, language, religion, political or other opinion, national or social origin, property, birth or other status.
2. When not already provided for by existing legislative or other measures, each State Party to the present Covenant undertakes to take the necessary steps, in accordance with its constitutional processes and with the provisions of the present Covenant, to adopt such legislative or other measures as may be necessary to give effect to the rights recognized in the present Covenant.

3. Each State Party to the present Covenant undertakes:
    (a) To ensure that any person whose rights or freedoms as herein recognized are violated shall have an effective remedy, notwithstanding that the violation has been committed by persons acting in an official capacity;
    (b) To ensure that any person claiming such a remedy shall have his right thereto determined by competent judicial, administrative or legislative authorities, or by any other competent authority provided for by the legal system of the State, and to develop the possibilities of judicial remedy;
    (c) To ensure that the competent authorities shall enforce such remedies when granted.

Article 3
The States Parties to the present Covenant undertake to ensure the equal right of men and women to the enjoyment of all civil and political rights set forth in the present Covenant.

PART III

Article 6
1. Every human being has the inherent right to life. This right shall be protected by law. No one shall be arbitrarily deprived of his life.
2. In countries which have not abolished the death penalty, sentence of death may be imposed only for the most serious crimes in accordance with the law in force at the time of the commission of the crime and not contrary to the provisions of the present Covenant and to the Convention on the Prevention and Punishment of the Crime of Genocide. This penalty can only be carried out pursuant to a final judgment rendered by a competent court.
3. When deprivation of life constitutes the crime of genocide, it is understood that nothing in this article shall authorize any State Party to the present Covenant to derogate in any way from any obligation assumed under the provisions of the Convention on the Prevention and Punishment of the Crime of Genocide.
4. Anyone sentenced to death shall have the right to seek pardon or commutation of the sentence. Amnesty, pardon or commutation of the sentence of death may be granted in all cases.
5. Sentence of death shall not be imposed for crimes committed by persons below eighteen years of age and shall not be carried out on pregnant women.
6. Nothing in this article shall be invoked to delay or to prevent the abolition of capital punishment by any State Party to the present Covenant.

Article 7
No one shall be subjected to torture or to cruel, inhuman or degrading treatment or punishment. In particular, no one shall be subjected without his free consent to medical or scientific experimentation.

Article 8

1. No one shall be held in slavery; slavery and the slave-trade in all their forms shall be prohibited.
2. No one shall be held in servitude.

Article 9

1. Everyone has the right to liberty and security of person. No one shall be subjected to arbitrary arrest or detention. No one shall be deprived of his liberty except on such grounds and in accordance with such procedure as are established by law.
2. Anyone who is arrested shall be informed, at the time of arrest, of the reasons for his arrest and shall be promptly informed of any charges against him.
3. Anyone arrested or detained on a criminal charge shall be brought promptly before a judge or other officer authorized by law to exercise judicial power and shall be entitled to trial within a reasonable time or to release. It shall not be the general rule that persons awaiting trial shall be detained in custody, but release may be subject to guarantees to appear for trial at any other stage of the judicial proceedings, and, should occasion arise, for execution of the judgment.
4. Anyone who is deprived of his liberty by arrest or detention shall be entitled to take proceedings before a court, in order that that court may decide without delay on the lawfulness of his detention and order his release if the detention is not lawful.
5. Anyone who has been the victim of unlawful arrest or detention shall have an enforceable right to compensation.

Article 12

1. Everyone lawfully within the territory of a State shall, within that territory, have the right to liberty of movement and freedom to choose his residence.
2. Everyone shall be free to leave any country, including his own.
3. The above-mentioned rights shall not be subject to any restrictions except those which are provided by law, are necessary to protect national security, public order (ordre public), public health or morals or the rights and freedoms of others, and are consistent with the other rights recognized in the present Covenant.
4. No one shall be arbitrarily deprived of the right to enter his own country.

Article 14

1. All persons shall be equal before the courts and tribunals. In the determination of any criminal charge against him, or of his rights and obligations in a suit at law, everyone shall be entitled to a fair and public hearing by a competent, independent and impartial tribunal established by law. The Press and the public may be excluded from all or part of a trial for reasons of morals, public order (ordre public) or national security in a democratic society, or when the interests of the private lives of the parties so requires, or to the extent strictly necessary in the opinion of the court in special circumstances where publicity

would prejudice the interests of justice; but any judgment rendered in a criminal case or in a suit at law shall be made public except where the interest of juvenile persons otherwise requires or the proceedings concern matrimonial disputes or the guardianship of children.

2. Everyone charged with a criminal offence shall have the right to be presumed innocent until proved guilty according to law.

3. In the determination of any criminal charge against him, everyone shall be entitled to the following minimum guarantees, in full equality:

   (a) To be informed promptly and in detail in a language which he understands of the nature and cause of the charge against him;

   (b) To have adequate time and facilities for the preparation of his defence and to communicate with counsel of his own choosing;

   (c) To be tried without undue delay;

   (d) To be tried in his presence, and to defend himself in person or through legal assistance of his own choosing; to be informed, if he does not have legal assistance, of this right; and to have legal assistance assigned to him, in any case where the interests of justice so require, and without payment by him in any such case if he does not have sufficient means to pay for it;

   (e) To examine, or have examined, the witnesses against him and to obtain the attendance and examination of witnesses on his behalf under the same conditions as witnesses against him;

   (f) To have the free assistance of an interpreter if he cannot understand or speak the language used in court;

   (g) Not to be compelled to testify against himself or to confess guilt.

Article 16
Everyone shall have the right to recognition everywhere as a person before the law.

Article 17
1. No one shall be subjected to arbitrary or unlawful interference with his privacy, family, home or correspondence, nor to unlawful attacks on his honour and reputation.

2. Everyone has the right to the protection of the law against such interference or attacks.

Article 18
1. Everyone shall have the right of freedom of thought, conscience and religion. This right shall include freedom to have or to adopt a religion or belief of his choice, and freedom, either individually or in community with others and in public or private, to manifest his religion or belief in worship, observance, practice and teaching.

2. No one shall be subject to coercion which would impair his freedom to have or to adopt a religion or belief of his choice.

3. Freedom to manifest one's religion or beliefs may be subject only to such limitations as are prescribed by law and are necessary to protect public safety,

order, health, or morals or the fundamental rights and freedoms of others.
4. The States Parties to the present Covenant undertake to have respect for the liberty of parents and, when applicable, legal guardians to ensure the religious and moral education of their children in conformity with their own convictions.

Article 19

1. Everyone shall have the right to hold opinions without interference.
2. Everyone shall have the right to freedom of expression; this right shall include freedom to seek, receive and impart information and ideas of all kinds, regardless of frontiers, either orally, in writing or in print, in the form of art, or through any other media of his choice.

Article 20

1. Any propaganda for war shall be prohibited by law.
2. Any advocacy of national, racial or religious hatred that constitutes incitement to discrimination, hostility or violence shall be prohibited by law.

Article 21

The right of peaceful assembly shall be recognized. No restrictions may be placed on the exercise of this right other than those imposed in conformity with the law and which are necessary in a democratic society in the interests of national security or public safety, public order (ordre public), the protection of public health or morals or the protection of the rights and freedoms of others.

Article 23

1. The family is the natural and fundamental group unit of society and is entitled to protection by society and the State.
2. The right of men and women of marriageable age to marry and to found a family shall be recognized.
3. No marriage shall be entered into without the free and full consent of the intending spouses.
4. States Parties to the present Covenant shall take appropriate steps to ensure equality of rights and responsibilities of spouses as to marriage, during marriage and at its dissolution. In the case of dissolution, provision shall be made for the necessary protection of any children.

Article 24

1. Every child shall have, without any discrimination as to race, colour, sex, language, religion, national or social origin, property or birth, the right to such measures of protection as are required by his status as a minor, on the part of his family, society and the State.
2. Every child shall be registered immediately after birth and shall have a name.
3. Every child has the right to acquire a nationality.

Article 25

Every citizen shall have the right and the opportunity, without any of the distinctions mentioned in Article 2 and without unreasonable restrictions;

(a) To take part in the conduct of public affairs, directly or through freely chosen representatives;

(b) To vote and to be elected at genuine periodic elections which shall be by universal and equal suffrage and shall be held by secret ballot, guaranteeing the free expression of the will of the electors;

(c) To have access, on general terms of equality, to public service in his country.

Article 26

All persons are equal before the law and are entitled without any discrimination to the equal protection of the law. In this respect, the law shall prohibit any discrimination and guarantee to all persons equal and effective protection against discrimination on any ground such as race, colour, sex, language, religion, political or other opinion, national or social origin, birth or other status.

Article 27

In those States in which ethnic, religious or linguistic minorities exist, persons belonging to such minorities shall not be denied the right, in community with the other members of their group, to enjoy their own culture, to profess and practise their own religion, or to use their own language.

Comprehensive table of countries assessed

Countries assessed in questionnaire form

Page	Country	Capital	Human rights rating		Signed/ratified UN Covenant** (see page 18)
	WORLD AVERAGE		*(above)* 64%	*(below)*	
32	**Algeria**	Algiers		62%	**
96	**Argentina**	Buenos Aires		44%	**
116	**Australia**	Canberra	93%		**
174	**Austria**	Vienna	92%		**
118	**Bangladesh**	Dacca	64%		
176	**Belgium**	Brussels	92%		**
98	**Brazil**	Brasilia	70%		
178	**Bulgaria**	Sofia		37%	**
78	**Canada**	Ottawa	94%		**
100	**Chile**	Santiago		37%	**
120	**China**	Beijing		32%	
102	**Colombia**	Bogota		62%	**
80	**Cuba**	Havana		30%	
180	**Czechoslovakia**	Prague		36%	**
182	**Denmark**	Copenhagen	96%		**
104	**Ecuador**	Quito	85%		**
34	**Egypt**	Cairo	64%		**
36	**Ethiopia**	Addis Ababa		17%	
184	**Finland**	Helsinki	96%		**
186	**France**	Paris	88%		**
188	**German Dem. Rep.**	East Berlin		35%	**
190	**German Fed. Rep.**	Bonn	91%		**
192	**Greece**	Athens	80%		
122	**Hong Kong**	Victoria	86%		
194	**Hungary**	Budapest		54%	**
124	**India**	New Delhi	70%		**
126	**Indonesia**	Jakarta		53%	
128	**Iraq**	Baghdad		27%	**
196	**Ireland**	Dublin	86%		**
130	**Israel***	Jerusalem	73%		**
198	**Italy**	Rome	88%		**
132	**Japan**	Tokyo	92%		**
38	**Kenya**	Nairobi		58%	**

Page	Country	Capital	Human rights rating	Signed/ratified UN Covenant** (see page 18)
	WORLD AVERAGE		*(above)* 64% *(below)*	
134	**Korea (North)**	Pyongyang	22%	
136	**Korea (South)**	Seoul	51%	
138	**Malaysia**	Kuala Lumpur	54%	
82	**Mexico**	Mexico City	67%	**
40	**Morocco**	Rabat	57%	**
42	**Mozambique**	Maputo	38%	
200	**Netherlands**	Amsterdam	94%	**
140	**New Zealand**	Wellington	96%	**
44	**Nigeria**	Abuja	69%	
202	**Norway**	Oslo	95%	**
142	**Pakistan**	Islamabad	42%	
84	**Panama**	Panama City	84%	**
144	**Papua New Guinea**	Port Moresby	93%	
106	**Peru**	Lima	81%	**
146	**Philippines**	Quezon City	51%	**
204	**Poland**	Warsaw	36%	**
206	**Portugal**	Lisbon	86%	**
208	**Romania**	Bucharest	32%	**
148	**Saudi Arabia**	Riyadh	29%	
46	**Senegal (Senegambia)**	Dakar	89%	**
150	**Singapore**	Singapore	61%	
48	**South Africa**	Pretoria/Capetown	30%	
210	**Spain**	Madrid	78%	**
152	**Sri Lanka**	Colombo	75%	**
52	**Sudan**	Khartoum	55%	
212	**Sweden**	Stockholm	94%	**
214	**Switzerland**	Bern	92%	
154	**Syria**	Damascus	34%	**
156	**Taiwan**	Taipeh	53%	
54	**Tanzania**	Dar es Salaam	62%	**
158	**Thailand**	Bangkok	64%	
56	**Tunisia**	Tunis	62%	**
216	**Turkey**	Ankara	43%	
218	**United Kingdom**	London	95%	**
86	**USA**	Washington D.C.	92%	**
220	**USSR**	Moscow	27%	**
108	**Venezuela**	Caracas	89%	**
160	**Vietnam**	Hanoi	29%	
222	**Yugoslavia**	Belgrade	55%	**
58	**Zaire**	Kinshasa	41%	**
60	**Zambia**	Lusaka	58%	
62	**Zimbabwe**	Harare	68%	

Countries assessed in summary form

Page	Country	Capital	Fair	Poor	Bad	Signed/ratified Un Covenant (see page 18)
162	**Afghanistan**	Kabul			X	
224	**Albania**	Tirana			X	
64	**Angola**	Luanda		X		
110	**Bolivia**	Sucre		X		
163	**Burma**	Rangoon		X		
65	**Cameroon**	Yaounde		X		
88	**Dominican Republic**	Santo Domingo	X			**
89	**El Salvador**	San Salvador			X	**
66	**Ghana**	Accra		X		
90	**Guatemala**	Guatemala City			X	
67	**Guinea**	Conakry		X		**
91	**Haiti**	Port-au-Prince			X	
92	**Honduras**	Tegucigalpa	X			**
164	**Iran**	Teheran			X	**
68	**Ivory Coast**	Abidjan	X			
165	**Jordan**	Amman		X		**
166	**Kampuchea**	Phnom Penh			X	
167	**Kuwait**	Kuwait		X		
168	**Laos**	Vientiane			X	
69	**Libya**	Tripoli			X	**
70	**Madagascar**	Tananarive		X		**
71	**Malawi**	Lilongwe		X		
169	**Nepal**	Kathmandu		X		
93	**Nicaragua**	Managua		X		**
111	**Paraguay**	Asuncion			X	
72	**Rwanda**	Kigali		X		**
73	**Sierra Leone**	Freetown	X			
74	**Somalia**	Mogadishu		X		
75	**Uganda**	Kampala		X		
112	**Uruguay**	Montevideo		X		**
170	**Yemen Arab Republic**	Sana'a			X	
171	**Yemen, South**	Aden			X	

* For the purposes of this Guide, Israel has been assessed excluding the Occupied Territories.

Notes on questionnaire

UN non-members. Four countries are not member states of the United Nations. They are Korea North and South, Switzerland and Taiwan (technically part of China).

Income per capita. In most cases this is the gross national product (GNP) per head but both are misleading indicators of how the wealth of a country is shared out. Distinctions between rich and poor and between urban and rural, to mention only two extremes, can be very great.

Question 20. The term 'civilian trials', for the sake of brevity, has been used instead of civil and criminal trials.

Questions 31 to 45. Where these cannot be answered on the YES/NO scale, the method adopted has been that of assessing the degree of severity.

Maximum punishments. This section has three questions (38–40) which are included in the human rights rating. Questions 41 to 45, however, are not and are given simply as an indication of the severity or otherwise of the penal code.

African countries. Officials and others are now substituting the term 'traditional peoples' for 'tribes' or 'tribal peoples'. In most instances, while appreciating the sensitivity of certain African countries, this guide adheres to the conventional designation.

Early abortion. This term has been used without specifying a minimum period of weeks. The questionnaire is concerned with the principle of abortion, a principle being more widely adopted by governments.

Police and military forces. Many countries avoid publishing statistics. The figures given in this guide are drawn, in such cases, from a number of informed unofficial sources. Where countries are involved in wars, insurrections or emergencies, the size of forces may be temporarily expanded. A second difficulty related to the inclusion of police and military forces in the human rights rating is that many countries, because of their geographical position near more belligerent states, have felt it prudent to increase their own strength. This may be seen as unfairly affecting the percentage of their rating but the guide is obliged to quote the figures as they exist. To do otherwise would invite the criticism of arbitrarily interpreting the motives of governments.

Corporal punishment. There may be much brutality and torture by security forces at local level but only where it is clearly practised with the complicity or consent of the government is it brought into the rating scale of question 23. The

Guide also regards corporal punishment as coming under Article 7 of the *International Covenant on Civil and Political Rights* ('No one shall be subject to ... degrading punishment').

Capital punishment. This is not outlawed by the United Nations but Article 6 of the Covenant, after mentioning a number of safeguards for those sentenced to death, states: 'Nothing in this article shall be invoked to delay or to prevent the abolition of capital punishment by any State Party to the present Covenant.'

Covenant. Unless stated otherwise, reference to 'the Covenant' shall mean the *International Covenant on Civil and Political Rights*. Only a very few countries have failed to ratify the Covenant after the act of signing but a signature should be seen as denoting an intention to respect the Articles.

IMPORTANT

The information in this Guide covers the period
to April, 1983

Numbers in **bold type** on the questionnaire are
drawn from or relate to the United Nations
Covenant on Civil and Political Rights. They are:
Nos. **1** to **24** and **31** to **33**. Numbers in roman type
are non-United Nations questions. They are:
Nos. 25 to 30 and 34 to 50.

For future editions of this work, relevant
information and comments from statistical
services or similar authorities would be welcomed

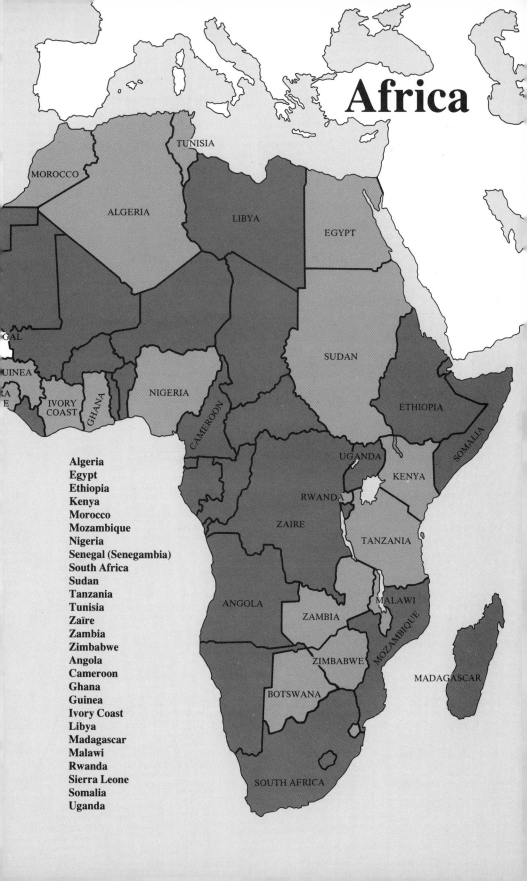

Africa

MOROCCO

TUNISIA

ALGERIA

LIBYA

EGYPT

GAL

UINEA

IVORY
COAST

GHANA

NIGERIA

CAMEROON

SUDAN

ETHIOPIA

SOMALIA

UGANDA

KENYA

RWANDA

ZAIRE

TANZANIA

ANGOLA

MALAWI

ZAMBIA

MOZAMBIQUE

ZIMBABWE

MADAGASCAR

BOTSWANA

SOUTH AFRICA

Algeria
Egypt
Ethiopia
Kenya
Morocco
Mozambique
Nigeria
Senegal (Senegambia)
South Africa
Sudan
Tanzania
Tunisia
Zaïre
Zambia
Zimbabwe
Angola
Cameroon
Ghana
Guinea
Ivory Coast
Libya
Madagascar
Malawi
Rwanda
Sierra Leone
Somalia
Uganda

Human rights rating: 62%

Population: 19,330,000
Life expectancy: 57
Infant mortality (0–1 year) per 1000 births: 110

Form of government: socialist one-party state
Income per capita: US$ 1935

Observations: Within the political constraints of a one-party system, limited freedom of speech and ideas are tolerated. Algeria has signed but not yet ratified the UN Covenant on civil and political rights.

FREEDOM/RIGHTS		Further comments	
1. Of movement in own country	YES		○
2. To leave own country	YES		○
3. From deprivation of nationality	YES		○
4. To seek information and teach ideas	yes	But degree of political conformity in academic circles considered prudent	◑
5. From serfdom, slavery, forced or child labour	yes	Child labour follows traditional regional pattern	○
6. Of peaceful political opposition	NO	No opposition to state party	●
7. Of peaceful assembly and association	no	Security police surveillance of meetings for hostility to government	◑
8. Of women to equal rights	yes	Legal equality but women, in general, still follow traditional and Islamic roles	○
9. From directed employment or work permits	YES		○
10. Of inter-racial, inter-religious and civil marriage	YES		○
11. To practise any religion	yes	But Islamic fundamentalists seeking changes less tolerant to others	◑
12. From compulsory religion or state ideology in schools	YES		○
13. From political press censorship	no	Government control or guidance. Nothing to conflict with state 'socialism'	◑
14. From police detention without charge	yes	48 hours by urban police. Security forces up to 1 month	◑
15. From police searches of home without warrant	yes	Security forces may act independently but not during the hours of darkness	◑
16. From torture or coercion by state	yes	But local abuses	◐
17. Of assumption of innocence until guilt proved	YES	Though less tolerance when military take over civil cases	○
18. Of accused to be promptly brought before judge or court	yes	But overworked system may mean many months' delay	◑
19. Of all courts to total independence	yes	Rare instances of military taking over cases	◑
20. From civilian trials in secret	YES		○
21. For independent trade unions	NO	Only one national union which is government controlled	●
22. From censorship of mail	yes	Except for political suspects under surveillance	◑
23. To publish and educate in ethnic languages	no	Protests at restrictions by Berber minority (15%)	◑
24. From deliberate state policies to control artistic works	YES		○

25. From compulsory military service	no	6 months' military service
26. To purchase and drink alcohol	**YES**	
27. To practise homosexuality between consenting adults	no	Illegal but no strict police action
28. To use contraceptive pills and devices	**YES**	
29. Of early abortion	no	Strict medical reasons only
30. Of divorce (for men and women equally)	yes	But Muslim majority subject to Sharia law

STATE POWER
31. Corporal punishment by state — None
32. Radio and TV broadcasts — Government-controlled and owned
33. Book publishing — State organization has replaced all private publishers
34. Number of police and military per 100,000 citizens — 1295
35. % of national income spent on above — 4%
36. Weapons normally carried by civil police — Sidearms
37. Capital punishment by state — Crimes against state security, murder, drug-smuggling etc. but present policy favours commuting penalty

MAXIMUM PUNISHMENTS IN PENAL CODE FOR:
(Freedom-related offences)
38. Non-violent anti-government activities — 10 years for political opposition
39. Possession of banned political literature — As 38. Depending on motives
40. Refusing compulsory national service — 1 year's prison

(Criminal offences)
41. Unlawful possession of 'hard' drugs — Minimum 5 years
42. Trading in pornography — Punishment at discretion of court
43. Illegal abortion — 5 years' prison
44. Bigamy — Islamic polygamous practice but foreigners judged by own country's laws
45. Rape without other injury — 10 years' prison

COMPULSORY DOCUMENTS FOR CITIZENS
46. Legally required at all times — ID card
47. For employment — None
48. When applying for passport — ID card, Nationality Certificate, father's birth certificate etc.
49. Period of validity of passport — 5 years
50. Countries forbidden to holder — Israel, South Africa

Human rights rating: 64%

Population: 43,190,000
Life expectancy: 56
Infant mortality (0–1 year) per 1000 births: 108

Form of government: republic with executive president
Income per capita: US$ 450

Observations: 'State of emergency' granting president full powers. Renewed October 1982

FREEDOM/RIGHTS		Further comments	
1. Of movement in own country	YES	Except for military zones	○
2. To leave own country	YES		○
3. From deprivation of nationality	YES		○
4. To seek information and teach ideas	no	Ethics law prohibits teaching of atheism, communism etc.	◐
5. From serfdom, slavery, forced or child labour	yes	But child labour follows regional pattern	◑
6. Of peaceful political opposition	no	Prosecution to defend 'social values'. Parties strictly controlled	◐
7. Of peaceful assembly and association	yes	But not when volatile religious groups are fomenting conflict and tensions	◑
8. Of women to equal rights	yes	But Islamic traditions limit constitutional freedoms	◑
9. From directed employment or work permits	YES		○
10. Of inter-racial, inter-religious and civil marriage	no	Civil marriages not recognized by Muslim courts. Advantages for males	◐
11. To practise any religion	YES		○
12. From compulsory religion or state ideology in schools	no	Schools of all denominations insist on religious instruction	◐
13. From political press censorship	no	Government guidance, particularly during periods of social tension. 7 papers banned in 1981	◐
14. From police detention without charge	yes	But present state of emergency has provoked indiscriminate arrests	◑
15. From police searches of home without warrant	yes	But constitution not always honoured in over-zealous searches	◑
16. From torture or coercion by state	yes	Local abuses only	◑
17. Of assumption of innocence until guilt proved	YES	But present martial law affects security cases	○
18. Of accused to be promptly brought before judge or court	yes	Article 42 allows 4 days but present martial law more severe	◑
19. Of all courts to total independence	yes	Except in martial law situation. Special courts try security cases	◑
20. From civilian trials in secret	yes	But mostly to protect juveniles ('security' trials usually in camera)	◑
21. For independent trade unions	no	Denied right to strike	◐
22. From censorship of mail	yes	Authorities check mail to suspected 'subversives'	◑
23. To publish and educate in ethnic languages	YES		○
24. From deliberate state policies to control artistic works	YES		○
25. From compulsory military service	no	Selective 1-year conscription	◐
26. To purchase and drink alcohol	YES	Opposed by orthodox Muslims	○

27. To practise homosexuality between consenting adults	no	Illegal but tolerated over 21. However, 10 years' prison for master forcing servant and teacher forcing male pupil
28. To use contraceptive pills and devices	**YES**	Government support
29. Of early abortion	no	Only when mother's life at risk. But Muslims claim less need for it
30. Of divorce (for men and women equally)	**YES**	Sharia law

STATE POWER
31. Corporal punishment by state — None
32. Radio and TV broadcasts — State-run. More liberal under new president
33. Book publishing — Relatively free
34. Number of police and military per 100,000 citizens — 1157
35. % of national income spent on above — 15%
36. Weapons normally carried by civil police — Pistols, rifles and unarmed
37. Capital punishment by state — Shooting for military, hanging for civilians. For numerous crimes

MAXIMUM PUNISHMENTS IN PENAL CODE FOR:
(Freedom-related offences)
38. Non-violent anti-government activities — 3 years with hard labour. Life imprisonment in extreme cases
39. Possession of banned political literature — 3 years if 'spreading hatred'
40. Refusing compulsory national service — 3 years' prison

(Criminal offences)
41. Unlawful possession of 'hard' drugs — 1 year. Trafficking life imprisonment
42. Trading in pornography — 3 years' prison. Salacious books banned
43. Illegal abortion — 3 years when self-induced. Longer for procurer.
44. Bigamy — 4 wives for men maximum. Women may be taken to court
45. Rape without other injury — 3–7 years' hard labour. Life when master violates servant or teacher with pupil

COMPULSORY DOCUMENTS FOR CITIZENS
46. Legally required at all times — ID card
47. For employment — ID card
48. When applying for passport — ID card and employment certificate
49. Period of validity of passport — 3 years
50. Countries forbidden to holder — None

Human rights rating: 17%

Population: 32,600,000
Life expectancy: 39
Infant mortality (0–1 year) per 1000 births: 155

Form of government: military Marxist
Income per capita: US$ 120

Observations: The disregard for human rights is worsened by the revolts and wars involving Eritreans, Somalis etc.

FREEDOM/RIGHTS		Further comments	
1. Of movement in own country	no	Local *Kebele* (parishes) issue permits for zones of secessionist unrest	◑
2. To leave own country	no	Husband and wife cannot travel together. Dissidents not at all	◑
3. From deprivation of nationality	NO	Arbitrary ruling by military government	●
4. To seek information and teach ideas	NO	Strict Marxist controls within limits of under-developed country	●
5. From serfdom, slavery, forced or child labour	NO	Forced labour. 220,000 militia provide unpaid slave labour	●
6. Of peaceful political opposition	NO	Over 10,000 prisoners on political grounds	●
7. Of peaceful assembly and association	NO	Only in support of government	●
8. Of women to equal rights	no	Marxist-style improvements to women's political status.	◑
9. From directed employment or work permits	NO	Conscripted labour. Widespread poverty defies normal controls	●
10. Of inter-racial, inter-religious and civil marriage	YES		○
11. To practise any religion	NO	Some churches still practise	●
12. From compulsory religion or state ideology in schools	NO	Marxist-Leninism compulsory	●
13. From political press censorship	NO	No criticism of government permitted	●
14. From police detention without charge	NO	Disappearances numerous. No official accountability of prisoners	●
15. From police searches of home without warrant	NO	Round-up of youth for military service	●
16. From torture or coercion by state	NO	Slashing, beating etc. Particularly of secessionist minorities	●
17. Of assumption of innocence until guilt proved	NO		●
18. Of accused to be promptly brought before judge or court	NO		●
19. Of all courts to total independence	NO	No appeals permitted	●
20. From civilian trials in secret	NO		●
21. For independent trade unions	NO	Indirect Marxist controls	●
22. From censorship of mail	NO	Lawless situation. Political suspects most affected	●
23. To publish and educate in ethnic languages	NO	Secessionist tensions	●
24. From deliberate state policies to control artistic works	no	Marxist-Leninist policy against bourgeois self-indulgence	◑
25. From compulsory national service	NO	Indefinite conscription	●

26. To purchase and drink alcohol	**YES**		
27. To practise homosexuality between consenting adults	no	Official disapproval but practice usually ignored	
28. To use contraceptive pills and devices	yes	Limited government encouragement	
29. Of early abortion	no	Medical grounds only	
30. Of divorce (for men and women equally)	yes	But religious laws still apply to women	

STATE POWER

31. Corporal punishment by state — Beatings, hot oil, genital torture etc.
32. Radio and TV broadcasts — Instrument of government policy
33. Book publishing — State control
34. Number of police and military per 100,000 citizens — 2000 including para-military, People's Militia etc.
35. % of national income spent on above — 12%
36. Weapons normally carried by civil police — Pistols, sub-machine guns etc.
37. Capital punishment by state — By shooting or death by torture. Army officers have arbitrary powers

MAXIMUM PUNISHMENTS IN PENAL CODE FOR:
(Freedom-related offences)

38. Non-violent anti-government activities — Death penalty
39. Possession of banned political literature — Death penalty
40. Refusing compulsory national service — Death penalty

(Criminal offences)

41. Unlawful possession of 'hard' drugs — Legal procedures non-existent Punishment arbitrary
42. Trading in pornography — As previous question
43. Illegal abortion — State of country makes official action unlikely
44. Bigamy — Government campaigning against polygamy which is still widely practised.
45. Rape without other injury — Shot. But military offenders frequently avoid prosecution

COMPULSORY DOCUMENTS FOR CITIZENS

46. Legally required at all times — Internal travel permits from parish authority
47. For employment — As above when away from home
48. When applying for passport — Birth certificate, security clearance
49. Period of validity of passport — 1–3 years
50. Countries forbidden to holder — No consistent endorsements

Human rights rating: 58%

Population: 15,800,000
Life expectancy: 55
Infant mortality (0–1 year) per 1000 births: 85

Form of government: one-party state
Income per capita: US$ 380

Observations: The human rights position has worsened with recent threats to the present government and constitutional rights can be suspended without due process of law. Kenya has signed and ratified the UN Covenant.

FREEDOM/RIGHTS		Further comments	
1. Of movement in own country	yes	Restricted movement in Somali area	◗
2. To leave own country	yes	Some passports withdrawn	◗
3. From deprivation of nationality	YES		◑
4. To seek information and teach ideas	no	Restrictions on many political and social issues in universities etc.	◑
5. From serfdom, slavery, forced or child labour	yes	But tribal child labour still widely practised	◗
6. Of peaceful political opposition	NO	Declared a one-party state in June, 1982. Opposition banned in 1969	●
7. Of peaceful assembly and association	no	Meetings must be licensed. Wide police powers	◑
8. Of women to equal rights	no	Marked social inferiority. 2.2% female students at universities	◑
9. From directed employment or work permits	YES		○
10. Of inter-racial, inter-religious and civil marriage	YES		○
11. To practise any religion	YES		○
12. From compulsory religion or state ideology in schools	YES		○
13. From political press censorship	no	Government guidelines on sensitive issues. Isolated harassment of journalists	◑
14. From police detention without charge	no	Under PS Act indefinite detention for political prisoners but charge must be stated within 5 days.	◑
15. From police searches of home without warrant	yes	Usually obeyed	◗
16. From torture or coercion by state	yes	Isolated abuses at local level and prison hardships	◗
17. Of assumption of innocence until guilt proved	no	Public Security Act can suspend all laws	◑
18. Of accused to be promptly brought before judge or court	no	Public Security Act, revised 1978, supersedes constitutional safeguards	◑
19. Of all courts to total independence	no	Increasing evidence of government pressure and interference	◑
20. From civilian trials in secret	NO	Political detainees may be tried in camera	●
21. For independent trade unions	no	Most strikes illegal. Civil servants' union deregistered for political opposition	◑
22. From censorship of mail	yes	Mail checked for currency illegalities	◗
23. To publish and educate in ethnic languages	YES		○

24. From deliberate state policies to control artistic works	no	Anti- 'establishment' books seized, theatres closed etc.
25. From compulsory military service	YES	
26. To purchase and drink alcohol	YES	
27. To practise homosexuality between consenting adults	NO	5 years' prison with or without corporal punishment
28. To use contraceptive pills and devices	YES	Government support
29. Of early abortion	no	Risk to mother's life only
30. Of divorce (for men and women equally)	YES	

STATE POWER

31. Corporal punishment by state — Yes. By rod or cane

32. Radio and TV broadcasts — Direct state control. No anti-government broadcasts permitted

33. Book publishing — In private hands but publishers limit controversial works

34. Number of police and military per 100,000 citizens — 156

35. % of national income spent on above — 4.5%

36. Weapons normally carried by civil police — City police usually unarmed

37. Capital punishment by state — Under the Hanging Bill, for murder, robbery with violence, treason etc.

MAXIMUM PUNISHMENTS IN PENAL CODE FOR:

(Freedom-related offences)

38. Non-violent anti-government activities — Death for treasonable felonies. Sedition 10 years

39. Possession of banned political literature — 7 years' prison

40. Refusing compulsory national service — Not applicable

(Criminal offences)

41. Unlawful possession of 'hard' drugs — 10 years' prison and fine

42. Trading in pornography — 2 years' prison and fine

43. Illegal abortion — By mother 7 years. By others 14 years

44. Bigamy — 5 years' prison

45. Rape without other injury — Life imprisonment

COMPULSORY DOCUMENTS FOR CITIZENS

46. Legally required at all times — ID card

47. For employment — ID card to prove nationality

48. When applying for passport — Birth certificate

49. Period of validity of passport — 5 years

50. Countries forbidden to holder — None, but South Africa discouraged

Human rights rating: 57%

Population: 21,580,000
Life expectancy: 56
Infant mortality (0–1 year) per 1000 births: 130

Form of government: nominated by monarch
Income per capita: US$ 850

Observations: The damaging war with the Algerian and Libyan-backed forces of Polisario has worsened the already intolerant attitude towards human rights. The country has signed and ratified the UN Covenant.

FREEDOM/RIGHTS		Further comments	
1. Of movement in own country	YES		○
2. To leave own country	no	Passports withheld from political dissidents	◐
3. From deprivation of nationality	YES		○
4. To seek, receive and impart information and teach ideas	yes	Certain areas of knowledge considered seditious	◑
5. From serfdom, slavery, forced or child labour	no	Serfdom and child labour	◐
6. Of peaceful political opposition	no	200–300 people imprisoned for political crimes. Periodic royal amnesties	◐
7. Of peaceful assembly and association	no	Prison sentences for forming 'unlicensed' political associations. Disrespect towards authorities illegal	◐
8. Of women to equal rights	yes	Legally equal but Muslim societies adhere to women's traditional role	◑
9. From directed employment or work permits	YES		○
10. Of inter-racial, inter-religious and civil marriage	YES	Though for Muslim majority it would not be recognized as marriage	○
11. To practise any religion	YES	But proselytizing illegal	○
12. From compulsory religion or state ideology in schools	no	Compulsion in numerous orthodox Muslim schools	◐
13. From political press censorship	no	Censorship lifted in 1977 but no criticism of monarchy, religion or policy in Western Sahara	◐
14. From police detention without charge	NO	Long periods of incommunicado detention. Sometimes resulting in deaths	●
15. From police searches of home without warrant	no	Law frequently disregarded in checking of dissidents	◐
16. From torture or coercion by state	yes	Local abuses	◑
17. Of assumption of innocence until guilt proved	NO	Arrests of political suspects. 1981 riots and Western Sahara war have exacerbated position	●
18. Of accused to be promptly brought before judge or court	no	Inconsistencies when dealing with political suspects	◐
19. Of all courts to total independence	YES		○
20. From civilian trials in secret	yes	Except when concerned with security or Western Sahara	◑
21. For independent trade unions	yes	Strong union movement but in 1981 a general strike led to crowd violence and the shooting of 600 strikers by authorities	◑

22. From censorship of mail	no	Constitutional guarantees no protection for mail of dissidents	
23. To publish and educate in ethnic languages	YES		
24. From deliberate state policies to control artistic works	yes	Distribution of certain artistic works held up by government	
25. From compulsory military service	NO	18 months' military service	
26. To purchase and drink alcohol	YES		
27. To practise homosexuality between consenting adults	NO	Law rigorous	
28. To use contraceptive pills and devices	YES		
29. Of early abortion	no	Only when mother's life at risk	
30. Of divorce (for men and women equally)	YES	Permitted by secular law. Divorce by Islamic law favours men	

STATE POWER

31. Corporal punishment by state	None	
32. Radio and TV broadcasts	Partly government controlled. No criticism of monarchy or 'sensitive' issues	
33. Book publishing	Publications not to criticize monarchy, religion etc.	
34. Number of police and military per 100,000 citizens	900 (including para-military)	
35. % of national income spent on above	10%	
36. Weapons normally carried by civil police	Variety of firearms	
37. Capital punishment by state	No admitted executions since 1973 though death sentences frequent for murder, treason, arson etc.	

MAXIMUM PUNISHMENTS IN PENAL CODE FOR:
(Freedom-related offences)

38. Non-violent anti-government activities	Indefinite detention, disappearances etc. (secret detention centres)	
39. Possession of banned political literature	6 months' prison	
40. Refusing compulsory national service	1 year peacetime, 10 years wartime	

(Criminal offences)

41. Unlawful possession of 'hard' drugs	10 years' prison
42. Trading in pornography	2 years' prison
43. Illegal abortion	5 years' prison
44. Bigamy	4 wives permitted
45. Rape without other injury	10 years' prison

COMPULSORY DOCUMENTS FOR CITIZENS

46. Legally required at all times	ID card
47. For employment	Work permit (issued by Ministry)
48. When applying for passport	ID card, certificate of residence
49. Period of validity of passport	5 years
50. Countries forbidden to holder	Israel and South Africa

Human rights rating: 38%

Population: 12,130,000
Life expectancy: 46
Infant mortality (0–1 year) per 1000 births: 148

Form of government: Marxist (Frelimo) state
Income per capita: US$ 250

Observations: Regional civil unrest and what is regarded as a threat from South Africa have exacerbated the human rights situation which, in any case, is subordinated to Marxist-Leninist policies and ideology.

FREEDOM/RIGHTS		Further comments	
1. Of movement in own country	no	Subject to security checks and permits	◗
2. To leave own country	NO	Only if one has an approved reason	●
3. From deprivation of nationality	YES		○
4. To seek, receive and impart information and teach ideas	NO	Only pro-Frelimo education and ideas permitted	●
5. From serfdom, slavery, forced or child labour	no	'Re-education camps' seen as forced labour. Detainees reported to number 10,000	◗
6. Of peaceful political opposition	NO	Frelimo only	●
7. Of peaceful assembly and association	NO	Party only	●
8. Of women to equal rights	yes	Political ideology overcoming traditional inequalities	◖
9. From directed employment or work permits	NO		●
10. Of inter-racial, inter-religious and civil marriage	YES	Traditional tribal marriages from age 10	○
11. To practise any religion	yes	More tolerant attitude following 1975 independence when many churches were closed	◗
12. From compulsory religion or state ideology in schools	NO	Marxist-Leninism a compulsory subject	●
13. From political press censorship	NO	Controlled by party and state	●
14. From police detention without charge	NO	Detention without trial for prolonged periods	●
15. From police searches of home without warrant	no	Number of arrests without warrants	◗
16. From torture or coercion by state	no	Used to obtain information or confessions during interrogation	◗
17. Of assumption of innocence until guilt proved	no	Civil unrest and incursions from South Africa give military power to arrest arbitrarily	◗
18. Of accused to be promptly brought before judge or court	NO	Long delays for political prisoners	●
19. Of all courts to total independence	yes	For non-political offences. Also village trials with local 'assessors'	◗
20. From civilian trials in secret	no	Some political offences tried in camera and by military officers	◗
21. For independent trade unions	NO	'No recognizable trade unions'	●
22. From censorship of mail	no	Wide surveillance, particularly connections with South Africa	◗
23. To publish and educate in ethnic languages	YES		○
24. From deliberate state policies to control artistic works	no	Marxist conservatism hostile towards 'bourgeois' creativity	◗

25. From compulsory military service	**NO**	2 years (including women)	●
26. To purchase and drink alcohol	**YES**		○
27. To practise homosexuality between consenting adults	yes	Tolerated despite party disapproval	◑
28. To use contraceptive pills and devices	**YES**	State-aided campaign	○
29. Of early abortion	no	Only when mother's life at risk	◑
30. Of divorce (for men and women equally)	**YES**		○

STATE POWER

31. Corporal punishment by state	Flogging for black-marketing	◑
32. Radio and TV broadcasts	State-controlled and run	●
33. Book publishing	State-owned and controlled	●
34. Number of police and military per 100,000 citizens	350	○
35. % of national income spent on above	14%	◑
36. Weapons normally carried by civil police	Pistols	◑
37. Capital punishment by state	Execution for 'crimes against the people', murder, political opposition etc.	●

MAXIMUM PUNISHMENTS IN PENAL CODE FOR:
(Freedom-related offences)

38. Non-violent anti-government activities	Death penalty if considered sedition	●
39. Possession of banned political literature	Varying periods of re-education in labour camps	○
40. Refusing compulsory national service	As 39	◑

(Criminal offences)

41. Unlawful possession of 'hard' drugs	None
42. Trading in pornography	None
43. Illegal abortion	None
44. Bigamy	Government attempting to limit polygamy among practising tribes
45. Rape without other injury	None

COMPULSORY DOCUMENTS FOR CITIZENS

46. Legally required at all times	ID card
47. For employment	ID card
48. When applying for passport	ID card/birth certificate
49. Period of validity of passport	Varies with purpose of journey
50. Countries forbidden to holder	None

NIGERIA

Human rights rating: 64%

Population: 82,503,000
Life expectancy: 48
Infant mortality (0–1 year) per 1000 births: 163

Form of government: federal parliament
Income per capita: US$ 1000

Observations: The 1979 constitution, after 12 years of martial law, contains most human rights guarantees. Violations are usually at local level or related to the diverse ethnic groups and customs of the country.

FREEDOM/RIGHTS		Further comments	
1. Of movement in own country	YES		○
2. To leave own country	YES		○
3. From deprivation of nationality	YES		○
4. To seek, receive and impart information and teach ideas	YES		○
5. From serfdom, slavery, forced or child labour	no	Traditional tribal patterns persist	◑
6. Of peaceful political opposition	YES	'Secret societies' prohibited. Political party headquarters must be in capital	○
7. Of peaceful assembly and association	YES		○
8. Of women to equal rights	NO	Varies by area and customary laws. Husband's permission required to obtain passport, property etc.	●
9. From directed employment or work permits	YES		○
10. Of inter-racial, inter-religious and civil marriage	YES	Muslim north of country adheres to religious marriages	○
11. To practise any religion	YES		○
12. From compulsory religion or state ideology in schools	YES		○
13. From political press censorship	yes	Self-censorship on sensitive issues. Reporters occasionally restricted	◑
14. From police detention without charge	no	Illegal violations at local level and overcrowded prisons create unpredictable problems	◑
15. From police searches of home without warrant	YES		○
16. From torture or coercion by state	NO	1 m. Ghanaians expelled (1983)	◑
17. Of assumption of innocence until guilt proved	yes		◑
18. Of accused to be promptly brought before judge or court	no	13,784 in overcrowded prisons awaiting trial (1980)	●
19. Of all courts to total independence	yes	Corrupt high officials frequently avoid prosecution. Islamic courts in north of country may prevail over secular.	◑
20. From civilian trials in secret	yes	Very occasional secret trials	◑
21. For independent trade unions	yes	Except those in 'essential services'	◑
22. From censorship of mail	no	No mail allowed from South Africa and occasional 'security' checks	◑
23. To publish and educate in ethnic languages	YES		○

24. From deliberate state policies to control artistic works	**YES**		○
25. From compulsory military service	**YES**		◐
26. To purchase and drink alcohol	yes	Restrictions in Muslim areas	◑
27. To practise homosexuality between consenting adults	**NO**	Strictly illegal	●
28. To use contraceptive pills and devices	yes	Limited government support	◑
29. Of early abortion	no	Only when mother's life at risk	◑
30. Of divorce (for men and women equally)	yes	Limits on divorced women's right to remarry. Muslim laws in northern states	◐

STATE POWER

31. Corporal punishment by state	Caning, male and female up to age 45. 12 strokes maximum	◑
32. Radio and TV broadcasts	All broadcasting state-owned and controlled	◑
33. Book publishing	Relatively free of control	○
34. Number of police and military per 100,000 citizens	230	○
35. % of national income spent on above	4%	○
36. Weapons normally carried by civil police	Usually unarmed but some firearms and anti-riot gear etc.	○
37. Capital punishment by state	Many offences including kidnapping, armed smuggling. By shooting, sometimes in public	●

MAXIMUM PUNISHMENTS IN PENAL CODE FOR:
(Freedom-related offences)

38. Non-violent anti-government activities	10 years for state servants taking bribes	◑
39. Possession of banned political literature	3 years' prison	◑
40. Refusing compulsory national service	None	○

(Criminal offences)

41. Unlawful possession of 'hard' drugs	10 years' prison
42. Trading in pornography	3 years' prison
43. Illegal abortion	14 years' prison
44. Bigamy	7 years' prison
45. Rape without other injury	14 years' prison

COMPULSORY DOCUMENTS FOR CITIZENS

46. Legally required at all times	None. But subject under review
47. For employment	None
48. When applying for passport	Birth certificate
49. Period of validity of passport	5 years
50. Countries forbidden to holder	South Africa

Human rights rating: 89%

Population: 5,509,000
Life expectancy: 43
Infant mortality (0–1 year) per 1000 births: 128

Form of government: multi-party system
Income per capita: US$ 500

Observations: The leading African supporter of human rights and the original sponsor of OAU Human Rights Charter (1981).

	FREEDOM/RIGHTS		Further comments	
1.	Of movement in own country	YES		
2.	To leave own country	YES		
3.	From deprivation of nationality	YES		
4.	To seek information and teach ideas	YES		
5.	From serfdom, slavery, forced or child labour	yes	But areas of traditional child labour	
6.	Of peaceful political opposition	yes	But certain opposition politicians have been detained on 'security' grounds	
7.	Of peaceful assembly and association	YES		
8.	Of women to equal rights	YES		
9.	From directed employment or work permits	YES		
10.	Of inter-racial, inter-religious and civil marriage	YES	Muslim majority adheres to strict opposition to inter-marriage	
11.	To practise any religion	YES		
12.	From compulsory religion or state ideology in schools	YES		
13.	From political press censorship	YES		
14.	From police detention without charge	YES	Except when identity has to be proved	
15.	From police searches of home without warrant	YES		
16.	From torture or coercion by state	YES		
17.	Of assumption of innocence until guilt proved	YES		
18.	Of accused to be promptly brought before judge or court	yes	Maximum 72 hours but rare cases of preventive detention	
19.	Of all courts to total independence	YES		
20.	From civilian trials in secret	YES		
21.	For independent trade unions	YES		
22.	From censorship of mail	YES		
23.	To publish and educate in ethnic languages	YES		
24.	From deliberate state policies to control artistic works	YES		
25.	From compulsory military service	YES		
26.	To purchase and drink alcohol	YES		
27.	To practise homosexuality between consenting adults	no	Illegal but punishment limited to modest fines	
28.	To use contraceptive pills and devices	yes	But strong religious opposition at local level	
29.	Of early abortion	no		
30.	Of divorce (for men and women equally)	YES	Civil and religious courts follow independent procedures	

STATE POWER

31. Corporal punishment by state Prison inmates may be whipped for ◐
 unruly behaviour

32. Radio and TV broadcasts State-run. Minimum of restrictions ◐
33. General book publishing Obscenity restrictions only ○
34. Number of police and military per 100,000 300 ○
 citizens
35. % of national income spent on above 2.5% ○
36. Weapons normally carried by civil police Normally unarmed ○
37. Capital punishment by state By firing squad. Very rare ●

MAXIMUM PUNISHMENTS IN PENAL CODE FOR:

(Freedom-related offences)

38. Non-violent anti-government activities None ○
39. Possession of banned political literature None ○
40. Refusing compulsory military service None ○

(Criminal offences)

41. Unlawful possession of 'hard' drugs 10 years' prison
42. Trading in pornography Confiscation of material
43. Illegal abortion 5 years' prison
44. Bigamy 2 years' prison
45. Rape without other injury Life imprisonment for rape of children.
 15 years when woman is over 16

COMPULSORY DOCUMENTS FOR CITIZENS

46. Legally required at all times ID card
47. For employment None
48. When applying for passport ID card and police clearance
49. Period of validity of passport 3 years and renewal of 3 years
50. Countries forbidden to holder South Africa

Human rights rating: 30%

Population: 29,030,000 (see Obs.)
Life expectancy: whites 70, blacks 53
**Infant mortality (0–1 year) per 1000
 births:** whites 15, Africans 200

Form of government: parliamentary
 republic
Income per capita: gap between
 different racial groups makes figure
 unrealistic

Observations: Human rights, because of discrimination against non-white races, vary between extremes. The answers given below, contrary to the assumptions of government and constitution, make no distinctions between the races. Black inhabitants are not treated as citizens or legally regarded as such and the number of full citizens should therefore drop to 8,000,000.

FREEDOM/RIGHTS		Further comments	
1. Of movement in own country	NO	70% of population are Africans needing permits (under 'pass' system). 200,000 arrests in 1982	●
2. To leave own country	NO	Passports 'a privilege'. Political opponents of regime usually denied them	●
3. From deprivation of nationality	NO	Remaining in exile in exchange for passport	●
4. To seek information and teach ideas	NO	Black education subject to limitations of curricula and books, state of surveillance etc.	●
5. From serfdom, slavery, forced or child labour	no	Cheap 'parole labour system' a form of forced black labour. The UN equate apartheid with 'slave-like practices'	◑
6. Of peaceful political opposition	NO	Anything that conflicts with policy of white supremacy comes under 'security' laws	●
7. Of peaceful assembly and association	NO	As 6	●
8. Of women to equal rights	NO	Discrimination apparent among all races	●
9. From directed employment or work permits	NO	Law restricts numbers and trades of blacks in many industries	●
10. Of inter-racial, inter-religious and civil marriage	NO	Banned under Immorality and Mixed Marriage Act	●
11. To practise any religion	yes	But no intruding into political or social controversy	◖
12. From compulsory religion or state ideology in schools	YES		○
13. From political press censorship	no	Over 100 laws restrict reporting. But significant section of white liberal press maintain opposition to government	◑
14. From police detention without charge	NO	Usually non-European suspects, including children under 16	●
15. From police searches of home without warrant	NO	Particularly during police checks in black areas or searching for blacks in unauthorized areas	●

16.	From torture or coercion by state	NO	Assaults on detainees frequent under interrogation. Law demands 'satisfactory replies'	●
17.	Of assumption of innocence until guilt proved	NO	Under Terrorism Act must prove that the offence did not come under such vague categories as 'prejudice to industry'	●
18.	Of accused to be promptly brought before judge or court	NO	Indefinite delays under Terrorism Act	●
19.	Of all courts to total independence	NO	No court can order release of individuals detained by security forces	●
20.	From civilian trials in secret	NO	Many 'security' trials in camera	●
21.	For independent trade unions	NO	Most strikes by non-Europeans regarded as political threat. No union for black farmworkers	●
22.	From censorship of mail	NO	Opponents of regime subject to mail interception	●
23.	To publish and educate in ethnic languages	yes	Subject to racial and educational laws and limitations	◑
24.	From deliberate state policies to control artistic works	yes	Laws that enforce ideas of social and racial inferiority may inhibit artists' work	◑
25.	From compulsory military service	NO	24 months' (whites) military service	●
26.	To purchase and drink alcohol	YES	Liquor stores divided for separate races	○
27.	To practise homosexuality between consenting adults	yes	Legal over 19 years but a crime to cross colour barriers	◑
28.	To use contraceptive pills and devices	YES	All races	○
29.	Of early abortion	yes	Broad medical/social reasons	◑
30.	Of divorce (for men and women equally)	YES		○

STATE POWER

31.	Corporal punishment by state	15 lashes (officially)	◑
32.	Radio and TV broadcasts	Controlled and operated by national corporation	●
33.	Book publishing	Privately owned publishing subject to security and racial laws	◐
34.	Number of police and military per 100,000 citizens	830 (including Commandos)	○
35.	% of national income spent on above	9%	◑
36.	Weapons normally carried by civil police	9mm Parabellum pistols	◑
37.	Capital punishment by state	Execution for political crimes, murder, rape, 'embarrassment to the state' (130 in 1980)	●

MAXIMUM PUNISHMENTS IN PENAL CODE FOR:
(Freedom-related offences)

38.	Non-violent anti-government activities	Indefinite detention under Terrorism Act on grounds of 'endangering maintenance of law and order'	◐
39.	Possession of banned political literature	As 38	◑
40.	Refusing compulsory national service	2 to 3 years' prison and/or R2000 fine. Reimposable if refusal continues	◐

(Criminal offences)

41. Unlawful possession of 'hard' drugs	15 years' prison
42. Trading in pornography	6 months' prison
43. Illegal abortion	5 years' prison and/or R5000 fine. Doctors 3 months and R250 fine
44. Bigamy	Discretion of court
45. Rape without other injury	Death penalty (usually when accused is a non-European)

COMPULSORY DOCUMENTS FOR CITIZENS

46. Legally required at all times	Collected identity details (Book of Life) which includes race classification
47. For employment	Book of Life. Blacks require 'passes' which also legitimize presence in country
48. When applying for passport	Book of Life (whites only). Blacks must also produce police and poll tax clearance etc. but issuing of passports rare
49. Period of validity of passport	5 years
50. Countries forbidden to holder	East European bloc, China, Cuba, Vietnam, N. Korea, S. Korea

Human rights rating: 55%

Population: 18,371,000
Life expectancy: 49
Infant mortality (0–1 year) per 1000 births: 120

Form of government: one-party state
Income per capita: US$ 370

Observations: Unsatisfactory. The State Security Law is invoked whenever the one-party government is challenged or feels threatened.

FREEDOM/RIGHTS		Further comments	
1. Of movement in own country	yes	Government attempting to reduce internal migrations	◖
2. To leave own country	yes	Exit permits are more restricted for much-needed qualified professionals	◖
3. From deprivation of nationality	YES		○
4. To seek, receive and impart information and teach ideas	no	Nothing prejudicial to state or president to be taught etc.	◑
5. From serfdom, slavery, forced or child labour	yes	Child labour within regional traditional practices	◖
6. Of peaceful political opposition	NO	Only Sudanese Socialist Party legal. Arrests of Communist Party members	●
7. Of peaceful assembly and association	no	Certain tolerance of criticism but not when openly challenging the party	◑
8. Of women to equal rights	no	Regional and religious traditions persist. Female circumcision in south	◖
9. From directed employment or work permits	YES		○
10. Of inter-racial, inter-religious and civil marriage	yes	Islamic majority may not inter-marry. Islamic fundamentalism increasing	◖
11. To practise any religion	YES		○
12. From compulsory religion or state ideology in schools	no	Islam a compulsory subject in most schools	◑
13. From political press censorship	yes	Journalists adhere to understood guidelines, avoiding direct criticism of president	◖
14. From police detention without charge	NO	Arbitrary and long detention for many political dissidents	●
15. From police searches of home without warrant	yes	Usually respected except for security or black-market reasons	◖
16. From torture or coercion by state	no	Occasional reports of torture. Pro-Libya elements may face harsh interrogation	◑
17. Of assumption of innocence until guilt proved	no	Numerous instances of arrests without adequate evidence	◑
18. Of accused to be promptly brought before judge or court	yes	Delays when military decide to intervene. Otherwise 24 hours	◖
19. Of all courts to total independence	NO	Special military courts may try profiteers, black-marketeers etc. for damage to economy	●
20. From civilian trials in secret	no	'In camera' if case taken over by military tribunal	◑
21. For independent trade unions	no	Strikes illegal. Long prison sentences	◑
22. From censorship of mail	yes	Occasional security checks only	◔
23. To publish and educate in ethnic languages	YES	Many ethnic groups without a written language	○

24. From deliberate state policies to control artistic works	**YES**		○
25. From compulsory military service	**YES**	Minimal selective scheme	◐
26. To purchase and drink alcohol	**YES**	From age 18 but not for orthodox Muslims	◐
27. To practise homosexuality between consenting adults	**NO**	Up to 10 years' prison	●
28. To use contraceptive pills and devices	yes	No state support	◑
29. Of early abortion	no	Only when mother's life at risk	◑
30. Of divorce (for men and women equally)	**YES**	But secular law not accepted by large Muslim majority	○

STATE POWER

31. Corporal punishment by state	By lashing. A 'common and swift punishment'	◑
32. Radio and TV broadcasts	State-controlled. No anti-state or anti-Islam comments	◑
33. Book publishing	Understood guidelines to prevent criticisms of president and religions	◑
34. Number of police and military per 100,000 citizens	450	○
35. % of national income spent on above	5%	◑
36. Weapons normally carried by civil police	Pistols	◑
37. Capital punishment by state	By hanging or firing squad. For trying to overthrow president, murder, organizing strikes etc.	●

MAXIMUM PUNISHMENTS IN PENAL CODE FOR:
(Freedom-related offences)

38. Non-violent anti-government activities	Death penalty if 'stability of the state' is threatened	●
39. Possession of banned political literature	Long detention if Communist Party member. Otherwise nominal fine	◑
40. Refusing compulsory national service	None	○

(Criminal offences)

41. Unlawful possession of 'hard' drugs	10–15 years' prison
42. Trading in pornography	Discretion of court
43. Illegal abortion	5 years' prison
44. Bigamy	Majority of men allowed 4 wives
45. Rape without other injury	15 years' prison

COMPULSORY DOCUMENTS FOR CITIZENS

46. Legally required at all times	ID cards
47. For employment	Card from employer's office
48. When applying for passport	Birth and nationality certificates
49. Period of validity of passport	10 years
50. Countries forbidden to holder	South Africa and Israel

Human rights rating: 62%

Population: 19,120,000
Life expectancy: 51
Infant mortality (0–1 year) per 1000 births: 175

Form of government: one-party state
Income per capita: US$ 300

Observations: Under the Preventive Detention Act (1962) the president may detain indefinitely any individual regarded as 'dangerous' to public order or security. The UN Covenant has been signed and ratified.

	FREEDOM/RIGHTS		Further comments	
1.	Of movement in own country	YES	Passports difficult to obtain.	○
2.	To leave own country	no	Currency shortages given as explanation	◑
3.	From deprivation of nationality	YES		○
4.	To seek information and teach ideas	yes	Government educational institutions conform to understood guidelines on public affairs	◑
5.	From serfdom, slavery, forced or child labour	yes	Regional pattern of child labour	◐
6.	Of peaceful political opposition	no	One-party system but greater degree of tolerance becoming evident	◑
7.	Of peaceful assembly and association	NO	If political, only in support of government	●
8.	Of women to equal rights	yes	Though many traditional (tribal) inequalities persist	◐
9.	From directed employment or work permits	YES		○
10.	Of inter-racial, inter-religious and civil marriage	YES		○
11.	To practise any religion	YES		○
12.	From compulsory religion or state ideology in schools	YES		○
13.	From political press censorship	NO	Government-owned. 'Nothing against the national interest'	●
14.	From police detention without charge	NO	Indefinite detention if regarded as dangerous to public order	●
15.	From police searches of home without warrant	no	Illegal searches for regime's opponents not always disciplined	◑
16.	From torture or coercion by state	yes	Local abuses on minor scale	◐
17.	Of assumption of innocence until guilt proved	no	Area of 'subversion' may permit abuses by police	◑
18.	Of accused to be promptly brought before judge or court	no	Under Detention Act rare cases where no recourse to judicial system	◑
19.	Of all courts to total independence	yes	A written order from president under Detention Act may override court ruling	◐
20.	From civilian trials in secret	YES		○
21.	For independent trade unions	NO	Strikes prohibited. Government-controlled	●
22.	From censorship of mail	no	Surveillance for currency irregularities and 'subversion'	◑
23.	To publish and educate in ethnic languages	YES		○
24.	From deliberate state policies to control artistic works	YES		○

25. From compulsory military service	**YES**		○
26. To purchase and drink alcohol	**YES**		○
27. To practise homosexuality between consenting adults	no	Illegal but authorities tolerant	◑
28. To use contraceptive pills and devices	**YES**		○
29. Of early abortion	no	Only when mother's life at risk	◑
30. Of divorce (for men and women equally)	**YES**		○

STATE POWER

31. Corporal punishment by state	Caning in penal code but rarely administered	◖
32. Radio and TV broadcasts	Government-owned and controlled. No TV on mainland (Zanzibar only)	●
33. Book publishing	Nothing directly subversive	◑
34. Number of police and military per 100,000 citizens	320	○
35. % of national income spent on above	7%	◖
36. Weapons normally carried by civil police	Batons	○
37. Capital punishment by state	By hanging. Treason, murder, intimidating judiciary etc.	●

MAXIMUM PUNISHMENTS IN PENAL CODE FOR:
(Freedom-related offences)

38. Non-violent anti-government activities	Indefinite detention for 'disrespect' towards president, state etc.	◑
39. Possession of banned political literature	Theoretical offence in practice	◖
40. Refusing compulsory national service	None	○

(Criminal offences)

41. Unlawful possession of 'hard' drugs	10 years' prison and/or heavy fine
42. Trading in pornography	Rare. Discretion of court
43. Illegal abortion	Discretion of court
44. Bigamy	Wronged party may sue. Polygamy legal for Muslims and 'traditional' marriages
45. Rape without other injury	Life sentence with or without corporal punishment

COMPULSORY DOCUMENTS FOR CITIZENS

46. Legally required at all times	ID card
47. For employment	None
48. When applying for passport	Birth certificate or affidavit
49. Period of validity of passport	5 years
50. Countries forbidden to holder	South Africa, Taiwan, S. Korea etc.

Human rights rating: 62%

Population: 6,392,000
Life expectancy: 59
Infant mortality (0–1 year) per 1000 births: 90

Form of government: one-party state (life-president)
Income per capita: US$ 1400

Observations: The UN Covenant was ratified in 1969 but violations of human rights occur in cases of serious opposition to the one-party government.

	FREEDOM/RIGHTS		Further comments	
1.	Of movement in own country	YES		◗
2.	To leave own country	yes	Passports sometimes withheld from critics of regime	◗
3.	From deprivation of nationality	YES		○
4.	To seek, receive and impart information and teach ideas	yes	Academics and universities display prudence on political and other issues	◗
5.	From serfdom, slavery, forced or child labour	yes	Child labour follows regional pattern	◗
6.	Of peaceful political opposition	no	Nominal opposition only. Communist Party illegal	◑
7.	Of peaceful assembly and association	no	No public opposition to president	◑
8.	Of women to equal rights	yes	By law but Islam is state religion and 99% are Muslims	◗
9.	From directed employment or work permits	YES		○
10.	Of inter-racial, inter-religious and civil marriage	YES		○
11.	To practise any religion	YES		○
12.	From compulsory religion or state ideology in schools	no	Islamic schools regard Islam as the basis of all education	◑
13.	From political press censorship	NO	Censorship. No criticism of president or senior officials	●
14.	From police detention without charge	NO	No time limit to bring charges	●
15.	From police searches of home without warrant	YES		○
16.	From torture or coercion by state	yes	Local abuses only though torture not directly prohibited	◗
17.	Of assumption of innocence until guilt proved	yes	Constitutional protection but wide interpretation of 'arrests on suspicion'	◗
18.	Of accused to be promptly brought before judge or court	NO	Indefinite period	●
19.	Of all courts to total independence	yes	Political and security cases may be influenced by higher authority	◗
20.	From civilian trials in secret	yes	Occasional security trials in camera	◗
21.	For independent trade unions	yes	Strikes technically illegal but little government interference	◑
22.	From censorship of mail	no	Political suspects subject to surveillance	◑
23.	To publish and educate in ethnic languages	YES		○
24.	From deliberate state policies to control artistic works	yes	But nothing that insults or satirizes president or religion	◗

25. From compulsory military service	no	12 months' selective	◑
26. To purchase and drink alcohol	**YES**	Some stores refuse to sell to Muslims	○
27. To practise homosexuality between consenting adults	no	But little harassment	◑
28. To use contraceptive pills and devices	**YES**		○
29. Of early abortion	**YES**	Up to 3 months	○
30. Of divorce (men and women equally)	**YES**	But overwhelming majority live by Sharia law	○

STATE POWER

31. Corporal punishment by state	None	○
32. Radio and TV broadcasts	State-owned and controlled	●
33. Book publishing	All publications need government authorization	◑
34. Number of police and military per 100,000 citizens	500	○
35. % of national income spent on above	3.5%	○
36. Weapons normally carried by civil police	Pistols	◑
37. Capital punishment by state	By hanging. Murder, treason, arson etc.	●

MAXIMUM PUNISHMENTS IN PENAL CODE FOR:
(Freedom-related offences)

38. Non-violent anti-government activities	Indefinite detention if threat to authority of president	◑
39. Possession of banned political literature	5 years' prison	●
40. Refusing compulsory national service	Limited detention	◑

(Criminal offences)

41. Unlawful possession of 'hard' drugs	5 years' prison
42. Trading in pornography	16 days to 5 years maximum
43. Illegal abortion	5 years' prison
44. Bigamy	6 months (by 1956 law)
45. Rape without other injury	5 years' prison

COMPULSORY DOCUMENTS FOR CITIZENS

46. Legally required at all times	ID card
47. For employment	None
48. When applying for passport	ID card, birth certificate
49. Period of validity of passport	5 years
50. Countries forbidden to holder	None

ZAIRE

Human rights rating: 41%

Population: 28,000,000
Life expectancy: 48
Infant mortality (0–1 year) per 1000 births: 171

Form of government: one-party state (executive president)
Income per capita: US$ 300

Observations: Little respect is paid to human rights despite the country having ratified the UN Covenant. The president has arbitrary powers, executions are numerous, and mostly occur in regions regarded as rebellious.

FREEDOM/RIGHTS		Further comments	
1. Of movement in own country	no	Banishment to own village a punishment for prisoners. Soldiers at some checkpoints demand money to augment low pay	◑
2. To leave own country	no	Exit visa needed. Bribes facilitate clearance	◑
3. From deprivation of nationality	NO	May be deprived on 'ethnic' grounds	●
4. To seek, receive and impart information and teach ideas	NO	One-party system dictates curricula. Non-conformist teachers arrested	●
5. From serfdom, slavery, forced or child labour	no	Forced and child labour common. For political or traditional reasons	◑
6. Of peaceful political opposition	NO	Formation of parties illegal. Citizens are assumed to belong to the single state party	●
7. Of peaceful assembly and association	no	Only permitted to favoured groups	◑
8. Of women to equal rights	no	Traditional social and domestic roles despite equality under law. Husband's permission needed to open bank account, own real estate etc.	◑
9. From directed employment or work permits	YES	Bribes and corruption dominate appointments to lucrative state posts	○
10. Of inter-racial, inter-religious and civil marriage	YES		○
11. To practise any religion	YES	But frequent tensions between president and Churches	○
12. From compulsory religion or state ideology in schools	YES		○
13. From political press censorship	NO	Government-controlled and censored. President may promulgate laws by decree	●
14. From police detention without charge	no	Legally 24 hours but extends to many months. Opportunities for seizing valuables by underpaid officers	◑
15. From police searches of home without warrant	NO	Excuse of 'national security' covers illegal entry. Property frequently stolen	●
16. From torture or coercion by state	NO	Routine torture and beatings to extort money from prisoners. Death sometimes follows	●
17. Of assumption of innocence until guilt proved	NO	Random arrests for political or security reasons	●
18. Of accused to be promptly brought before judge or court	NO	Arbitrary situation worsened by bribery and extortion practices	●

19. Of all courts to total independence	no	Corruption and bribery of judges a major factor. President may order military to take over civil courts	◑
20. From civilian trials in secret	NO	Arbitrary powers with president and appointees	●
21. For independent trade unions	NO	Only one government union, with restrictions on strikes	●
22. From censorship of mail	NO	Arbitrary powers to open mail	●
23. To publish and educate in ethnic languages	yes	Certain tribal groups have no written language	○
24. From deliberate state policies to control artistic works	yes	Care needed not to provoke authorities with works of critical social comment	◔
25. From compulsory military service	yes	Small-scale selective system	◔
26. To purchase and drink alcohol	YES		○
27. To practise homosexuality between consenting adults	NO	Illegal. Blackmail a common hazard	●
28. To use contraceptive pills and devices	YES		○
29. Of early abortion	no	Only when mother's life at risk	◐
30. Of divorce (men and women equally)	no	Men favoured in divorce settlements. Also in traditional tribal customs	◑

STATE POWER

31. Corporal punishment by state	Flogging	○
32. Radio and TV broadcasts	Government-controlled	●
33. Book publishing	Nothing critical of president	◔
34. Number of police and military per 100,000 citizens	220 (approx.)	○
35. % of national income spent on above	3%	○
36. Weapons normally carried by civil police	Sidearms	◔
37. Capital punishment by state	For treason, murder, embezzlement of public funds, arson etc.	●

MAXIMUM PUNISHMENTS IN PENAL CODE FOR:
(Freedom-related offences)

38. Non-violent anti-government activities	Death penalty for political opposition; embezzlement of public funds etc.	●
39. Possession of banned political literature	Indefinite detention while motives for possession examined.	◑
40. Refusing compulsory national service	None	○

(Criminal offences)

41. Unlawful possession of 'hard' drugs	5 years' prison
42. Trading in pornography	None
43. Illegal abortion	2 years' prison
44. Bigamy	Varies with traditional tribal customs
45. Rape without other injury	15 years' prison

COMPULSORY DOCUMENTS FOR CITIZENS

46. Legally required at all times	ID card
47. For employment	None
48. When applying for passport	ID card, identity affidavit etc.
49. Period of validity of passport	3 years
50. Countries forbidden to holder	South Africa

Human rights rating: 58%

Population: 6,020,000
Life expectancy: 49
**Infant mortality (0–1 year) per 1000
  births:** 144

Form of government: one-party state
Income per capita: US$ 550

Observations: Since 1964, the president has had special powers to detain, restrict etc., and parliament may suspend constitutional guarantees. As a one-party state, the human rights situation varies with the government's need to protect itself.

FREEDOM/RIGHTS		Further comments	
1. Of movement in own country	no	'State of emergency' since 1964 (Independence). Restrictions on dissidents	◑
2. To leave own country	NO	Passports of dissidents can be withheld	●
3. From deprivation of nationality	YES		○
4. To seek information and teach ideas	yes	But pressures on universities to support party and system	○
5. From serfdom, slavery, forced or child labour	yes	Child labour customs conform to regional traditions	◖
6. Of peaceful political opposition	NO	Opposition UP Party banned in 1972. Several hundred dissidents detained	●
7. Of peaceful assembly and association	NO	Only in support of government	●
8. Of women to equal rights	yes	Matters of inheritance, sterilization – under husband's control	◖
9. From directed employment or work permits	YES		○
10. Of inter-racial, inter-religious and civil marriage	YES		○
11. To practise any religion	yes	Except Jehovah's Witnesses	◑
12. From compulsory religion or state ideology in schools	YES		○
13. From political press censorship	no	Government-owned or 'guided'. Circumspection on president and ideology	◑
14. From police detention without charge	NO	Unlimited detention of political opponents on president's personal orders	●
15. From police searches of home without warrant	no	Broad powers of search when 'subversion' suspected	◑
16. From torture or coercion by state	yes	Many local abuses overlooked by authorities	◖
17. Of assumption of innocence until guilt proved	yes	Inconsistencies in practice contradict constitution	◖
18. Of accused to be promptly brought before judge or court	yes	Within 14 days but not always honoured in practice	◖
19. Of all courts to total independence	no	Subordinate to government but non-political trials fairly conducted	◑
20. From civilian trials in secret	yes	President may personally intervene in 'security' cases	◖
21. For independent trade unions	no	Unions form part of ruling party. Leaders compliant	◑
22. From censorship of mail	yes	But political suspects under surveillance	◖

23. To publish and educate in ethnic languages	YES		○
24. From deliberate state policies to control artistic works	YES		○
25. From compulsory military service	YES		○
26. To purchase and drink alcohol	YES	From age 16	○
27. To practise homosexuality between consenting adults	NO	14 years' gaol (maximum if charged). Visitors deported	●
28. To use contraceptive pills and devices	YES	State encouragement	○
29. Of early abortion	yes	Medical and social reasons but not on demand	◑
30. Of divorce (for men and women equally)	yes	Husbands favoured in divorce settlements	◑

STATE POWER

31. Corporal punishment by state	Caning for theft/burglary etc.	◑
32. Radio and TV broadcasts	All broadcasting subject to presidential decrees	◐
33. Book publishing	Many publications prohibited by presidential decrees	◐
34. Number of police and military per 100,000 citizens	120 police, 280 military	○
35. % of national income spent on above	15% (special economic factors)	◑
36. Weapons normally carried by civil police	Batons or sidearms	◑
37. Capital punishment by state	By hanging. Treason, murder, theft with violence etc.	●

MAXIMUM PUNISHMENTS IN PENAL CODE FOR:
(Freedom-related offences)

38. Non-violent anti-government activities	Indefinite detention under Preservation of Public Security Regulations	◐
39. Possession of banned political literature	2 years' prison for anti-presidential or seditious literature	◑
40. Refusing compulsory national service	None	○

(Criminal offences)

41. Unlawful possession of 'hard' drugs	3 years' prison and/or fine
42. Trading in pornography	2 years' prison
43. Illegal abortion	7 years' prison
44. Bigamy	5 years' prison
45. Rape without other injury	Life imprisonment

COMPULSORY DOCUMENTS FOR CITIZENS

46. Legally required at all times	None
47. For employment	National Registration Card
48. When applying for passport	NRC and proof of nationality
49. Period of validity of passport	5 years
50. Countries forbidden to holder	None

Human rights rating: 68%

Population: 7,600,000
Life expectancy: 55
Infant mortality (0–1 year) per 1000 births: 120

Form of government: parliamentary system
Income per capita: US$ 700

Observations: The Temporary Emergency Powers Act gives the government ultimate authority in most areas. In practice this is confined to security but a worsening of regional opposition could lead to more human rights violations. Executive rule by decree ignores parliament.

FREEDOM/RIGHTS		Further comments	
1. Of movement in own country	yes	Security risks occasionally limit free movement	◐
2. To leave own country	yes	Emergency Powers Act covers list of prohibited dissidents (passports withdrawn)	◐
3. From deprivation of nationality	YES		○
4. To seek, receive and impart information and teach ideas	YES		○
5. From serfdom, slavery, forced or child labour	yes	Regional pattern of child labour	◐
6. Of peaceful political opposition	yes	Evidence of a less tolerant attitude by government, which favours a one-party state	◐
7. Of peaceful assembly and association	yes	Written authority from Ministry of Home Affairs for political rallies	◐
8. Of women to equal rights	yes	Areas of traditional roles still persist	◐
9. From directed employment or work permits	YES		○
10. Of inter-racial, inter-religious and civil marriage	YES		○
11. To practise any religion	YES		○
12. From compulsory religion or state ideology in schools	YES		○
13. From political press censorship	yes	Degree of inhibition. Press very conscious of 'official line'. Government owns major newspapers	◐
14. From police detention without charge	NO	Indefinite detention under renewed Emergency Powers Act	●
15. From police searches of home without warrant	no	Emergency Act may dispense with warrant when 'reasonably justified'	◑
16. From torture or coercion by state	no	Local abuses by over-zealous police	◑
17. Of assumption of innocence until guilt proved	no	But application of Emergency Powers may be arbitrary	◑
18. Of accused to be promptly brought before judge or court	yes	'As soon as reasonably practical'. This is usually honoured	○
19. Of all courts to total independence	no	Subject to ultimate Emergency Powers. From 1981 village courts deal with minor cases	○
20. From civilian trials in secret	no	In camera only for protection of minors but Emergency Act may be enforced	◑
21. For independent trade unions	yes	Government restrictions only when strikes considered to be over-disruptive	◐

22. From censorship of mail	yes	Occasionally. Covered by Law and Order Maintenance Act	◖
23. To publish and educate in ethnic languages	**YES**	Encouraged	○
24. From deliberate state policies to control artistic works	**YES**		○
25. From compulsory military service	**YES**		○
26. To purchase and drink alcohol	**YES**	From 18 years	○
27. To practise homosexuality between consenting adults	**YES**	Over 18 (but under old constitution, which may be changed)	○
28. To use contraceptive pills and devices	**YES**	State-aided	○
29. Of early abortion	no	Only when mother's life at risk	◑
30. Of divorce (men and women equally)	**YES**		○

STATE POWER

31. Corporal punishment by state	Cane	◐
32. Radio and TV broadcasts	Government-controlled but not a party propaganda machine	◐
33. Book publishing	Recent banning orders	◐
34. Number of police and military per 100,000 citizens	600	◐
35. % of national income spent on above	16% (post-Independence factors)	◑
36. Weapons normally carried by civil police	Batons	◐
37. Capital punishment by state	Death penalty resumed after 2 years' respite	◑

MAXIMUM PUNISHMENTS IN PENAL CODE FOR:
(Freedom-related offences)

38. Non-violent anti-government activities	10 years' prison for 'anti-government activities'	◑
39. Possession of banned political literature	2 years' prison and/or fine	◐
40. Refusing compulsory national service	None	○

(Criminal offences)

41. Unlawful possession of 'hard' drugs	10 years' prison and/or heavy fine for either possession or trafficking
42. Trading in pornography	2 years' prison and/or $1000 fine
43. Illegal abortion	10 years' prison
44. Bigamy	Discretion of court
45. Rape without other injury	No maximum. Possibly death penalty

COMPULSORY DOCUMENTS FOR CITIZENS

46. Legally required at all times	None but National Registration Scheme being introduced
47. For employment	None
48. When applying for passport	Birth certificate, proof of citzenship
49. Period of validity of passport	10 years
50. Countries forbidden to holder	None

Human rights rating: POOR

Population: 7,600,000
Life expectancy: 43
Infant mortality (0–1 year) per 1000
  births: 192

Form of government: one-party state
Income per capita: US$ 700

Observations: With the country divided by civil war it would be unrealistic to infer that the Guide's questionnaire could apply to the whole population.

Summary

The prolonged civil war, in which the government is fighting the powerful UNITA movement, has meant a continuation of restrictions on political freedom, travel within and outside the country, and on all forms of independent social expression.

The position is further complicated by the presence of a large force of Cuban and Soviet-bloc advisers to reinforce both the political and military purpose of the Angolan government. Torture is frequently reported to have taken place, summary executions of UNITA prisoners or supporters are commonplace, and the number of people in detention is understood to be large.

The new constitution guarantees most human rights but there is the qualification that the honouring of these rights depends on whether they help 'realize the fundamental objectives of the People's Republic of Angola' and are 'in the national interest'.

Trade unions are controlled and strikes forbidden but women are gaining more freedom and equality. This is also true for many ethnic groups previously oppressed under colonial rule or by each other. With UNITA receiving considerable support and arms from South Africa, it is difficult to predict the course of events or when the country will be at peace and in a position to improve the human rights situation.

Human rights rating: POOR

Population: 8,503,000
Life expectancy: 46
Infant mortality (0–1 year) per 1000
  births: 157

Form of government: one-party state
Income per capita: US$ 300

Observations: There has been continuity of one-party civilian rule since 1960 and human rights violations have decreased.

Summary

The joining of ex-British and ex-French colonies in 1961 to form the country has given a policy of national unity the highest priority but this is imposed under a one-party system. The result has been severe restrictions on assembly and association, on press freedom and on political opposition. An exit visa is necessary for foreign travel (women can only leave with their husbands' permission) and a state of emergency in a limited area of the country prevents total internal freedom of movement. Charges of torture have been brought against the police, interrogation of dissidents is occasionally harsh and followed by 'administrative detention' in special camps.

The death penalty exists for armed robbery as well as treason and murder, and for 'possessing in suspicious circumstances tools for opening locks'.

Broadcasting is controlled, academic life subject to surveillance, and books critical of the government banned. The role of women in social and national affairs is improving and some hold cabinet positions. Freedom of religion is permitted, though the Jehovah's Witnesses are proscribed, and animism is the belief of a section of the population. The government has powers under the law to imprison those practising witchcraft and sorcery.

Human rights rating: POOR

Population: 11,450,000
Life expectancy: 49
Infant mortality (0–1 year) per 1000 births: 115

Form of government: military junta
Income per capita: US$ 500

Observations: After the second seizure of power in three years by an air-force officer (civilian rule had been restored after the first) and with the constitution temporarily suspended, a detailed completion of the Guide's questionnaire would have only a brief relevancy.

Summary

The last decade has seen a succession of civilian and military governments, the latest being led by an air-force officer who seized power at the end of 1981.

The constitution was immediately suspended, parliament dismissed and all political-party and opposition activities banned. The press, radio and television are totally controlled, police power alternates in its severity with the changing governments as does the degree of torture and the ignoring of legal safeguards for those arrested.

Departure from the country is subject to strict scrutiny and an opposition in exile is regarded as a threat by the government.

If the constitution is restored and honoured, as was briefly the situation, the human rights position should improve significantly.

Human rights rating: POOR

Population: 5,014,000
Life expectancy: 45
Infant mortality (0–1 year) per 1000
　births: 175 (1972)

Form of government: one-party
Marxist state
Income per capita: US$ 300

Observations: Despite having ratified the UN Covenant, most human rights are violated. Torture is not by law prohibited.

Summary

The regime of President Sekou Toure, unchanged since independence from France in 1958, appears more assured of its survival and there has been a reduction of political prisoners under detention. Nevertheless, security is strict and the population is expected to follow the single-party policies.

Opponents may suffer preventive detention, torture and general police brutality. There have also been cases of execution for political offences. There is complete control over the press and other media, the police are empowered to enter homes arbitrarily and the president is reported to have exhorted both national and foreign residents to 'kill all thieves with any means at their disposal'.

Travel abroad and public assembly are controlled and suspects can be held without charge, but since many tribal groups inhabit both sides of the state frontiers, free movement is usually tolerated in these regions. Trade unions are a political arm of the government and do not enjoy independence.

Efforts have been made to improve the status of women and overcome traditional customs that limit their role. They now hold senior state positions and are allowed careers in politics, the military and the police.

Human rights rating: FAIR

Population: 8,400,000
Life expectancy: 48
Infant mortality (0–1 year) per 1000
   births: 127

Form of government: one-party state
Income per capita: US$ 1400

Observations: The country has not signed the UN Covenant but the human rights situation, related to its geographical position, is reasonable.

Summary

Despite the restrictions of a single-party government intolerant of opposition, a degree of freedom of speech, of assembly and of travel within the country and abroad is permitted. The media are government-controlled and there is occasional suppression of critical literature. Religions are free to practise and human rights groups are permitted to operate.

Capital punishment has not been inflicted since 1960 and has been abolished for political crimes. Nevertheless, no political opposition can be formed and the police are sometimes over-zealous in enforcing conformity. In the case of house searches without warrants, for example, breaches are covered by a vague 'police must have reason for searching . . .'

The legal system, although having to conform to party 'guidance', grants a fair public trial to the accused, but tribal courts at village level are subject to traditional customs. The device of threatening to conscript strikers is used, trade unions and the government being closely associated.

About one quarter of the population is of foreign African descent and the government's policy of Ivorianization is frequently to their disadvantage. Large resources are being devoted to education but in the underprivileged Muslim north of the country, boys are given preference for school places.

Human rights rating: BAD

Population: 2,850,000
Life expectancy: 55
**Infant mortality (0–1 year) per 1000
 births:** 53

Form of government: Islamic socialist
 regime
Income per capita: US$ 8500

Observations: This country is presented in summary form because of conflicting information and the refusal of official sources to reply to inquiries. The country has ratified the UN Covenant.

Summary

The human rights position is best related to a statement by the country's leader, Colonel Gaddafi: 'It is a matter of honour to jail or liquidate the enemies of the authorities.' This principle is being energetically pursued, the 'liquidation' extending even to dissidents living abroad.

Summary executions of both political and religious opponents occur frequently, large numbers being arrested without further information being given, and there is widespread evidence of torture. Ratification of human rights agreements has been accompanied by increased violations.

Court procedures now include the establishment of People's Courts, trials also being held in camera and with fewer safeguards for the accused. Some trials, with a view to warning the opposition, have been televised. Broadcasting is an instrument of government, newspapers adhere to official policy, and editorials and similar comments are discouraged.

As a 'Republic of the Masses', trade unions and local committees are pressed to participate in workers' control and management and, following state policy, are attempting to achieve a fusion of national socialism and orthodox Islamic beliefs.

MADAGASCAR

Human rights rating: POOR

Population: 8,742,000
Life expectancy: 43
Infant mortality (0–1 year) per 1000 births: 160

Form of government: one-party state
Income per capita: US$ 325

Observations: This country is presented in summary form because of the unreliability of information and the failure of official sources to reply to inquiries. Madagascar has ratified the UN Covenant.

Summary

Political activity, after the 1975 referendum, is prohibited if it conflicts with the National Front for the Defence of the Republic. This has meant limitation of free speech and assembly and pre-publication censorship of the press. The penal code in the style of the previous French colonial power has been retained but capital punishment has not been implemented since 1958.

The influence of women is an unusual feature of society and they make up a third of the country's magistrates as well as being active in political and party life.

Court procedures are not repressive though dissidents can be held incommunicado for long periods. Several foreigners and military officers have been imprisoned without trial and accusations of torture have been made against police at local level. The major area of violence, however, does not relate to human rights but to traditional ethnic conflicts between tribes. This occurs despite the constitutional prohibition of 'tribalism'.

75% of the country's economy has been nationalized and trade unions which are not affiliated to acceptable political groups suffer harassment.

MALAWI

Human rights rating: POOR

Population: 6,100,000
Life expectancy: 48
Infant mortality (0–1 year) per 1000 births: 172

Form of government: one-party state
Income per capita: US$ 220

Observations: Information on political detainees is difficult to obtain and official sources failed to reply satisfactorily to inquiries. Malawi accused by UN of gross abuses of civil rights.

Summary

Since independence in 1964, the Malawi Congress Party and its leader Life-President Banda have ruled the country. There is little political opposition within Malawi, the small group of dissidents preferring to live abroad. The president's present security of authority has encouraged the release from detention of opponents arrested earlier – to be replaced in prison by more recent dissidents.

A secure paternalist rule extends to full control of broadcasting and to recognized guidelines for the single national newspaper. A puritanical view is taken of printed matter of a sexually explicit or prurient nature. Strikes do not occur because the trade unions are associated with the ruling political party but students are permitted to read what would normally be regarded as radical literature on the understanding that their interest remains academic.

Law courts are both modern and African-traditional, for criminal and civil cases respectively, and there are few abuses though some administrative delays in the system. Women enjoy greater equality than in most countries of the region.

Special permission is needed for foreign journalists visiting Malawi. To attend school, children must join the party and pay a small annual subscription.

Human rights rating: POOR

Population: 5,000,000
Life expectancy: 48
Infant mortality (0–1 year) per 1000
  births: 160 (approx.)

Form of government: one-party state
Income per capita: US$ 250

Observations: Rwanda has ratified the UN Covenant. Geographical remoteness, poverty, and the recent evolution from a backward feudal system have made it inadvisable, on the information available, to complete the Guide's questionnaire.

Summary

In 1973, the majority Hutu tribe (80%) overthrew the Tutsi (14%), who had previously dominated the country. Since the coup d'état, the present president and his National Revolutionary Movement have been in power. A competent administration in this emergent state is still in the process of formation and although the constitution declares its intention to conform to the UN *Universal Declaration of Human Rights*, there have been reports of various violations.

The State Security Court has sentenced to death a number of political opponents for plotting the government's fall or the president's assassination, and the penal code permits prison sentences for anyone distributing leaflets inciting public dissatisfaction. A legal system which is generally impartial (apart from security and public order cases) is handicapped by the shortage of trained professionals. The radio and an infrequent national newspaper are government-owned and controlled.

The constitution permits the establishment of unions and the right to strike but, in practice, there are no unions. Freedom of movement is not always easy; passports are difficult to obtain and a deposit of US$ 400 has to be paid for them.

Every citizen is automatically made a member of the National Revolutionary Movement although women do not enjoy either equal rights or opportunities.

SIERRA LEONE

Human rights rating: FAIR

Population: 3,474,000
Life expectancy: 47.5
Infant mortality (0–1 year) per 1000
  births: 136

Form of government: one-party state
Income per capita: US$ 250

Observations: Dissident groups in the US and the UK still challenge the All People's Congress, the single ruling party. The country has not signed the UN Covenant.

Summary

A one-party state promulgated in 1978, the president has power to call for repressive measures or for a state of emergency. The opposition, both at home and abroad, has not been on a scale to call for such action.

The state of emergency powers, if exercised, could extend to indefinite detention of dissidents, the deregistering of critical newspapers and the control of a loosely-formed trade union movement. Travel inside the country and abroad is generally unrestricted and there is little interference with the many minority tribes and religious bodies.

The position of women is guaranteed in the constitution but because of the country's recent independence (1961), after more than a hundred years of colonial rule, their roles vary from traditional rural styles to high political and professional positions in the capital.

As a poor country, with the position worsened by widespread corruption at all levels, the government has been unable to implement its social welfare programme. However, the National Population Commission was established in 1982 for the purpose of planning future population growth and increasing the people's awareness of related issues.

Human rights rating: POOR

Population: 4,637,000

Life expectancy: 43

Infant mortality (0–1 year) per 1000 births: 146

Form of government: one-party state

Income per capita: US$ 350

Observations: This country is presented in summary form because of the unreliability of information and the failure of official sources to reply to inquiries.

Summary

All authority rests in the hands of President Sidi Barre and a few close associates. In spite of constitutional guarantees most human rights are restricted. The press is entirely government-controlled and, while the constitution provides for freedom of speech and assembly, it adds that their exercise must not contravene the 'laws of the land, general morality and public order'.

Trade unions are part of the government apparatus and strikes are forbidden. The constitution stipulates that the state religion is Islam, and Muslims and others may practise their faiths so long as there is no challenge to the authorities.

All participation in public affairs is centrally directed and under the auspices of the only legal party, the Somali Socialist Revolutionary Party. Detention without charge or trial, harsh prison conditions and the use of the death penalty are commonplace, as well as allegations of torture.

The state of emergency of 1980 gives the president extra powers and a year later 5000 prisoners were released under an amnesty. On the other hand executions of embezzlers of public funds were reported, while political prisoners were denied visits from their families.

The viability of this impoverished country depends on extensive outside aid. The position is made even more critical by the continuing war against Ethiopia and the influx of large numbers of refugees.

UGANDA

Human rights rating: POOR

Population: 12,630,076
Life expectancy: 52
Infant mortality (0–1 year) per 1000 births: 120

Form of government: disputed parliamentary system
Income per capita: US$ 450

Observations: The anarchic state of the country, which is fragmented by armed and tribal disputes, makes it inadvisable to attempt to complete the Guide's questionnaire.

Summary

After the departure in 1979 of dictator Idi Amin, Ugandan politics and society were subjected to a number of successive governments and internal disputes. A period in which law and order broke down appears to be ending and the present president, Milton Obote, after being voted into power in an election which the opposition claimed to be fraudulent, is attempting to restore both the economy and normal social life. On the other hand, in view of the many unpredictable factors, including powerful opposition groups abroad, the prospect of stability may seem to be optimistic.

After the withdrawal of most Tanzanian troops in 1981 (following their victory over the Amin forces), it was left to an assortment of Ugandan military units to maintain order. The result, so far as human rights are concerned, has been a continuation of the catalogue of summary deaths, detention and imprisonment, torture and disappearances. The brutality of the instances of torture, with the military barracks in the vicinity of Kampala as favourite locations, frequently lead to death, with the bodies dumped into rivers and lakes. The government claims to be blameless for these excesses and powerless to stop them.

Constitutional guarantees are therefore of little value when the transgressions of the security forces go unchallenged. Villages are plundered, particularly when there are tribal hostilities, and houses and premises in towns are searched without warrants and frequently looted. Trade-union leadership is closely associated with the Obote government but the Law Society has managed to maintain a degree of independence.

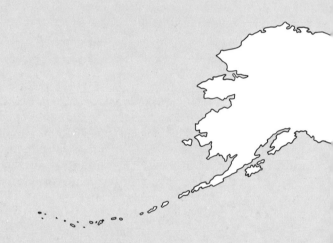

Most human rights respected
Many human rights denied
Most human rights denied

America, North and Central

CANADA

USA

MEXICO

CUBA

DOMINICAN
REP

HAITI

GUATEMALA

EL SALVADOR

HONDURAS

NICARAGUA

PANAMA

Canada
Cuba
Mexico
Panama
United States of America
Dominican Republic
El Salvador
Guatemala
Haiti
Honduras
Nicaragua

Human rights rating: 94%

Population: 24,350,000
Life expectancy: 74
Infant mortality (0–1 year) per 1000 births: 12

Form of government: federal parliamentary state
Income per capita: US$ 10,400

Observations: Satisfactory.

FREEDOM/RIGHTS		Further comments	
1. Of movement in own country	YES		○
2. To leave own country	YES		○
3. From deprivation of nationality	YES		○
4. To seek information and teach ideas	YES		○
5. From serfdom, slavery, forced or child labour	YES		○
6. Of peaceful political opposition	YES	Federal civil servants not to participate in political campaigns	○
7. Of peaceful assembly and association	YES	Subject to maintenance of law and order	○
8. Of women to equal rights	yes	New Charter of Rights strengthens equality. Minor violations in pay/pensions	◑
9. From directed employment or work permits	YES		○
10. Of inter-racial, inter-religious and civil marriage	YES		○
11. To practise any religion	YES		○
12. From compulsory religion or state ideology in schools	YES		○
13. From political press censorship	YES	117 daily newspapers (1980)	○
14. From police detention without charge	YES		○
15. From police searches of home without warrant	yes	Local police abuses under guise of security checks	◑
16. From torture or coercion by state	YES		○
17. Of assumption of innocence until guilt proved	YES		○
18. Of accused to be promptly brought before judge or court	YES		○
19. Of all courts to total independence	YES		○
20. From civilian trials in secret	YES	Espionage trials may be in camera	○
21. For independent trade unions	YES		○
22. From censorship of mail	YES		○
23. To publish and educate in ethnic languages	YES	New constitution corrects French/English language anomalies. Commissioner reviews violations	○
24. From deliberate state policies to control artistic works	YES		○
25. From compulsory military service	YES		○
26. To purchase and drink alcohol	YES	Minimum age varies with provincial laws	○
27. To practise homosexuality between consenting adults	YES	Over 21 years. No encouraging of minors	○
28. To use contraceptive pills and devices	YES		○

29. Of early abortion	no	Medical reasons only	
30. Of divorce (for men and women equally)	yes	Slight discrimination in divorce settlements favour men	

STATE POWER
31. Corporal punishment by state — None
32. Radio and TV broadcasts — No political controls or bias in national and private networks
33. Book publishing — No state control
34. Number of police and military per 100,000 citizens — 275 police 335 military
35. % of national income spent on above — 3.5%
36. Weapons normally carried by civil police — .38 revolvers
37. Capital punishment by state — Abolished 1976 except for military in time of war

MAXIMUM PUNISHMENTS IN PENAL CODE FOR:
(Freedom-related offences)
38. Non-violent anti-government activities — None
39. Possession of banned political literature — None
40. Refusing compulsory national service — None

(Criminal offences)
41. Unlawful possession of 'hard' drugs — 7 years' prison. 14 for trafficking
42. Trading in pornography — 2 years' prison
43. Illegal abortion — Self-induced by mother 2 years; maximum of life for others
44. Bigamy — 5 years' prison
45. Rape without other injury — Life imprisonment

COMPULSORY DOCUMENTS FOR CITIZENS
46. Legally required at all times — None
47. For employment — Insurance card
48. When applying for passport — Birth certificate and verification of photo
49. Period of validity of passport — 5 years
50. Countries forbidden to holder — None

Human rights rating: 30%

Population: 10,000,000
Life expectancy: 72
Infant mortality (0–1 year) per 1000 births: 25

Form of government: one-party Marxist state
Income per capita: US$ 1400

Observations: Despite the importance of human rights in the 1976 constitution, the government retains the power to ban all activities it claims to be in opposition to state and party.

	FREEDOM/RIGHTS		Further comments	
1.	Of movement in own country	YES		○
2.	To leave own country	NO	Exit visa required	●
3.	From deprivation of nationality	NO	Dissidents have been subjected to forced emigration	●
4.	To seek information and teach ideas	NO	Teaching and textbooks must be approved	●
5.	From serfdom, slavery, forced or child labour	NO	Forced labour for political prisoners	●
6.	Of peaceful political opposition	NO	Constitution states that no freedoms can be exercised which are 'contrary to the building of Socialism and Communism'	●
7.	Of peaceful assembly and association	NO		●
8.	Of women to equal rights	yes	Constitutional equality but no women in top politburo	◑
9.	From directed employment or work permits	NO	Permits denied to many former political prisoners who are left without means of support	●
10.	Of inter-racial, inter-religious and civil marriage	YES		○
11.	To practise any religion	yes	But harassment of beliefs 'opposed to the constitution'	◑
12.	From compulsory religion or state ideology in schools	NO	Marxist-Leninism compulsory in schools	●
13.	From political press censorship	NO	Total party/state control. No dissent permitted	●
14.	From police detention without charge	NO	Arbitrary powers despite constitutional protection	●
15.	From police searches of home without warrant	no	Security services' request for warrants a formality	◑
16.	From torture or coercion by state	no	Significant decrease in cases of torture but 'intransigents' denied facilities in prison	◑
17.	Of assumption of innocence until guilt proved	NO	'Counter-revolutionary' suspects denied legal safeguards	●
18.	Of accused to be promptly brought before judge or court	NO	Indefinite period before being brought to trial	●
19.	Of all courts to total independence	NO	All lawyers controlled by guild. Certain cases prejudged	●
20.	From civilian trials in secret	NO	Arbitrary state decisions	●
21.	For independent trade unions	NO	Party-controlled Federation of Cuban Workers	●
22.	From censorship of mail	NO		●

23. To publish and educate in ethnic languages	YES		○
24. From deliberate state policies to control artistic works	no	Pressures to conform to social realism. 'Art must serve the people'	◑
25. From compulsory military service	NO	3 year conscription from age 17	●
26. To purchase and drink alcohol	YES		○
27. To practise homosexuality between consenting adults	NO	Fine US$ 270 (crime against morality)	●
28. To use contraceptive pills and devices	YES	Government support	○
29. Of early abortion	YES		○
30. Of divorce (for men and women equally)	YES		○

STATE POWER

31. Corporal punishment by state	Unlawful beatings tolerated by higher authorities	◑
32. Radio and TV broadcasts	Total state control	●
33. Book publishing	Total state control	●
34. Number of police and military per 100,000 citizens	4800 (including People's Militia)	●
35. % of national income spent on above	15%	◑
36. Weapons normally carried by civil police	Sidearms	◑
37. Capital punishment by state	By shooting. Many offences including treason, rape, arson, anti-state theft etc.	●

MAXIMUM PUNISHMENTS IN PENAL CODE FOR:
(Freedom-related offences)

38. Non-violent anti-government activities	Indefinite detention	◑
39. Possession of banned political literature	30 years' prison if intentions are 'anti-state'	◑
40. Refusing compulsory national service	Indefinite detention if regarded as an 'anti-state action'	◑

(Criminal offences)

41. Unlawful possession of 'hard' drugs	10 years' prison
42. Trading in pornography	1 year's prison
43. Illegal abortion	1 year when self-induced, 2 years for other parties
44. Bigamy	2–6 years' prison
45. Rape without other injury	10 years' prison

COMPULSORY DOCUMENTS FOR CITIZENS

46. Legally required at all times	ID card (carnet)
47. For employment	ID card
48. When applying for passport	ID card, birth certificate, police clearance
49. Period of validity of passport	3 to 5 years
50. Countries forbidden to holder	None

Human rights rating: 67%

Population: 69,200,000
Life expectancy: 67
Infant mortality (0–1 year) per 1000 births: 52

Form of government: one-party state
Income per capita: US$ 2720

Observations: Despite having recently signed the UN Covenant, the human rights situation is unsatisfactory, a contradiction that is blamed on the existence of 'terrorist' groups.

FREEDOM/RIGHTS		Further comments	
1. Of movement in own country	YES		◐
2. To leave own country	YES		◐
3. From deprivation of nationality	YES		◐
4. To seek, receive and impart information and teach ideas	yes	Universities avoid offending authorities in political and other sensitive areas	◑
5. From serfdom, slavery, forced or child labour	yes	Child labour in rural areas	◐
6. Of peaceful political opposition	no	Token presidential candidates and nine opposition parties but government PRI has real and absolute control	◑
7. Of peaceful assembly and association	yes	Occasional police restrictions	◐
8. Of women to equal rights	yes	Legally equal but tradition and customs still strong	◐
9. From directed employment or work permits	YES		○
10. Of inter-racial, inter-religious and civil marriage	YES		○
11. To practise any religion	yes	Clergy must avoid politics and not criticize social practices	◐
12. From compulsory religion or state ideology in schools	YES		○
13. From political press censorship	yes	Circumspection necessary. No criticism of president. Newsprint a state monopoly	◐
14. From police detention without charge	NO	Despite constitution, 500 possible dissidents declared missing in 1981	●
15. From police searches of home without warrant	no	Political and 'hot pursuit' searches without warrant but seizing remote homes and land of peasants is a better indication of rural police practices	◑
16. From torture or coercion by state	no	Prohibited by law but terrorists, drug-traffickers etc. subject to severe torture. Deaths and disappearances have followed interrogation	◑
17. Of assumption of innocence until guilt proved	no	Wide police powers to arrest political or guerrilla suspects	◑
18. Of accused to be promptly brought before judge or court	no	Long delays may relate to too many arrests on suspicion of *planning* crimes	◑
19. Of all courts to total independence	no	Only in nominal sense. Ultimate authority with president	◑

20. From civilian trials in secret	yes	Security cases. Definition decided by police
21. For independent trade unions	no	95% of workers in party-affiliated unions. Extreme unions not allowed to register
22. From censorship of mail	yes	Except in security cases
23. To publish and educate in ethnic languages	**YES**	
24. From deliberate state policies to control artistic works	**YES**	
25. From compulsory military service	yes	Small selective intake by lottery system at age 18
26. To purchase and drink alcohol	**YES**	
27. To practise homosexuality between consenting adults	**NO**	6 months' – 5 years' prison for 'immoral behaviour'
28. To use contraceptive pills and devices	**YES**	
29. Of early abortion	no	Only when mother's life at risk
30. Of divorce (for men and women equally)	**YES**	

STATE POWER

31. Corporal punishment by state	Forbidden but see 16
32. Radio and TV broadcasts	Most censorship is on moral grounds
33. Book publishing	No criticism of incumbent president
34. Number of police and military per 100,000 citizens	350 (not including part-time conscripts)
35. % of national income spent on above	3%
36. Weapons normally carried by civil police	Sidearms
37. Capital punishment by state	Recently abolished

MAXIMUM PUNISHMENTS IN PENAL CODE FOR:

(Freedom-related offences)

38. Non-violent anti-government activities	40 years' prison ('acts against integrity of Mexican nation')
39. Possession of banned political literature	5 years' prison
40. Refusing compulsory national service	Many civil rights withdrawn. Passport, social security etc.

(Criminal offences)

41. Unlawful possession of 'hard' drugs	10 years' prison
42. Trading in pornography	5 years' prison
43. Illegal abortion	1 year when self-induced
44. Bigamy	5 years' prison
45. Rape without other injury	16 years' prison

COMPULSORY DOCUMENTS FOR CITIZENS

46. Legally required at all times	ID card
47. For employment	Military Service card, Social Security number
48. When applying for passport	Birth certificate, Military Service card
49. Period of validity of passport	5 years
50. Countries forbidden to holder	None

PANAMA

Human rights rating: 84%

Population: 2,000,000
Life expectancy: 71
Infant mortality (0–1 year) per 1000 births: 21

Form of government: parliamentary democracy
Income per capita: US$ 1550

Observations: After the military coup of 1968, political activity was inhibited until Legislative Council elections in 1980. General elections with full party participation are planned for 1984.

	FREEDOM/RIGHTS		Further comments
1.	Of movement in own country	YES	
2.	To leave own country	YES	
3.	From deprivation of nationality	YES	
4.	To seek information and teach ideas	YES	
5.	From serfdom, slavery, forced or child labour	yes	Regional pattern of casual child labour
6.	Of peaceful political opposition	yes	But the National Guard continues to be active though not oppressive in politics
7.	Of peaceful assembly and association	yes	The qualification of a 'legitimate' purpose gives authorities arbitrary powers.
8.	Of women to equal rights	yes	Constitutional rights are not always enjoyed socially or in employment
9.	From directed employment or work permits	YES	
10.	Of inter-racial, inter-religious and civil marriage	YES	
11.	To practise any religion	YES	
12.	From compulsory religion or state ideology in schools	YES	
13.	From political press censorship	yes	But occasional government restrictions on public order and security issues
14.	From police detention without charge	YES	
15.	From police searches of home without warrant	YES	
16.	From torture or coercion by state	yes	Local abuses only
17.	Of assumption of innocence until guilt proved	yes	A few summary hearings before 'night court' judges limit proper defence for accused
18.	Of accused to be promptly brought before judge or court	YES	
19.	Of all courts to total independence	yes	Military intelligence permitted to review court procedures
20.	From civilian trials in secret	YES	
21.	For independent trade unions	YES	
22.	From censorship of mail	YES	
23.	To publish and educate in ethnic languages	YES	
24.	From deliberate state policies to control artistic works	YES	
25.	From compulsory military service	YES	
26.	To purchase and drink alcohol	YES	

27. To practise homosexuality between consenting adults	**NO**	Short prison sentence	●
28. To use contraceptive pills and devices	**YES**		○
29. Of early abortion	**NO**	Illegal for any reason	●
30. Of divorce (for men and women equally)	**YES**	But majority of population devout Catholics	○

STATE POWER

31. Corporal punishment by state	None	○
32. Radio/TV companies and broadcasts	Part government-owned and occasional pressures on other stations	○
33. General book publishing	Penalties when government feels publication against public interest	○
34. Number of police and military per 100,000 population	700 National Guard includes both the military and police	○
35. % of national income spent on above	2%	○
36. Weapons normally carried by civil police	Pistols	○
37. Capital punishment by state	No death penalty. Constitution limits punishments to 20 years' prison	○

MAXIMUM PUNISHMENTS IN PENAL CODE FOR:
(Freedom-related offences)

38. Non-violent anti-government activities	2 years' prison if 'affecting public order'	○
39. Possession of banned political literature	None	○
40. Refusing compulsory national service	None	○

(Criminal offences)

41. Unlawful possession of 'hard' drugs	15 years' prison
42. Trading in pornography	Fines and confiscation
43. Illegal abortion	2 years' prison
44. Bigamy	18 months' 'arresto' but second marriage 'impossible' for Catholic population
45. Rape without other injury	5 years' prison (under review)

COMPULSORY DOCUMENTS FOR CITIZENS

46. Legally required at all times	ID card
47. For employment	Nothing
48. When applying for passport	ID card/proof of nationality
49. Period of validity of passport	5 years
50. Countries forbidden to holder	None

Human rights rating: 92%

Population: 229,805,000
Life expectancy: 73
Infant mortality (0–1 year) per 1000 births: 13

Form of government: federal democracy
Income per capita: US$ 12,000

Observations: Satisfactory. Each of 50 states has a different penal code. For this reason the maximum punishments of the District of Columbia (Washington), which is most influenced by Federal law, has been quoted as representing an approximate consensus.

FREEDOM/RIGHTS		Further comments
1. Of movement in own country	YES	
2. To leave own country	YES	
3. From deprivation of nationality	YES	
4. To seek information and teach ideas	YES	
5. From serfdom, slavery, forced or child labour	YES	
6. Of peaceful political opposition	YES	
7. Of peaceful assembly and association	YES	Police permits required and invariably granted though some states less liberal
8. Of women to equal rights	YES	Certain women's groups allege areas of inequality
9. From directed employment or work permits	YES	
10. Of inter-racial, inter-religious and civil marriage	YES	
11. To practise any religion	YES	
12. From compulsory religion or state ideology in schools	YES	
13. From political press censorship	YES	
14. From police detention without charge	yes	Limited investigative detention varies from state to state
15. From police searches of home without warrant	YES	Except when in 'hot pursuit'
16. From torture or coercion by state	yes	Rare local abuses. Such cases investigated by FBI
17. Of assumption of innocence until guilt proved	YES	
18. Of accused to be promptly brought before judge or court	YES	Law states: 'without unnecessary delay'
19. Of all courts to total independence	YES	
20. From civilian trials in secret	YES	Restrictions when minors need to be protected
21. For independent trade unions	YES	
22. From censorship of mail	YES	
23. To publish and educate in ethnic languages	YES	
24. From deliberate state policies to control artistic works	YES	
25. From compulsory military service	YES	Registration only for possible future service
26. To purchase and drink alcohol	YES	Ages 18–21 depending on state. Insignificant cases of local prohibition

27. To practise homosexuality between consenting adults	yes	State law varies between extremes but more often legal .	◑
28. To use contraceptive pills and devices	**YES**		◯
29. Of early abortion	yes	Generally on request but certain states have conservative laws	◑
30. Of divorce (for men and women equally)	**YES**		◯

STATE POWER

31. Corporal punishment by state	None	◯
32. Radio and TV broadcasts	No intrusive controls	◯
33. Book publishing	No controls	◯
34. Number of police and military per 100,000 citizens	All police/military 1200 (approx.)	◐
35. % of national income spent on above	8%	◑
36. Weapons normally carried by civil police	.38 revolvers in most states. Other firearms used elsewhere	◯
37. Capital punishment by state	Frequent Supreme Court sessions to consider constitutional validity of death penalty. Many states sentence but rarely execute for murder	◑

MAXIMUM PUNISHMENTS IN PENAL CODE FOR:
(Freedom-related offences)

38. Non-violent anti-government activities	None	◯
39. Possession of banned political literature	None	◯
40. Refusing compulsory national service	None	◯

(Criminal offences)

41. Unlawful possession of 'hard' drugs	1 years' jail and/or fine. 2 years' jail second offence
42. Trading in pornography	1 year and/or $3000 fine. 3 years and $5000 fine if previous conviction
43. Illegal abortion	10 years' prison but influenced by US Supreme Court decision of 1973
44. Bigamy	7 years' jail
45. Rape without other injury	Any term of years up to life imprisonment

COMPULSORY DOCUMENTS FOR CITIZENS

46. Legally required at all times	None
47. For employment	Social Security number (card)
48. When applying for passport	Birth certificate, proof of citizenship
49. Period of validity of passport	5 years
50. Countries forbidden to holder	Temporary ban (1982) to Libya

Human rights rating: FAIR

Population: 5,500,000
Life expectancy: 60
Infant mortality (0–1 year) per 1000
  births: 96

Form of government: parliamentary
  democracy
Income per capita: US$ 1000

Observations: The country is one of the freer of the West Indies but harsh economic conditions and erratic administrative restrictions influence the human rights situation. It has ratified the UN Covenant.

Summary

Since the overthrow of the Trujillo dynasty in 1961 and the end of the subsequent US military intervention, the Dominican Republic has slowly and unsurely moved towards a form of democracy. But endemic poverty, unemployment and illiteracy continue to act as restraints on social and economic improvements for the great majority.

Although human rights are guaranteed by the 1966 constitution, the police continue to enjoy arbitrary powers. Freedom of speech, press, religion and public assembly are permitted and, to a growing extent, practised. Labour unions exist but are weak, only 12 per cent of the work force being organized.

Movement within the country is unrestricted but foreign travel can be curtailed for a number of legal reasons. A ban on entry has been applied to certain leftist activists and on a few members of the Trujillo family.

There is a wide range of political parties and these are generally permitted to operate freely. Despite the announced recognition of women's rights, traditional ideas continue to limit their claims to equality. There is a sizeable minority from neighbouring Haiti. Although the Dominican Republic has been a traditional refuge for dissident Haitians, there have recently been charges of forcible repatriation.

EL SALVADOR

Human rights rating: BAD

Population: 4,650,000
Life expectancy: 63
Infant mortality (0–1 year) per 1000 births: 53

Form of government: elected coalition (nominal)
Income per capita: US$ 550

Observations: This country is presented in summary form because of the unreliability of information and the refusal of official sources to reply to inquiries. A state of civil war exists.

Summary

The replacement of one authoritarian government by another in the 1982 elections, which were boycotted by moderate and left-wing parties, is not expected to change a human rights situation made worse by the continuation of civil war.

The insurgents include a broad spectrum of political dissidents and peasants, and exercise intermittent or permanent control over large areas of the countryside. Villages are destroyed by government forces, resulting in the deaths of women and children, and prisoners of both sides are subjected to extreme atrocities. Killings are not limited to the civil war, and include priests, academics, journalists, trade unionists, foreign news reporters and many other categories considered to be hostile to the regime.

The violence committed by guerrilla forces is also considerable and government officials, landowners, right-wing sympathizers and state employees are often murdered or kidnapped. Almost 10,000 are calculated to have been killed during 1980.

The judicial system, the press, radio, television and the trade-union movement, are all subject to pressures and intimidation which restrict their free and normal functioning.

Efforts are frequently made by mediators, particularly the US government, to end the civil war, and guerrilla forces are understood to be ready to negotiate a 'satisfactory' peace.

Human rights rating: BAD

Population: 7,477,427
Life expectancy: non-Indians 60,
Indians 50
**Infant mortality (0–1 year) per 1000
births:** 66 (urban) 120 (rural)

Form of government: military junta (de
facto)
Income per capita: US$ 1060

Observations: This country is presented in summary form because of the unreliability of information and the refusal of official sources to reply to inquiries.

Summary

After an election in 1982 in which only right-wing parties participated, a new military junta seized power in a bloodless coup. It has promised extensive reforms, but in the light of previous experience a continuation of the problems and human rights violations must be expected.

The extent of these violations should be seen against a background of extraordinary violence in which over a hundred politically motivated deaths have occurred each month, in which 'death squads' belonging to the security forces are employed to eliminate opponents of the regime, and in which a strong peasant movement has conducted a rural-based insurgency for over 20 years. Murder, disappearances and torture are therefore features of a continuing conflict.

In court trials, judges and lawyers are often intimidated and some have been found murdered after 'unsatisfactory' verdicts. Journalists risking official disapproval have suffered the same fate, and the paramilitary 'death squads' have not refrained from killing priests who spoke up for oppressed peasants and workers.

The National University has also been a target and in recent years nearly a hundred academics and students have lost their lives. Trade unions are restricted, with public sector strikes illegal, and in 1980 more than 80 union leaders and militants were murdered or disappeared. The killings continue.

Human rights rating: BAD

Population: 4,918,695
Life expectancy: 53
Infant mortality (0–1 year) per 1000 births: 130

Form of government: executive life-president
Income per capita: US$ 340

Observations: This country is presented in summary form because of the unreliability of information and the failure of official sources to reply to inquiries.

Summary

Following a very brief and limited relaxation in a long history of repression, the government in 1980 again imposed authoritarian rule. Dissidents, journalists, lawyers and human rights activists were arrested or banished. Interrogation of prisoners is accompanied by beatings, electric shocks and other tortures, the law being very explicit that those holding 'communist' beliefs or aiding such individuals are subject to trial by court martial and the death penalty. Execution is by firing squad, on occasion in public squares.

The report on Haiti of the Inter-American Commission of Human Rights (1980) stated: 'It may be said that freedom of inquiry, opinion, speech and dissemination of thought does not exist. There are taboo questions which cannot be discussed such as all matters concerning the President's family, the dictatorship . . .' etc.

Although the constitution accords equal rights to women, once married they are compelled to live in the husband's home and need his permission to apply for a passport and exit visa. Trade unions, even when officially recognized, choose to avoid open conflict with the authorities, and since Appeal Court judges are directly appointed by the president, verdicts and sentences in political cases inevitably meet with his approval.

Human rights rating: POOR

Population: 3,693,000
Life expectancy: 59
Infant mortality (0–1 year) per 1000
  births: 105

Form of government: parliamentary
  system (nominal)
Income per capita: US$ 620

Observations: A common border with El Salvador and Guatemala has meant that Honduras has been drawn into the regional unrest. Maltreatment of refugees or handing them back to their countries of origin is common practice. In frontier areas the army frequently misuses its arbitrary powers.

Summary

Although a civilian government came to power in 1981 in a general election, the armed forces still maintain their political influence. With this element dominant both inside and outside the government, limitations continue on freedom of speech, the press, public assemblies and trade-union activities. The judicial administration suffers from corrupt traditional influences; political prisoners are occasionally tortured and prison conditions are harsh.

Federations representing the large peasant population claim intimidation by the authorities when trying to protect their rights against the large landowners.

There were a number of 'disappearances' during 1981, including non-Hondurans believed to be political opponents, and the cooperation with neighbouring armies in combating left-wing insurgents has brought charges of calculated suppression of 'freedom movements'. There has certainly been much bloodshed in the name of 'border control'.

Some progress is being made to return to constitutional government though a gradual improvement in the human rights position is dependent on the military accepting civilian rule.

NICARAGUA

Human rights rating: POOR

Population: 2,732,520
Life expectancy: 56
Infant mortality (0–1 year) per 1000 births: 90

Form of government: parliamentary system
Income per capita: US$ 760

Observations: In 1981 the government declared a state of social and economic emergency. It has ratified the UN Covenant. It is being presented in summary form because of the failure of official sources to reply to inquiries.

Summary

The end of a 50-year reign by the Somoza family after a civil war was followed by the forming in 1979 of the Government of National Reconstruction. Although committing itself to a human rights programme as well as to a fairer distribution of wealth, the threat of outside military invasion has possibly prevented much progress towards these laudable aims.

The Sandinista National Liberation Front has taken over as the dominant party in Nicaraguan politics and its authority is becoming oppressive. Numerous supporters of the Somoza regime remain in detention and have suffered retributive torture, and there are many arrests on the grounds of 'counter-revolutionary' activities.

Much of the previous regime's security practices of mail and telephone checking, searches without warrants and causing opponents to 'disappear' have continued. Sections of the press and all of the television network are controlled by the government which has enacted a decree authorizing it to clear all news items on 'sensitive' topics. The long Somoza dictatorship left the country without an acceptable constitution, and elections promised for 1985 have been delayed until then 'to enable a higher literacy rate and standard of living to be enjoyed by the people'.

The government has, however, allowed human rights groups to visit the country and monitor court trials, though seldom acting on the eventual recommendations.

America, South

VENEZUELA

COLOMBIA

ECUADOR

PERU

B R A Z I L

BOLIVIA

PARAGUAY

C H I L E

URUGUAY

ARGENTINA

Argentina
Brazil
Chile
Colombia
Ecuador
Peru
Venezuela
Bolivia
Paraguay
Uruguay

Human rights rating: 44%

Population: 26,740,000
Life expectancy: 71
Infant mortality (0–1 year) per 1000 births: 40

Form of government: military junta
Income per capita: US$ 2500

Observations: 'State of siege' prohibitions have been in force since 1974. The military junta has promised free elections in 1983–4. The human rights position is poor.

FREEDOM/RIGHTS		Further comments	
1. Of movement in own country	YES		◐
2. To leave own country	yes	Unaccompanied wives with children must have husband's permission (passport issued by police)	◑
3. From deprivation of nationality	no	Certain categories of political detainees can choose self-exile instead of prison	◐
4. To seek, receive and impart information and teach ideas	no	Restrictions on extreme left teaching etc.	◐
5. From serfdom, slavery, forced or child labour	yes	Traditional labour abuses at local level	◖
6. Of peaceful political opposition	NO	Disappearances continuing	●
7. Of peaceful assembly and association	NO	Rights suspended since 1976	●
8. Of women to equal rights	yes	Inequalities of tradition and custom still strong. Legal marriage ages 14F, 16M	◖
9. From directed employment or work permits	YES		○
10. Of inter-racial, inter-religious and civil marriage	YES		○
11. To practise any religion	YES		○
12. From compulsory religion or state ideology in schools	YES		○
13. From political press censorship	no	Government-imposed guidelines	◕
14. From police detention without charge	NO	Permissible under constitution	●
15. From police searches of home without warrant	no	But violations of law decreasing	◐
16. From torture or coercion by state	NO	Beatings, electric shocks, removal of nails, teeth, eyes etc. (despite prohibition under constitution)	●
17. Of assumption of innocence until guilt proved	NO	Unsubstantiated charges enough for indefinite detention	●
18. Of accused to be promptly brought before judge or court	NO	Law ignored. 10,000 missing	●
19. Of all courts to total independence	NO	Position improving. Defending lawyers no longer disappearing	●
20. From civilian trials in secret	no	When political, taken over by secret military tribunals	◐
21. For independent trade unions	no	Strikes prohibited	◕
22. From censorship of mail	NO	'Security' considerations give authorities full powers	●
23. To publish and educate in ethnic languages	YES		○

24.	From deliberate state policies to control artistic works	YES	○
25.	From compulsory military service	NO	Military service of up to 14 months ●
26.	To purchase and drink alcohol	YES	○
27.	To practise homosexuality between consenting adults	YES	Over age of 22 ○
28.	To use contraceptive pills and devices	yes	◐
29.	Of early abortion	no	Limited medical reasons – life in danger, pregnancy after rape etc. ◐
30.	Of divorce (for men and women equally)	NO	●

STATE POWER

31.	Corporal punishment by state	Extent of state complicity in frequent torture cannot be ignored	◐
32.	Radio and TV broadcasts	Certain political controls but these are lessening	◐
33.	Book publishing	Army and state power extends to banning and book burning	◐
34.	Number of police and military per 100,000 citizens	1100 (including conscripts but not reservists)	◐
35.	% of national income spent on above	8%	○
36.	Weapons normally carried by civil police	9mm pistols. Women .38 revolvers	○
37.	Capital punishment by state	By firing squad. Usually political offences	●

MAXIMUM PUNISHMENTS IN PENAL CODE FOR:
(Freedom-related offences)

38.	Non-violent anti-government activities	Death penalty	●
39.	Possession of banned political literature	6 years' prison	◐
40.	Refusing compulsory national service	3 years' prison	◐

(Criminal offences)

41.	Unlawful possession of 'hard' drugs	2 years' prison. Traffickers up to 12 years
42.	Trading in pornography	1 year's prison
43.	Illegal abortion	4 years. If woman dies, 6 years
44.	Bigamy	4 years' prison
45.	Rape without other injury	6 years' prison

COMPULSORY DOCUMENTS FOR CITIZENS

46.	Legally required at all times	ID card, citizen's and marriage pass books
47.	For employment	ID card and citizen's book
48.	When applying for passport	ID card and citizen's book
49.	Period of validity of passport	3 years since 1978
50.	Countries forbidden to holder	Cuba and other communist countries

BRAZIL

Human rights rating: 70%

Population: 120,000,000
Life expectancy: 63
Infant mortality (0–1 year) per 1000 births: 82

Form of government: federal republic with executive president
Income per capita: US$ 1995

Observations: The country has not signed the UN Covenant. Following the November 1982 elections for state governors and senators, further progress on human rights is anticipated.

FREEDOM/RIGHTS		Further comments	
1. Of movement in own country	YES		○
2. To leave own country	YES		○
3. From deprivation of nationality	YES		○
4. To seek information and teach ideas	YES		○
5. From serfdom, slavery, forced or child labour	no	Large landowners in remote interior impose near-serfdom. Child labour common in rural areas	◑
6. Of peaceful political opposition	no	Communist Party and National Union of Students illegal	◑
7. Of peaceful assembly and association	yes	Strict controls when law and order threatened	○
8. Of women to equal rights	yes	Inequalities mostly in rural areas where traditional attitudes prevail	○
9. From directed employment or work permits	YES		○
10. Of inter-racial, inter-religious and civil marriage	YES		○
11. To practise any religion	YES		○
12. From compulsory religion or state ideology in schools	YES		○
13. From political press censorship	no	Election ban on radio and TV discussions by candidates during campaigns. Minor actions against leftist papers.	◑
14. From police detention without charge	yes	Scattered local abuses	○
15. From police searches of home without warrant	yes	But occasional instances of illegal police entry	○
16. From torture or coercion by state	yes	With redemocratization (*abertura*), abuses diminished	○
17. Of assumption of innocence until guilt proved	yes	But police in distant interior may exercise arbitrary powers	○
18. Of accused to be promptly brought before judge or court	yes	Except cases contravening National Security Law. Custody 30 days and renewable	○
19. Of all courts to total independence	yes	Cases under National Security Law heard by military court	○
20. From civilian trials in secret	YES		○
21. For independent trade unions	no	Law of National Security limits strikes. Prison sentences for leaders.	◑
22. From censorship of mail	yes	Checks of mail and telexes usually relate to financial illegalities	○
23. To publish and educate in ethnic languages	YES		○

24. From deliberate state policies to control artistic works	**YES**		○
25. From compulsory military service	no	1-year military service for 18-year-olds chosen by 'random method'	◑
26. To purchase and drink alcohol	**YES**		○
27. To practise homosexuality between consenting adults	**YES**	Soliciting forbidden	○
28. To use contraceptive pills and devices	yes	Limited government support	◑
29. Of early abortion	no	Except when life at risk or on juridical grounds (rape etc.)	◑
30. Of divorce (for men and women equally)	**NO**	Marriage indissoluble. Divorce only recognized for foreign spouse	●

STATE POWER

31. Corporal punishment by state	Illegal but minor abuses at local level	◐
32. Radio and TV broadcasts	Political controls lessening but subject to sudden changes despite constitutional freedom	◐
33. Book publishing	State strict on security and race affairs	◐
34. Number of police and military per 100,000 citizens	350	○
35. % of national income spent on above	4%	○
36. Weapons normally carried by civil police	.38 revolvers, tear gas etc.	◐
37. Capital punishment by state	None in peacetime	○

MAXIMUM PUNISHMENTS IN PENAL CODE FOR:
(Freedom-related offences)

38. Non-violent anti-government activities	'Subversive activities' – 5 years' prison	◑
39. Possession of banned political literature	'Subversive activities' – 5 years' prison	◑
40. Refusing compulsory national service	5 years' prison	◑

(Criminal offences)

41. Unlawful possession of 'hard' drugs	10 years' prison
42. Trading in pornography	3 years' prison
43. Illegal abortion	5 years' prison
44. Bigamy	10 years' prison
45. Rape without other injury	15 years' prison

COMPULSORY DOCUMENTS FOR CITIZENS

46. Legally required at all times	ID card
47. For employment	ID card, work permit, military service card
48. When applying for passport	As above
49. Period of validity of passport	4 years
50. Countries forbidden to holder	Cuba

CHILE

Human rights rating: 37%

Population: 11,198,000
Life expectancy: 67
Infant mortality (0–1 year) per 1000 births: 27

Form of government: military junta
Income per capita: US$ 2000

Observations: Severe curtailment of human rights despite having signed and ratified the UN Covenant.

FREEDOM/RIGHTS		Further comments	
1. Of movement in own country	no	Political dissidents may suffer 3-month periods of local confinement	◑
2. To leave own country	yes	Wife needs husband's consent when taking children abroad	◐
3. From deprivation of nationality	no	Expulsion of political opponents	◑
4. To seek information and teach ideas	NO	Severe limitations under 1980 constitution. University rectors are military men	●
5. From serfdom, slavery, forced or child labour	yes	Limited rural child labour	◐
6. Of peaceful political opposition	NO	Anything contrary to 'the interests of Chile' harassed or banned	●
7. Of peaceful assembly and association	NO	Police permission limited to pro-government meetings. Strict new constitution	●
8. Of women to equal rights	no	Traditional inequalities still persist	◑
9. From directed employment or work permits	YES		○
10. Of inter-racial, inter-religious and civil marriage	YES		○
11. To practise any religion	YES		○
12. From compulsory religion or state ideology in schools	YES		○
13. From political press censorship	no	Government warnings to papers rather than direct censorship. Parochial criticisms permitted	◑
14. From police detention without charge	NO	Under Decree 3451 up to 20 days. Sometimes extended. 100 detained on average per month	●
15. From police searches of home without warrant	NO	Legal requirements frequently violated with connivance of superiors	●
16. From torture or coercion by state	NO	Beatings, electric shocks etc. by CNI or DINA (secret police)	●
17. Of assumption of innocence until guilt proved	NO	Sentences of internal exile without trial or appeal	●
18. Of accused to be promptly brought before judge or court	NO	As above	●
19. Of all courts to total independence	NO	Courts are beginning to be less coerced by government	●
20. From civilian trials in secret	NO	And disappearances can follow	●
21. For independent trade unions	no	Labour rights restricted, uncooperative leaders arrested	◐
22. From censorship of mail	NO	All dissidents subject to checks	●
23. To publish and educate in ethnic languages	YES		○

24.	From deliberate state policies to control artistic works	**YES**		○
25.	From compulsory military service	**NO**	1 year at age 19	●
26.	To purchase and drink alcohol	**YES**		○
27.	To practise homosexuality between consenting adults	**NO**	Illegal	●
28.	To use contraceptive pills and devices	**YES**	Active state encouragement	○
29.	Of early abortion	no	Only when risk to mother's life	◑
30.	Of divorce (for men and women equally)	**NO**	System of annulment (*nulidad*) complex and infrequent	●

STATE POWER

31. Corporal punishment by state — Usually in form of torture ●
32. Radio and TV broadcasts — National network state-controlled by local stations run by universities etc. ◑
33. Book publishing — Publishers forbidden to issue pro-Marxist or anti-government works ◑
34. Number of police and military per 100,000 citizens — 1785 (including para-military) ◑
35. % of national income spent on above — 8% ◑
36. Weapons normally carried by civil police — Revolvers. Carbines when mounted ◑
37. Capital punishment by state — By shooting for treason, parricide etc. Sentenced often by military rather than by courts ●

MAXIMUM PUNISHMENTS IN PENAL CODE FOR:
(*Freedom-related offences*)

38. Non-violent anti-government activities — Death penalty if considered treason ●
39. Possession of banned political literature — 10 years' prison if against 'interests of Chile' or public order ◑
40. Refusing compulsory national service — Short prison sentences and fines ○

(*Criminal offences*)

41. Unlawful possession of 'hard' drugs — 15 years' prison (being reviewed)
42. Trading in pornography — 540 days' prison plus fine
43. Illegal abortion — 3–5 years if self-induced and 5 years for 'physician'
44. Bigamy — 5 years' prison
45. Rape without other injury — 15 years' prison

COMPULSORY DOCUMENTS FOR CITIZENS

46. Legally required at all times — ID card
47. For employment — ID card
48. When applying for passport — ID card, birth certificate
49. Period of validity of passport — 2–3 years
50. Countries forbidden to holder — None

Human rights rating: 62%

Population: 26,122,000
Life expectancy: 62
Infant mortality (0–1 year) per 1000 births: 75

Form of government: parliamentary system
Income per capita: US$ 1200

Observations: A constitutional 'state of siege' curtails certain freedoms and rights. The severity of this varies with the degree of threat to the government. At present this is posed by active guerrilla groups.

FREEDOM/RIGHTS		Further comments	
1. Of movement in own country	no	Measures against rural guerrilla groups mean frequent zonal restrictions	◑
2. To leave own country	YES		○
3. From deprivation of nationality	YES		○
4. To seek information and teach ideas	yes	Except for wide interpretation of seditious teachings	◑
5. From serfdom, slavery, forced or child labour	yes	Child labour abuses countrywide	◑
6. Of peaceful political opposition	yes	Constitutional 'state of siege' for last 20 years inhibits total freedom	◑
7. Of peaceful assembly and association	yes	But strict controls when violence feared	◑
8. Of women to equal rights	yes	Position improving. Traditional disadvantages in employment	◑
9. From directed employment or work permits	YES	Proof of having done military service necessary where applicable	○
10. Of inter-racial, inter-religious and civil marriage	YES		○
11. To practise any religion	YES		○
12. From compulsory religion or state ideology in schools	YES		○
13. From political press censorship	yes	But 'state of siege' means wide interpretation of sedition	◑
14. From police detention without charge	no	Many violations. Also 1200 detentions by 'security forces' in 1980	◐
15. From police searches of home without warrant	no	Many violations. Searches of premises of suspects' relatives	◐
16. From torture or coercion by state	no	Frequent and well-documented. Sometimes resulting in death. New penal code stresses illegality of torture	◐
17. Of assumption of innocence until guilt proved	no	Constitution frequently ignored	◐
18. Of accused to be promptly brought before judge or court	no	Accused subject to long periods of 'incommunicado'	◐
19. Of all courts to total independence	yes	But many civil cases are deferred to the military	◑
20. From civilian trials in secret	yes	But military courts can take over	◑
21. For independent trade unions	yes	Certain limits denied under 'state of siege' laws	◑
22. From censorship of mail	yes	Except for known dissidents	◑
23. To publish and educate in ethnic languages	YES		○
24. From deliberate state policies to control artistic works	YES		○

25. From compulsory military service	**NO**	2 years' military service	●
26. To purchase and drink alcohol	**YES**		○
27. To practise homosexuality between consenting adults	**NO**	2 years' prison	●
28. To use contraceptive pills and devices	**YES**	Wide state support	○
29. Of early abortion	no	Only when mother's life at risk	◐
30. Of divorce (for men and women equally)	yes	But under 'Concordata' with Holy See a Catholic marriage also needs annulment	◐

STATE POWER

31. Corporal punishment by state	By law illegal but record of torture a contradiction	◐
32. Radio and TV broadcasts	Government can ban broadcasts regarded as subversive	◐
33. Book publishing	Free but with 'understood' guidelines	◐
34. Number of police and military per 100,000 citizens	700 (including para-military reserves)	○
35. % of national income spent on above	6%	◐
36. Weapons normally carried by civil police	Variety of arms	◐
37. Capital punishment by state	None under constitution but many deaths unexplained	◐

MAXIMUM PUNISHMENTS IN PENAL CODE FOR:
(Freedom-related offences)

38. Non-violent anti-government activities	20 years' prison under 'state of siege'	◐
39. Possession of banned political literature	Seditious literature up to 3 years' prison	◐
40. Refusing compulsory national service	3 years' prison	◐

(Criminal offences)

41. Unlawful possession of 'hard' drugs	18 months' prison
42. Trading in pornography	1 year's prison plus fine
43. Illegal abortion	4 years' prison
44. Bigamy	2 years' prison
45. Rape without other injury	8 years' maximum but 10 years if victim a virgin or 'very virtuous woman'

COMPULSORY DOCUMENTS FOR CITIZENS

46. Legally required at all times	ID card
47. For employment	ID card and military service card ('tarjeta')
48. When applying for passport	ID card, birth certificate and 'tarjeta'
49. Period of validity of passport	7 years
50. Countries forbidden to holder	None

ECUADOR

Human rights rating: 85%

Population: 8,500,000
Life expectancy: 62
Infant mortality (0–1 year) per 1000 births: 66

Form of government: parliamentary republic
Income per capita: US$ 1200

Observations: Satisfactory except for minor regional problems.

FREEDOM/RIGHTS		Further comments	
1. Of movement in own country	YES		◐
2. To leave own country	yes	Exit permit depends on tax and military service clearance	◑
3. From deprivation of nationality	YES		○
4. To seek information and teach ideas	YES		○
5. From serfdom, slavery, forced or child labour	yes	Degree of child labour in rural areas	◑
6. Of peaceful political opposition	YES	12 political parties including communists	○
7. Of peaceful assembly and association	yes	Permission needed and usually granted. Slandering officials a punishable offence	◑
8. Of women to equal rights	yes	Traditional discrimination in pay and socially	◑
9. From directed employment or work permits	YES		○
10. Of inter-racial, inter-religious and civil marriage	YES		○
11. To practise any religion	YES		○
12. From compulsory religion or state ideology in schools	YES		○
13. From political press censorship	YES		○
14. From police detention without charge	YES	72 hours maximum	○
15. From police searches of home without warrant	YES	Except when in 'hot pursuit'	○
16. From torture or coercion by state	yes	Local police abuses	◑
17. Of assumption of innocence until guilt proved	YES		○
18. Of accused to be promptly brought before judge or court	no	Lengthy administrative delays – up to 2 years	◑
19. Of all courts to total independence	YES		○
20. From civilian trials in secret	YES		○
21. For independent trade unions	YES		○
22. From censorship of mail	YES		○
23. To publish and educate in ethnic languages	YES		○
24. From deliberate state policies to control artistic works	YES		○
25. From compulsory military service	NO	2 years' selective military service	●
26. To purchase and drink alcohol	YES	Above age 18	○
27. To practise homosexuality between consenting adults	NO	Prison sentences	●
28. To use contraceptive pills and devices	YES		○

29. Of early abortion	no	Only when mother's life at risk
30. Of divorce (for men and women equally)	YES	

STATE POWER
31. Corporal punishment by state   Prison punishments include beatings
32. Radio and TV broadcasts   Over 200 commercial stations
33. Book publishing   Privately owned and free
34. Number of police and military per 100,000 citizens   600
35. % of national income spent on above   3%
36. Weapons normally carried by civil police   Only officers carry revolvers
37. Capital punishment by state   Abolished 1897

MAXIMUM PUNISHMENTS IN PENAL CODE FOR:
(Freedom-related offences)
38. Non-violent anti-government activities   None
39. Possession of banned political literature None
40. Refusing compulsory national service   2 years' maximum

(Criminal offences)
41. Unlawful possession of 'hard' drugs   Minor offence but 12 years for trafficking
42. Trading in pornography   6 years for extreme cases
43. Illegal abortion   6 years' prison
44. Bigamy   2 years' prison
45. Rape without other injury   12 years' prison

COMPULSORY DOCUMENTS FOR CITIZENS
46. Legally required at all times   ID card
47. For employment   ID card. Occasionally police clearance
48. When applying for passport   ID card, tax and military clearance
49. Period of validity of passport   6 years (3 × 2 year renewals)
50. Countries forbidden to holder   None

Human rights rating: 81%

Population: 18,075,000
Life expectancy: 58
Infant mortality (0–1 year) per 1000 births: 92

Form of government: multi-party democracy
Income per capita: US$ 820

Observations: A satisfactory human rights position is being threatened by tougher measures against sporadic 'guerrilla' outbreaks. 60-day martial law is renewable.

FREEDOM/RIGHTS		Further comments	
1. Of movement in own country	YES		○
2. To leave own country	YES		○
3. From deprivation of nationality	YES		○
4. To seek information and teach ideas	YES		○
5. From serfdom, slavery, forced or child labour	yes	Child labour common in poor rural areas	◑
6. Of peaceful political opposition	yes	Paramilitary squads oppressive	◕
7. Of peaceful assembly and association	yes	Police permits needed	◕
8. Of women to equal rights	yes	Distinct social and economic disadvantages due to poverty etc.	◑
9. From directed employment or work permits	YES		○
10. Of inter-racial, inter-religious and civil marriage	YES		○
11. To practise any religion	YES		○
12. From compulsory religion or state ideology in schools	YES		○
13. From political press censorship	yes	1 year prison for defaming govt	◕
14. From police detention without charge	yes	Up to 15 days. But local abuses lengthen detention	◕
15. From police searches of home without warrant	yes	Local abuses	◑
16. From torture or coercion by state	yes	Position worsening with increase in terrorism. Many beatings in jails	◑
17. Of assumption of innocence until guilt proved	yes	Temporary declarations of state of emergency impose periodic harshness	◑
18. Of accused to be promptly brought before judge or court	yes	But long delays due to administrative limitations	◑
19. Of all courts to total independence	YES		○
20. From civilian trials in secret	YES		○
21. For independent trade unions	yes	Some restrictions	◕
22. From censorship of mail	YES		○
23. To publish and educate in ethnic languages	YES		○
24. From deliberate state policies to control artistic works	YES		○
25. From compulsory military service	NO	2 years' selective conscription for both sexes	●
26. To purchase and drink alcohol	YES	From age 18	○
27. To practise homosexuality between consenting adults	YES	Legal over 18 but strong social hostility	○
28. To use contraceptive pills and devices	yes	Limited government support	◑

29. Of early abortion	no	Only when mother's life at risk	◖
30. Of divorce (for men and women equally)	**YES**		○

STATE POWER

31. Corporal punishment by state	None	○
32. Radio and TV broadcasts	Negligible government control	○
33. Book publishing	No government control but in emergency president has decree powers	○
34. Number of police and military per 100,000 citizens	Police and military (inc. Guardia Civil) 1000	◖
35. % of national income spent on above	4.5% (approx.)	○
36. Weapons normally carried by civil police	Pistols	◗
37. Capital punishment by state	Restored 1982 for terrorist acts of murder	●

MAXIMUM PUNISHMENTS IN PENAL CODE FOR:
(Freedom-related offences)

38. Non-violent anti-government activities	None	○
39. Possession of banned political literature	None	○
40. Refusing compulsory national service	2 years' prison and/or fine	◖

(Criminal offences)

41. Unlawful possession of 'hard' drugs	Minor sentence for possessing but up to 15 years for trafficking etc.
42. Trading in pornography	3 days to 5 years depending on category
43. Illegal abortion	4 years when self-induced, 6 years for accomplices
44. Bigamy	4 years' prison
45. Rape without other injury	2 years' prison. 10 years when victim is of unsound mind

COMPULSORY DOCUMENTS FOR CITIZENS

46. Legally required at all times	Various proofs of electoral, military and tax clearances
47. For employment	None
48. When applying for passport	Birth, marriage, 'good conduct' certificate etc.
49. Period of validity of passport	1–2 years
50. Countries forbidden to holder	None

Human rights rating: 89%

Population: 16,458,502
Life expectancy: 66
Infant mortality (0–1 year) per 1000 births: 45

Form of government: multi-party democracy
Income per capita: US$ 4700

Observations: Satisfactory, though occasional abuses for 'security' reasons.

FREEDOM/RIGHTS		Further comments	
1. Of movement in own country	YES		○
2. To leave own country	YES		○
3. From deprivation of nationality	YES		○
4. To seek, receive and impart information and teach ideas	YES		○
5. From serfdom, slavery, forced or child labour	YES		○
6. Of peaceful political opposition	YES		○
7. Of peaceful assembly and association	YES		○
8. Of women to equal rights	yes	Bill to protect women's rights pending. Discrimination in wages	◐
9. From directed employment or work permits	YES		○
10. Of inter-racial, inter-religious and civil marriage	YES		○
11. To practise any religion	YES		○
12. From compulsory religion or state ideology in schools	YES		○
13. From political press censorship	yes	Rare instances of investigation by the military	◐
14. From police detention without charge	yes	24 hours. But occasional major abuses	◐
15. From police searches of home without warrant	YES	Except when in 'hot pursuit'	○
16. From torture or coercion by state	yes	Isolated cases of beatings during interrogation	◐
17. Of assumption of innocence until guilt proved	YES		○
18. Of accused to be promptly brought before judge or court	YES	Within 8 days. Occasional delays due to 'lethargy'	○
19. Of all courts to total independence	YES		○
20. From civilian trials in secret	YES	Occasionally in camera to protect identity of minors	○
21. For independent trade unions	YES		○
22. From censorship of mail	YES		○
23. To publish and educate in ethnic languages	YES		○
24. From deliberate state policies to control artistic works	YES		○
25. From compulsory military service	NO	18 months' selective service	●
26. To purchase and drink alcohol	YES	Legal age 18	○
27. To practise homosexuality between consenting adults	YES	Legal over 18 years	○

28. To use contraceptive pills and devices	**YES**	Family planning programme	○
29. Of early abortion	no	Only when mother's life at risk	◐
30. Of divorce (for men and women equally)	yes	Inequalities suffered by women now under review	◐

STATE POWER

31. Corporal punishment by state	None	○
32. Radio and TV broadcasts	Free but occasional directives from government	◐
33. Book publishing	No direct state interference	○
34. Number of police and military per 100,000 citizens	500	○
35. % of national income spent on above	3%	○
36. Weapons normally carried by civil police	.38 revolvers	◐
37. Capital punishment by state	Abolished 1863	○

MAXIMUM PUNISHMENTS IN PENAL CODE FOR:
(Freedom-related offences)

38. Non-violent anti-government activities	None	○
39. Possession of banned political literature	None	○
40. Refusing compulsory national service	Punishment takes form of job and social restrictions	◐

(Criminal offences)

41. Unlawful possession of 'hard' drugs	8 years' prison
42. Trading in pornography	Local area laws decide penalties
43. Illegal abortion	Self-induced 2 years. By others up to 30 years
44. Bigamy	4 years' prison
45. Rape without other injury	5 years' prison

COMPULSORY DOCUMENTS FOR CITIZENS

46. Legally required at all times	ID card
47. For employment	Nothing
48. When applying for passport	ID card, birth certificate
49. Period of validity of passport	5 years
50. Countries forbidden to holder	None

Human rights rating: POOR

Population: 5,444,000
Life expectancy: 53
Infant mortality (0–1 year) per 1000 births: 148

Form of government: civilian multi-party
Income per capita: US$ 630

Observations: In October 1982 the military junta which had seized power after the 1980 general election at last stepped down in favour of the president-elect. This recent event, and the impossibility of predicting how it will affect one of the worst human rights situations in South America, makes it inadvisable to complete the Guide's questionnaire.

Summary

The spectacle of a military junta voluntarily handing over power to a civilian government in South America is rare but the real test will be whether the military stays out of politics should the social and administrative changes seem too extreme. During their two years in power, the military junta had shown little respect for human rights. Torture, detentions and death penalties were widely practised and hundreds of political and trade-union leaders were exiled, their passports being stamped to prevent re-entry. Radio and television are state-controlled, the news service provided only by the government and newspapers closed when their criticisms are too damaging. It is too early in the life of the civilian government, which in fact is a minority coalition, to decide how much of the old oppressive state apparatus is needed to maintain it in power.

The human rights rating of POOR relates more to the past than the future, which should improve if the new government holds to its promises and policies.

PARAGUAY

Human rights rating: BAD

Population: 3,167,985
Life expectancy: 64
Infant mortality (0–1 year) per 1000 births: 58

Form of government: military junta
Income per capita: US$ 1200

Observations: The failure of official sources to reply to inquiries and misleading government statements made it inadvisable to complete the Guide's questionnaire.

Summary

A 'state of siege', a provision of the constitution, has been in force since 1929. The present president, General Stroessner, came to power in 1954 and has ruled by the same provision ever since.

The majority political movement, the Colorado Party, and the military and police have combined during this period to maintain his dictatorial authority. This necessitates the arrest, forcible interrogation and frequent summary executions of those disagreeing with the regime. Similar treatment is inflicted on a dissatisfied peasantry, the great majority of the population, some of whom have been shot when in dispute with large landowners.

A 1980 report of the International League for Human Rights stated that the courts did not hold fair trials, that the judges acted lawlessly and that they were influenced by 'superior executive power'. This lack of respect for human rights extends to all law enforcement agencies who act under the 'legal' umbrella of 'state of siege' provisions, and permits indefinite detention, torture, searches of homes, the seizing of personal possessions and forcing political opponents into exile.

Although there is a degree of freedom for the press and other media, this must not extend to criticizing the president or the country's other leaders. Nominal general elections are held every five years but some parties, including the Communist Party, are banned from participating.

Human rights rating: POOR

Population: 2,899,000
Life expectancy: 71
Infant mortality (0–1 year) per 1000 births: 34

Form of government: military junta (de facto)
Income per capita: US$ 2100

Observations: The human rights record of Uruguay contravenes in many areas its ratification of the UN Covenant. Official sources failed to reply to inquiries needed to complete the Guide's questionnaire.

Summary

During the last ten years a national security law has been in force and though an ebb-and-flow in the activities of democratic institutions has been permitted, real control is still exercised by the military. The government held a plebiscite in 1980 on the issues of a new constitution and a return in the following year to democratic party politics but the electorate rejected the proposals which they felt were a device to give legitimacy to military rule.

The human rights situation varies with social tensions, and under the present emergency security measures the government has admitted the imprisonment of over a thousand dissidents with many cases still untried. Torture and harsh interrogation are widely practised and the families of those arrested are not always informed of such detentions. Many accused are tried by military courts which the Inter-American Human Rights Commission, in its 1980 report, described as 'failing to guarantee due process'.

The press, publishing, radio and television are restricted and cannot criticize the security forces or public order measures. There is also a ban on the reporting of the activities of political parties though in practice there is some tolerance of public assemblies with political objectives, and trade unions suffer less harassment than previously. Travel within the country and abroad is relatively unimpeded except for a few 'political undesirables', and women enjoy equality before the law.

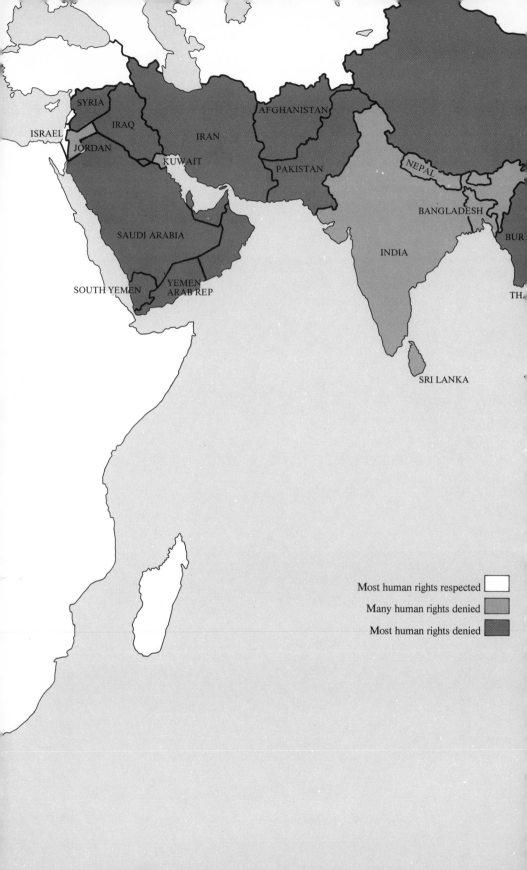

SYRIA

IRAQ

ISRAEL

JORDAN

KUWAIT

AFGHANISTAN

IRAN

PAKISTAN

NEPAL

BANGLADESH

BUR

SAUDI ARABIA

INDIA

TH.

SOUTH YEMEN

YEMEN
ARAB REP

SRI LANKA

Most human rights respected

Many human rights denied

Most human rights denied

Asia and Australasia

Australia
Bangladesh
China
Hong Kong
India
Indonesia
Iraq
Israel
Japan
North Korea
South Korea
Malaysia
New Zealand
Pakistan
Papua New Guinea
Philippines
Saudi Arabia
Singapore
Sri Lanka
Syria
Taiwan
Thailand
Vietnam
Afghanistan
Burma
Iran
Jordan
Kampuchea
Kuwait
Laos
Nepal
Yemen Arab Republic
South Yemen

NORTH KOREA
SOUTH KOREA
JAPAN
CHINA
TAIWAN
HONG KONG
VIETNAM
KAMPUCHEA
PHILIPPINES
MALAYSIA
SINGAPORE
INDONESIA
PAPUA NEW GUINEA
AUSTRALIA
NEW ZEALAND

Human rights rating: 93%

Population: 14,567,000
Life expectancy: 74
Infant mortality (0–1 year) per 1000 births: 12

Form of government: democratic federal commonwealth
Income per capita: US$ 10,500

Observations: Aborigines (1% of population) are subject to state and federal development policies. These are often regarded as controversial. Otherwise, the human rights position is satisfactory.

	FREEDOM/RIGHTS		Further comments	
1.	Of movement in own country	YES		○
2.	To leave own country	YES		○
3.	From deprivation of nationality	YES		○
4.	To seek information and teach ideas	YES		○
5.	From serfdom, slavery, forced or child labour	yes	Limitations on aborigines by Queensland government. No freehold land ownership within their reserves	◑
6.	Of peaceful political opposition	YES		○
7.	Of peaceful assembly and association	yes	Occasional repressive measures by Queensland government against aboriginal and trade-union demonstrations	◑
8.	Of women to equal rights	YES	Minor violations	○
9.	From directed employment or work permits	YES	Influx of immigrants subject to temporary permits	○
10.	Of inter-racial, inter-religious and civil marriage	YES	Mixed marriages occasionally encounter social prejudices	○
11.	To practise any religion	YES		○
12.	From compulsory religion or state ideology in schools	YES	Though parent's letter may be necessary to obtain exemption	○
13.	From political press censorship	YES		○
14.	From police detention without charge	YES	Within 24 hours	○
15.	From police searches of home without warrant	YES		○
16.	From torture or coercion by state	YES		○
17.	Of assumption of innocence until guilt proved	YES		○
18.	Of accused to be promptly brought before judge or court	YES	24 hours limit	○
19.	Of all courts to total independence	YES		○
20.	From civilian trials in secret	YES	State security and juvenile cases may be in camera to protect accused	○
21.	For independent trade unions	YES		○
22.	From censorship of mail	YES	But legal provision when state security is involved	○
23.	To publish and educate in ethnic languages	YES	Encouraged by government	○
24.	From deliberate state policies to control artistic works	YES	Development of arts a priority of recent governments	○
25.	From compulsory military service	YES		○

26. To purchase and drink alcohol	**YES**	But restrictions in aborigine areas on grounds of extreme effects of alcohol
27. To practise homosexuality between consenting adults	no	Occasional police actions to enforce law
28. To use contraceptive pills and devices	**YES**	Government encouragement
29. Of early abortion	yes	Broad medical/social reasons
30. Of divorce (for men and women equally)	**YES**	

STATE POWER

31. Corporal punishment by state — None though whipping still not deleted from all penal codes

32. Radio and TV broadcasts — No state control but commercial monopolies very powerful

33. Book publishing — No controls

34. Number of police and military per 100,000 citizens — 800

35. % of national income spent on above — 4.5%

36. Weapons normally carried by civil police — Pistols and batons

37. Capital punishment by state — Death penalty retained in three of the six states but last hanging in 1969

MAXIMUM PUNISHMENTS IN PENAL CODE FOR:
(Freedom-related offences)
38. Non-violent anti-government activities — None
39. Possession of banned political literature — None
40. Refusing compulsory national service — None

(Criminal offences)
41. Unlawful possession of 'hard' drugs — Life imprisonment with hard labour
42. Trading in pornography — 1 year's prison on 3rd offence
43. Illegal abortion — 14 years with hard labour
44. Bigamy — 7 years with hard labour
45. Rape without other injury — Life imprisonment with hard labour (Queensland penal code taken as example)

COMPULSORY DOCUMENTS FOR CITIZENS
46. Legally required at all times — None
47. For employment — None
48. When applying for passport — Birth certificate. Citizenship certificate for immigrants
49. Period of validity of passport — 5 years
50. Countries forbidden to holder — None

Human rights rating: 64%

Population: 92,900,000
Life expectancy: 49
Infant mortality (0–1 year) per 1000 births: 130

Form of government: parliamentary system (nominally)
Income per capita: US$ 110

Observations: The Special Powers Act (1974) may mean indefinite detention for any political or economic act that is considered 'prejudicial to the state'. In practice the human rights position is fair, but worsening.

FREEDOM/RIGHTS		Further comments	
1. Of movement in own country	yes	Except to insurgent 'Protected Areas'	◑
2. To leave own country	yes	Citizens of questionable loyalty denied passports	◐
3. From deprivation of nationality	YES		○
4. To seek information and teach ideas	YES		○
5. From serfdom, slavery, forced or child labour	NO	Bonded and child labour	●
6. Of peaceful political opposition	no	Martial law regulations	◑
7. Of peaceful assembly and association	yes	Many student clashes with police	◐
8. Of women to equal rights	no	Strong Muslim influences. Women usually confined to domestic role	◑
9. From directed employment or work permits	YES		○
10. Of inter-racial, inter-religious and civil marriage	yes	Secular law not accepted by large Muslim majority	◐
11. To practise any religion	YES		○
12. From compulsory religion or state ideology in schools	no	Compulsion in Muslim schools	◑
13. From political press censorship	yes	Government seldom uses broad controls over press	◑
14. From police detention without charge	NO	Under Special Powers Act indefinite detention for any 'prejudicial act'	●
15. From police searches of home without warrant	yes	Except for security suspects. 'Spreading fear and alarm' justifies detention	◑
16. From torture or coercion by state	yes	Local abuses by security forces	◑
17. Of assumption of innocence until guilt proved	no	Special Powers Act often used against black marketeers, smugglers etc.	◑
18. Of accused to be promptly brought before judge or court	yes	Overworked system prevents prompt appearance in court (80,000 cases pending)	◑
19. Of all courts to total independence	YES	Free of state pressures	○
20. From civilian trials in secret	yes	Except under Special Powers Act	◑
21. For independent trade unions	no	No strikes in essential industries	◑
22. From censorship of mail	yes	Occasional checking under Special Powers Act	◐
23. To publish and educate in ethnic languages	YES		○
24. From deliberate state policies to control artistic works	YES		○
25. From compulsory military service	YES		○

26. To purchase and drink alcohol	no	Device of 'health permits' for buying alcohol. Muslims but not Hindus pay for the permits	◑
27. To practise homosexuality between consenting adults	NO	7 years' prison	●
28. To use contraceptive pills and devices	YES		○
29. Of early abortion	no	Only when mother's life at risk	◑
30. Of divorce (for men and women equally)	yes	Muslim majority follow complex Sharia divorce laws	◐

STATE POWER

31. Corporal punishment by state	None	○
32. Radio and TV broadcasts	State-owned and directed	◑
33. Book publishing	Only occasional banning	◐
34. Number of police and military per 100,000 citizens	150 (including paramilitary)	○
35. % of national income spent on above	2.5%	○
36. Weapons normally carried by civil police	Bamboo rods. Armed police in reserve	○
37. Capital punishment by state	By hanging or shooting. For murder, treason, 'unlawful actions'	●

MAXIMUM PUNISHMENTS IN PENAL CODE FOR:
(Freedom-related offences)

38. Non-violent anti-government activities	Indefinite detention	◑
39. Possession of banned political literature	Theoretical offence under Special Powers Act	◐
40. Refusing compulsory national service	None	○

(Criminal offences)

41. Unlawful possession of 'hard' drugs	10 years' prison
42. Trading in pornography	3 years' prison
43. Illegal abortion	Up to 14 years
44. Bigamy	Most of population follow polygamous beliefs
45. Rape without other injury	14 years' prison

COMPULSORY DOCUMENTS FOR CITIZENS

46. Legally required at all times	None
47. For employment	None
48. When applying for passport	Birth certificate, police clearance
49. Period of validity of passport	5 years
50. Countries forbidden to holder	Israel and South Africa

CHINA

Human rights rating: 32%

Population: 1,032,000,000
Life expectancy: 68
Infant mortality (0–1 year) per 1000 births: 60

Form of government: communist republic
Income per capita: US$ 350

Observations: Little regard for human rights though the position has improved from the even harsher conditions of the previous three decades.

FREEDOM/RIGHTS		Further comments	
1. Of movement in own country	no	Controls take form of needing work, food ration and accommodation permits	◑
2. To leave own country	no	Limited relaxation permitting some joining of families abroad and emigration	◑
3. From deprivation of nationality	YES		○
4. To seek information and teach ideas	NO	Strict controls of reading and learning	◕
5. From serfdom, slavery, forced or child labour	yes	Penal labour camps on diminishing scale still exist	◑
6. Of peaceful political opposition	NO	Fate of many dissidents unknown	●
7. Of peaceful assembly and association	NO	Only in support of government	●
8. Of women to equal rights	yes	Constitution emphasizes equality but few women occupy senior positions. Legal marriage age: 20F, 22M	◑
9. From directed employment or work permits	NO	Work assigned at local authority level	●
10. Of inter-racial, inter-religious and civil marriage	YES		○
11. To practise any religion	yes	Provided not foreign-controlled	◑
12. From compulsory religion or state ideology in schools	NO	Marxist-Leninism a compulsory subject	●
13. From political press censorship	NO	Slight relaxation permitting criticism of bureaucratic functions	●
14. From police detention without charge	NO	Indefinite confinement	●
15. From police searches of home without warrant	NO		●
16. From torture or coercion by state	yes	Violations at local level	◑
17. Of assumption of innocence until guilt proved	NO		●
18. Of accused to be promptly brought before judge or court	NO	Should be charged within two months but detention can be extended by higher authority	●
19. Of all courts to total independence	no	Communist Party ultimate arbiter	◑
20. From civilian trials in secret	NO	Often resulting in maximum sentences or death penalty	◕
21. For independent trade unions	NO		●
22. From censorship of mail	NO	Dissidents under constant scrutiny	●
23. To publish and educate in ethnic languages	yes	Local autonomy in many minority areas	◑
24. From deliberate state policies to control artistic works	NO	Conformism both political and traditional. Slight improvement on doctrinaire 'art must serve the people'	●

25. From compulsory military service	NO	Military service up to 5 years but only 10% called up	●
26. To purchase and drink alcohol	YES		○
27. To practise homosexuality between consenting adults	NO	Considered a bourgeois perversion	●
28. To use contraceptive pills and devices	YES		○
29. Of early abortion	YES		○
30. Of divorce (for men and women equally)	YES		○

STATE POWER

31. Corporal punishment by state — Excesses by individual officers with state approval ◐

32. Radio and TV broadcasts — State-controlled but many stations run by communes, universities etc. ◐

33. Book publishing — State-controlled. 100 publishers out of 165 in Peking ●

34. Number of police and military per 100,000 citizens — 2000 (including para-military) ◐

35. % of national income spent on above — 20% of planned government expenditure ◐

36. Weapons normally carried by civil police — Local police frequently unarmed ◔

37. Capital punishment by state — By shooting in back of neck. Sometimes in public and on television. Numerous crimes, including bribery and black marketeering ●

MAXIMUM PUNISHMENTS IN PENAL CODE FOR:

(Freedom-related offences)

38. Non-violent anti-government activities — Death penalty. Counter-revolutionary propaganda etc. But less frequent ●

39. Possession of banned political literature — Death penalty if active anti-revolutionary but extreme punishments less common ●

40. Refusing compulsory national service — Period of 're-education' or land work ◖

(Criminal offences)

41. Unlawful possession of 'hard' drugs — 5 years' prison

42. Trading in pornography — 3 years' prison

43. Illegal abortion — Abortion encouraged

44. Bigamy — 2 years' prison

45. Rape without other injury — Death penalty for gang rape – sometimes in public squares

COMPULSORY DOCUMENTS FOR CITIZENS

46. Legally required at all times — ID card

47. For employment — System of comprehensive personal files available to employer

48. When applying for passport — ID card. Strict currency control and permission for trip

49. Period of validity of passport — Single trip permits

50. Countries forbidden to holder — Taiwan, South Africa and where diplomatic relations not established

Human rights rating: 86%

Population: 5,100,000
Life expectancy: 73
Infant mortality (0–1 year) per 1000 births: 12

Form of government: British Crown colony
Income per capita: US$ 3600

Observations: The alternative to colonial rule, being absorbed into China, has little popular support. Hong Kong, in practice, is governed by two advisory bodies and in general they respect human rights. No universal suffrage.

FREEDOM/RIGHTS		Further comments	
1. Of movement in own country	YES		○
2. To leave own country	YES		○
3. From deprivation of nationality	YES		○
4. To seek information and teach ideas	YES		○
5. From serfdom, slavery, forced or child labour	yes	Child labour problem related to mass immigration from China	◖
6. Of peaceful political opposition	yes	Minimal opposition to colonial rule which precludes normal democratic political system	◖
7. Of peaceful assembly and association	yes	Police permits required but invariably granted	◖
8. Of women to equal rights	YES	Confucian traditions still influence domestic life	○
9. From directed employment or work permits	no	Work permits recently adopted because of illegal immigration problem	◐
10. Of inter-racial, inter-religious and civil marriage	YES		○
11. To practise any religion	YES		○
12. From compulsory religion or state ideology in schools	YES		○
13. From political press censorship	YES	97 newspapers and 388 periodicals in circulation (1981)	○
14. From police detention without charge	YES	48-hour limit	○
15. From police searches of home without warrant	yes	Exceptions for illegal drugs, gambling, prostitution and checking ID cards	○
16. From torture or coercion by state	YES		○
17. Of assumption of innocence until guilt proved	yes	Anti-corruption legislation has meant tougher investigations, particularly for Crown servants	◖
18. Of accused to be promptly brought before judge or court	YES		○
19. Of all courts to total independence	YES		○
20. From civilian trials in secret	YES		○
21. For independent trade unions	YES		○
22. From censorship of mail	YES		○
23. To publish and educate in ethnic languages	YES		○
24. From deliberate state policies to control artistic works	YES	Rare instances of government banning films damaging to relations with China	○
25. From compulsory national service	YES		○

26. To purchase and drink alcohol	**YES**	◐
27. To practise homosexuality between consenting adults	**NO**	●
28. To use contraceptive pills and devices	**YES**	○
29. Of early abortion	yes	Broad social/medical reasons ◐
30. Of divorce (for men and women equally)	**YES**	○

STATE POWER

31. Corporal punishment by state	Caning (rarely used). 18 strokes maximum	◑
32. Radio and TV broadcasts	Evenly divided between publicly owned and commercial	○
33. Book publishing	No state interference	○
34. Number of police and military per 100,000 citizens	Police only: 588 (1980)	◑
35. % of national income spent on above	2.8% law and order plus defence contribution (to UK)	○
36. Weapons normally carried by civil police	.38 Colts and batons	◐
37. Capital punishment by state	Hanging for treason and murder but all commuted since 1966	◑

MAXIMUM PUNISHMENTS IN PENAL CODE FOR:
(Freedom-related offences)

38. Non-violent anti-government activities	None, but code could impose life imprisonment for published propaganda aimed at deposing Queen	◑
39. Possession of banned political literature	2 years/HK$ 5000 fine for having literature liable to disaffect HM Forces	◑
40. Refusing compulsory national service	None	○

(Criminal offences)

41. Unlawful possession of 'hard' drugs	Simple possession up to 3 years, trafficking life imprisonment and fines
42. Trading in pornography	3 years' prison and fines
43. Illegal abortion	Life imprisonment
44. Bigamy	7 years' prison
45. Rape without other injury	Life imprisonment

COMPULSORY DOCUMENTS FOR CITIZENS

46. Legally required at all times	ID card (introduced 1980 to control illegal immigration problem)
47. For employment	ID card
48. When applying for passport	ID card
49. Period of validity of passport	10 years
50. Countries forbidden to holder	None

Human rights rating: 70%

Population: 683,900,000
Life expectancy: 53
Infant mortality (0–1 year) per 1000 births: 125

Form of government: federal democracy (22 state governments)
Income per capita: US$ 190

Observations: The National Security Act (1980) gives the government ultimate authority to suspend normal constitutional law. The severity of this varies with what is regarded as an emergency.

FREEDOM/RIGHTS		Further comments	
1. Of movement in own country	YES	But limited border areas may be controlled	○
2. To leave own country	YES		○
3. From deprivation of nationality	YES		○
4. To seek information and teach ideas	YES		○
5. From serfdom, slavery, forced or child labour	no	Despite constitution, child labour (5–14 years) is largest proportion in world	◑
6. Of peaceful political opposition	yes	Despite constitution, students, trade unionists etc. sometimes regarded as public threat	◗
7. Of peaceful assembly and association	yes	These frequently become riots which police anticipate with precautionary arrests	◗
8. Of women to equal rights	yes	But social and religious inequalities widespread	◗
9. From directed employment or work permits	YES		○
10. Of inter-racial, inter-religious and civil marriage	YES		○
11. To practise any religion	YES		○
12. From compulsory religion or state ideology in schools	YES		○
13. From political press censorship	yes	Issues creating racial or social tensions seized or banned	◗
14. From police detention without charge	NO	NSA gives both central and state governments power to detain for 15 months without trial	●
15. From police searches of home without warrant	no	No warrant needed if officer decides prompt action required	◑
16. From torture or coercion by state	no	Despite constitution many serious local abuses. Also reports of deaths while in custody	◑
17. Of assumption of innocence until guilt proved	NO	Arbitrary 'preventive' detention sometimes extends to black marketeers	●
18. Of accused to be promptly brought before judge or court	yes	Under NSA (1980) must be brought before Advisory Board of 3 judges within 21 days	◗
19. Of all courts to total independence	yes	States vary but high degree of impartial justice	◗
20. From civilian trials in secret	no	Judiciary may close court on grounds of 'safety of the state'	◑
21. For independent trade unions	no	Strikes in essential industries illegal	◑

22. From censorship of mail	yes	But tension with Pakistan means security checks on mail	◖
23. To publish and educate in ethnic languages	**YES**		○
24. From deliberate state policies to control artistic works	**YES**		○
25. From compulsory military service	**YES**		○
26. To purchase and drink alcohol	**YES**	Small areas of state prohibition	◑
27. To practise homosexuality between consenting adults	**NO**	'Unnatural act'	●
28. To use contraceptive pills and devices	**YES**	Government actively seeking to reduce population	○
29. Of early abortion	yes	Medical/social grounds	◖
30. Of divorce (for men and women equally)	yes	Near equality for Hindus. Muslims subject to Sharia law	◑

STATE POWER

31. Corporal punishment by state	None	◖
32. Radio and TV broadcasts	Autonomous government corporation. Occasional charges of bias	◖
33. Book publishing	No direct censorship	○
34. Number of police and military per 100,000 citizens	270	○
35. % of national income spent on above	5%	◖
36. Weapons normally carried by civil police	Unarmed on routine duties with the Armed Police, a separate corps	○
37. Capital punishment by state	Treason, murder, abetting suicide etc. State variations	●

MAXIMUM PUNISHMENTS IN PENAL CODE FOR:
(Freedom-related offences)

38. Non-violent anti-government activities	Prolonged detention under NSA in a few volatile districts	◑
39. Possession of banned political literature	Limited detention in some states Charged with 'sabotaging democracy'	◖
40. Refusing compulsory national service	None	○

(Criminal offences)

41. Unlawful possession of 'hard' drugs	Multiplicity of heavy sentences
42. Trading in pornography	6 months' prison
43. Illegal abortion	10 years' prison
44. Bigamy	7 years' prison
45. Rape without other injury	12 years' prison

COMPULSORY DOCUMENTS FOR CITIZENS

46. Legally required at all times	None
47. For employment	None
48. When applying for passport	Application requires police verification
49. Period of validity of passport	5 years
50. Countries forbidden to holder	South Africa

Human rights rating: 53%

Population: 154,360,000
Life expectancy: 53
Infant mortality (0–1 year) per 1000 births: 120

Form of government: parliamentary system (nominally)
Income per capita: US$ 431

Observations: The representative government is dominated by the military. The human rights situation is improving outside those areas affected by military operations against secessionist groups.

FREEDOM/RIGHTS		Further comments	
1. Of movement in own country	yes	Except former political prisoners	◖
2. To leave own country	yes	'Black list' of opponents prevented from travelling. Exit permits required	◖
3. From deprivation of nationality	**YES**		◗
4. To seek, receive and impart information and teach ideas	no	Surveillance of teaching, some harassment of academics	◑
5. From serfdom, slavery, forced or child labour	yes	Labour camps for political prisoners. Child labour abuses	◖
6. Of peaceful political opposition	no	Not if policy is for secession of islands and areas seeking independence	◑
7. Of peaceful assembly and association	no	Controlled and limited to pro-government groups	◑
8. Of women to equal rights	yes	But law disregarded in pay, work, social and political areas	◖
9. From directed employment or work permits	yes	But discrimination against former political prisoners	◖
10. Of inter-racial, inter-religious and civil marriage	yes	Majority are Muslims who do not tolerate inter-marriage	◖
11. To practise any religion	**YES**		○
12. From compulsory religion or state ideology in schools	**NO**	Islam is state religion and compulsory in most schools	●
13. From political press censorship	no	Censorship of sensitive issues. Otherwise 'self-censorship' by journalists	◑
14. From police detention without charge	**NO**	Political detentions numerous and for long periods. No legal limits	●
15. From police searches of home without warrant	no	Exceptions include corruption, economic crimes etc.	◑
16. From torture or coercion by state	no	Police abuses against arrested opponents and criminals. Position improving	◑
17. Of assumption of innocence until guilt proved	no	Habeas corpus not practised. Summary executions in East Timor	◑
18. Of accused to be promptly brought before judge or court	**NO**	Detention without trial for subversion cases continuing after new (1981) criminal code	●
19. Of all courts to total independence	no	Judges are civil servants and influenced by higher authorities	◑
20. From civilian trials in secret	no	Left to discretion of court. Reasons include public order and propriety	◑
21. For independent trade unions	no	No strikes in 'vital' sectors. No unions in government service	◑
22. From censorship of mail	yes	Does not apply to political opponents of regime	◖

23. To publish and educate in ethnic languages	NO	No Chinese schools or press for 3 million minority	●
24. From deliberate state policies to control artistic works	yes	Censorship sometimes extends into the arts	◑
25. From compulsory military service	**YES**	Minimal selective scheme	○
26. To purchase and drink alcohol	**YES**	From 18 years. Muslims abstain	○
27. To practise homosexuality between consenting adults	no	Illegal but tolerated	◑
28. To use contraceptive pills and devices	**YES**	State support. Free vasectomy	○
29. Of early abortion	no	Only when mother's life at risk	◑
30. Of divorce (for men and women equally)	**YES**	Muslim divorces favour husbands but state law is secular	○

STATE POWER

31. Corporal punishment by state	None officially	○
32. Radio and TV broadcasts	State and private stations with careful 'guidelines' to be followed	◑
33. Book publishing	Severe limitations on political and sexually permissive publications	◑
34. Number of police and military per 100,000 citizens	Police 88, military 700	◑
35. % of national income spent on above	9%	◑
36. Weapons normally carried by civil police	Pistols	◑
37. Capital punishment by state	By firing squad for murder, subversion, drug-trafficking etc.	●

MAXIMUM PUNISHMENTS IN PENAL CODE FOR:
(Freedom-related offences)

38. Non-violent anti-government activities	20 years' prison under national 'subversion' law	◑
39. Possession of banned political literature	5 years' prison	◑
40. Refusing compulsory national service	None	○

(Criminal offences)

41. Unlawful possession of 'hard' drugs	10 years' prison
42. Trading in pornography	1–5 years' prison
43. Illegal abortion	20 years' prison
44. Bigamy	Laws on bigamy considered 'unnecessary' in view of Muslim polygamy
45. Rape without other injury	2–5 years' prison

COMPULSORY DOCUMENTS FOR CITIZENS

46. Legally required at all times	ID cards. Ex-political prisoners' cards have special markings
47. For employment	ID card
48. When applying for passport	ID card, tax clearance papers
49. Period of validity of passport	5 years
50. Countries forbidden to holder	Israel, Taiwan

Human rights rating: 27%

Population: 12,525,000
Life expectancy: 57
Infant mortality (0–1 year) per 1000 births: 88

Form of government: military government
Income per capita: US$ 2410

Observations: Severe curtailment of human rights despite having signed and ratified the UN Covenant. The conflict with Iran has added a 'wartime' dimension.

FREEDOM/RIGHTS		Further comments	
1. Of movement in own country	NO	A war situation limits movements to many frontier and sensitive areas	●
2. To leave own country	yes	But not for political opponents. Exit permits required	◐
3. From deprivation of nationality	NO	30,000 of Iranian descent expelled in 1980	●
4. To seek, receive and impart information and teach ideas	NO	Total conformity with political and social aims of government	●
5. From serfdom, slavery, forced or child labour	yes	Child labour a regional practice	○
6. Of peaceful political opposition	NO	Risk of death penalty. See 38	◕
7. Of peaceful assembly and association	NO	Must be approved. Only those favourable to regime permitted	◕
8. Of women to equal rights	yes	Constitutional equality but married women need husband's permission to travel abroad	○
9. From directed employment or work permits	yes	Certain 'wartime' controls	○
10. Of inter-racial, inter-religious and civil marriage	YES	But Muslim majority denied freedom of secular law	○
11. To practise any religion	yes	Proselytizing prohibited	◑
12. From compulsory religion or state ideology in schools	no	Recent attempt to introduce Koranic studies for non-Muslims abandoned 1980	◑
13. From political press censorship	NO	No contrary views permitted. No 'undermining national unity'	●
14. From police detention without charge	NO	For political detainees. Usually accompanied by torture during interrogation	●
15. From police searches of home without warrant	no	Occasional abuses but police prefer to make arrests outside home	◐
16. From torture or coercion by state	NO	Beatings, burns, electric shocks, sexual violations etc. Deaths frequently follow	●
17. Of assumption of innocence until guilt proved	NO	Many Kurds summarily executed. Opponents abroad risk assassination by government agents	●
18. Of accused to be promptly brought before judge or court	NO	Denied to political detainees	●
19. Of all courts to total independence	NO	Revolutionary Command Council often supersedes civil courts	●
20. From civilian trials in secret	NO	Revolutionary Courts deal in camera with treason, smuggling, drug-trafficking etc.	●
21. For independent trade unions	NO	Controlled by government. No strikes permitted	●

22. From censorship of mail	no	Surveillance of suspects	◑
23. To publish and educate in ethnic languages	yes	Government licence required but not always granted	○
24. From deliberate state policies to control artistic works	yes	Care needed by artists to avoid social provocation	◐
25. From compulsory military service	NO	2 years	●
26. To purchase and drink alcohol	yes	But not for essentially Muslim population	○
27. To practise homosexuality between consenting adults	NO	Strict Islamic application of law	●
28. To use contraceptive pills and devices	yes	No government encouragement	◑
29. Of early abortion	no	Only when mother's life at risk	◑
30. Of divorce (for men and women equally)	no	Civil divorce almost unknown in essentially Muslim country	◑

STATE POWER

31. Corporal punishment by state	Extent of condoned torture reflects government disregard of constitution	◑
32. Radio and TV broadcasts	Government-owned. Daily guidance of programmes	●
33. Book publishing	Censored and controlled	●
34. Number of police and military per 100,000 citizens	2000 (peacetime strength)	◑
35. % of national income spent on above	15%. Increased by war with Iran	◑
36. Weapons normally carried by civil police	Sidearms	○
37. Capital punishment by state	Approx. 20 offences carry mandatory death sentences. By hanging or firing squad	●

MAXIMUM PUNISHMENTS IN PENAL CODE FOR:
(Freedom-related offences)

38. Non-violent anti-government activities	Death penalty. Also for Ba'ath Party members leaving for another political association or party	●
39. Possession of banned political literature	Indefinite detention with torture a probability	◑
40. Refusing compulsory national service	Minimum 3 years' prison. Regarded as 'deserter'	◑

(Criminal offences)

41. Unlawful possession of 'hard' drugs	10 years' prison
42. Trading in pornography	None
43. Illegal abortion	1 year's prison when self-induced
44. Bigamy	Discretion of court
45. Rape without other injury	15 years' prison

COMPULSORY DOCUMENTS FOR CITIZENS

46. Legally required at all times	ID card
47. For employment	ID card
48. When applying for passport	ID card, proof of nationality etc.
49. Period of validity of passport	8 years
50. Countries forbidden to holder	Israel and South Africa

Human rights rating: 73%

Population: 3,700,000
Life expectancy: 71
Infant mortality (0–1 year) per 1000 births: 17

Form of government: parliamentary democracy
Income per capita: US$ 4900

Observations: The information below does not cover the Occupied Territories, which are under separate military government. Until there is an annexation by Israel, they cannot be considered part of the country. In the Occupied Territories the Fourth Geneva Convention on the protection of civilians in times of war is not always honoured.

	FREEDOM/RIGHTS		Further comments
1.	Of movement in own country	YES	
2.	To leave own country	YES	
3.	From deprivation of nationality	yes	Occasional deportation of 'hostile' Arabs
4.	To seek information and teach ideas	YES	
5.	From serfdom, slavery, forced or child labour	YES	
6.	Of peaceful political opposition	yes	Subject to Prevention of Terror Law
7.	Of peaceful assembly and association	yes	Subject to security and military considerations
8.	Of women to equal rights	YES	Though prevalent Religious Law exercises discrimination. Marriage age 16
9.	From directed employment or work permits	YES	
10.	Of inter-racial, inter-religious and civil marriage	NO	Marriage regarded by all faiths as their religious prerogative. Based on long tradition of sectarian elitism
11.	To practise any religion	YES	
12.	From compulsory religion or state ideology in schools	no	Compulsion in state religious schools but not in non-religious
13.	From political press censorship	yes	Censorship related to security and military considerations
14.	From police detention without charge	YES	
15.	From police searches of home without warrant	yes	Local abuses against Arabs
16.	From torture or coercion by state	yes	Local abuses against Arabs
17.	Of assumption of innocence until guilt proved	YES	
18.	Of accused to be promptly brought before judge or court	YES	
19.	Of all courts to total independence	YES	
20.	From civilian trials in secret	yes	Security trials and a few juvenile cases in camera
21.	For independent trade unions	YES	
22.	From censorship of mail	yes	Only intercepted on rare 'security' grounds
23.	To publish and educate in ethnic languages	YES	
24.	From deliberate state policies to control artistic works	YES	

25. From compulsory military service	**NO**	Up to 3 years' military service	●
26. To purchase and drink alcohol	**YES**		○
27. To practise homosexuality between consenting adults	no	Illegal but law not enforced	◐
28. To use contraceptive pills and devices	**YES**		○
29. Of early abortion	yes	Broad medical and social reasons	◐
30. Of divorce (for men and women equally)	yes	Always through Rabbinate or Sharia Courts. Tradition tends to favour men	○

STATE POWER

31. Corporal punishment by state	None	○
32. Radio and TV broadcasts	'State of siege' restrictions still in force	◐
33. Book publishing	Military can veto certain books. Religious parties strict on permissive works	○
34. Number of police and military per 100,000 citizens	500 police, 4000 military (not including reservists)	●
35. % of national income spent on above	30%	◐
36. Weapons normally carried by civil police	Pistols	◐
37. Capital punishment by state	By Military Courts for terrorist acts. Last civil hanging 1962 (Eichmann)	○

MAXIMUM PUNISHMENTS IN PENAL CODE FOR:
(Freedom-related offences)

38. Non-violent anti-government activities	Law and order considerations only	○
39. Possession of banned political literature	Only *Mein Kampf*, for Holocaust reasons; under scrutiny	○
40. Refusing compulsory national service	5 years' prison	◐

(Criminal offences)

41. Unlawful possession of 'hard' drugs	3–15 years' prison
42. Trading in pornography	3 years' prison
43. Illegal abortion	5 years' prison
44. Bigamy	5 years' prison
45. Rape without other injury	14 years' prison

COMPULSORY DOCUMENTS FOR CITIZENS

46. Legally required at all times	ID card (retained from British wartime regulations)
47. For employment	ID card
48. When applying for passport	ID card and proof of Israeli citizenship if born abroad
49. Period of validity of passport	5 years
50. Countries forbidden to holder	None

Human rights rating: 92%

Population: 115,000,000
Life expectancy: 76
Infant mortality (0–1 year) per 1000 births: 8.4

Form of government: parliamentary monarchy
Income per capita: US$ 9200

Observations: Satisfactory.

FREEDOM/RIGHTS		Further comments
1. Of movement in own country	YES	
2. To leave own country	YES	
3. From deprivation of nationality	YES	
4. To seek information and teach ideas	YES	
5. From serfdom, slavery, forced or child labour	yes	Certain small minorities suffer disadvantages
6. Of peaceful political opposition	YES	
7. Of peaceful assembly and association	YES	
8. Of women to equal rights	no	Major improvements overcoming old attitudes and customs. Legal marriage age: 16F, 18M
9. From directed employment or work permits	YES	
10. Of inter-racial, inter-religious and civil marriage	YES	Females 16–20 and males 18–20 still need parent's permission
11. To practise any religion	YES	
12. From compulsory religion or state ideology in schools	YES	
13. From political press censorship	YES	
14. From police detention without charge	YES	
15. From police searches of home without warrant	YES	
16. From torture or coercion by state	YES	
17. Of assumption of innocence until guilt proved	YES	
18. Of accused to be promptly brought before judge or court	YES	Held for 72-hour maximum
19. Of all courts to total independence	YES	
20. From civilian trials in secret	YES	
21. For independent trade unions	YES	
22. From censorship of mail	YES	
23. To publish and educate in ethnic languages	YES	
24. From deliberate state policies to control artistic works	YES	
25. From compulsory military service	YES	
26. To purchase and drink alcohol	YES	
27. To practise homosexuality between consenting adults	YES	Over age 18
28. To use contraceptive pills and devices	yes	But birth pill banned
29. Of early abortion	yes	Broad social and medical reasons
30. Of divorce (for men and women equally)	YES	

STATE POWER

31. Corporal punishment by state	None	○
32. Radio and TV broadcasts	No state control of non-commercial public corporation	○
33. Book publishing	No direct control by state	○
34. Number of police and military per 100,000 citizens	Police 208, military 460	◑
35. % of national income spent on above	1%	○
36. Weapons normally carried by civil police	Pistols and truncheons	◑
37. Capital punishment by state	By hanging. Death penalty for 13 categories of crime	●

MAXIMUM PUNISHMENTS IN PENAL CODE FOR:
(*Freedom-related offences*)

38. Non-violent anti-government activities	None	○
39. Possession of banned political literature	None	○
40. Refusing compulsory national service	None	○

(*Criminal offences*)

41. Unlawful possession of 'hard' drugs	10 years' prison
42. Trading in pornography	2 years' prison
43. Illegal abortion	1 year's prison
44. Bigamy	2 years' prison. Rare because of personal 'record' book
45. Rape without other injury	15 years' prison

COMPULSORY DOCUMENTS FOR CITIZENS

46. Legally required at all times	None, but *Koseki tohon* is an official personal record
47. For employment	None
48. When applying for passport	Birth certificate
49. Period of validity of passport	5 years
50. Countries forbidden to holder	North Korea

Human rights rating: 22%

Population: 18,500,000
Life expectancy: 65
Infant mortality (0–1 year) per 1000 births: 35

Form of government: one-party communist state
Income per capita: US$ 1300

Observations: Human rights are not respected and the country is not a member state of the United Nations

FREEDOM/RIGHTS		Further comments	
1. Of movement in own country	NO	Permits required. Frequent police checks on population	●
2. To leave own country	NO	Only officials and special cases	●
3. From deprivation of nationality	YES	Kinship with Fatherland an important national concept	○
4. To seek information and teach ideas	NO	All teaching must be directed towards the 'collective spirit'	●
5. From serfdom, slavery, forced or child labour	yes	Forced labour in prison camps. Children do 'educational' labour during holidays	◖
6. Of peaceful political opposition	NO	Strict suppression of opposition	◕
7. Of peaceful assembly and association	NO	Only in support of government policies	◕
8. Of women to equal rights	yes	Slight discrimination in pay and certain social practices	◔
9. From directed employment or work permits	NO	Controlled and directed labour	●
10. Of inter-racial, inter-religious and civil marriage	YES	But late marriages (28–30) part of government policy	○
11. To practise any religion	no	Repression severe but not total. Harassment by officials	◐
12. From compulsory religion or state ideology in schools	NO	Ideological instruction in schools. Personality cult round President Kim Il-sung	●
13. From political press censorship	NO	Controlled totally by party and state	●
14. From police detention without charge	NO	Indefinite detention frequent	●
15. From police searches of home without warrant	NO	Constitutional safeguards constantly violated	●
16. From torture or coercion by state	NO	Internal Security Forces have arbitrary powers of interrogation	●
17. Of assumption of innocence until guilt proved	NO	Arbitrary state powers	●
18. Of accused to be promptly brought before judge or court	NO	Security factors decide individual cases	●
19. Of all courts to total independence	NO	Despite constitution, concept of 'responsibility to the people' takes priority over law	●
20. From civilian trials in secret	NO	Internal security decides cases individually	●
21. For independent trade unions	NO	All government-controlled	●
22. From censorship of mail	NO	Arbitrary state powers	●
23. To publish and educate in ethnic languages	YES	No significant minorities	○
24. From deliberate state policies to control artistic works	NO	Only works of cultural and political orthodoxy. Satire banned	●

25. From compulsory military service	NO	5 years maximum
26. To purchase and drink alcohol	yes	Social prejudices against female drinkers
27. To practise homosexuality between consenting adults	NO	Official view is that practice 'does not exist'
28. To use contraceptive pills and devices	yes	But puritan policies discourage use for pre-marital sex
29. Of early abortion	yes	Broad medical/reasons but policy tending to be more restrictive
30. Of divorce (for men and women equally)	yes	Social pressures discourage constitutional freedom

STATE POWER

31. Corporal punishment by state	Local abuses only
32. Radio and TV broadcasts	State-controlled. Exclusion of anything conflicting with official policy
33. Book publishing	As 32
34. Number of police and military per 100,000 citizens	7000 (including Reserves)
35. % of national income spent on above	14.5% (official budget figure)
36. Weapons normally carried by civil police	Variety of firearms
37. Capital punishment by state	Treason, murder, serious 'economic' crimes etc.

MAXIMUM PUNISHMENTS IN PENAL CODE FOR:

(Freedom-related offences)

38. Non-violent anti-government activities	Death penalty for most serious
39. Possession of banned political literature	Long period in 're-education' camp
40. Refusing compulsory national service	Death penalty if motive considered counter-revolutionary

(Criminal offences)

41. Unlawful possession of 'hard' drugs	Long period of 're-education'
42. Trading in pornography	In category of 'does not exist' but 're-education' for culprits
43. Illegal abortion	'Re-education' rather than prison
44. Bigamy	Police records make this a rare offence. Short 're-education' period
45. Rape without other injury	Death penalty despite official 'does not exist' in 'perfect' society

COMPULSORY DOCUMENTS FOR CITIZENS

46. Legally required at all times	ID documents
47. For employment	Labour and ID documents
48. When applying for passport	Personal documents plus exit visa
49. Period of validity of passport	One-trip passport except for 'official' travellers
50. Countries forbidden to holder	Those not having diplomatic relations, which are many

Human rights rating: 51%

Population: 38,860,000
Life expectancy: 64
Infant mortality (0–1 year) per 1000 births: 35

Form of government: executive president
Income per capita: US$ 1650

Observations: Government policy is centred on defending the country from a possible attack from the north. This worsens an already unsatisfactory human rights situation.

	FREEDOM/RIGHTS		Further comments	
1.	Of movement in own country	yes	Except N. Korea frontier zone restrictions	◖
2.	To leave own country	yes	But denied to those regarded as politically suspect	◖
3.	From deprivation of nationality	YES		○
4.	To seek information and teach ideas	no	Government surveillance of universities' curricula and free-thinking students	◑
5.	From serfdom, slavery, forced or child labour	yes	Random child labour	◖
6.	Of peaceful political opposition	NO	All political opposition banned. Fear of N. Korean infiltration	●
7.	Of peaceful assembly and association	NO	Not for purpose of criticizing government	●
8.	Of women to equal rights	yes	1980 constitution grants equality but discrimination pay and socially	◖
9.	From directed employment or work permits	YES		○
10.	Of inter-racial, inter-religious and civil marriage	YES		○
11.	To practise any religion	YES		○
12.	From compulsory religion or state ideology in schools	YES		○
13.	From political press censorship	no	Severe guidelines. No criticism of foreign policy, the president etc.	◑
14.	From police detention without charge	no	Long detentions without families being notified	◑
15.	From police searches of home without warrant	yes	Constitution not always honoured	◖
16.	From torture or coercion by state	NO	Torture routine. Broken limbs, beatings. Victims sign paper certifying no torture	●
17.	Of assumption of innocence until guilt proved	no	Law suspended when government decides that offence is 'grave'	◑
18.	Of accused to be promptly brought before judge or court	NO	1572 arrested in 'purification' campaign of 1980	●
19.	Of all courts to total independence	no	President may overrule Supreme Court on political/security grounds	◑
20.	From civilian trials in secret	NO	Government decides on 'justifiable' reasons for secrecy	●
21.	For independent trade unions	NO	No strikes. Independence limited	●
22.	From censorship of mail	no	Dissidents and 'suspects' under constant surveillance	◑
23.	To publish and educate in ethnic languages	YES		○

24. From deliberate state policies to control artistic works	**YES**		○
25. From compulsory military service	**NO**	30–36 months	●
26. To purchase and drink alcohol	**YES**		○
27. To practise homosexuality between consenting adults	**NO**		●
28. To use contraceptive pills and devices	**YES**	Government support	○
29. Of early abortion	yes	Medical/juridical grounds	◐
30. Of divorce (for men and women equally)	yes	Areas of inequality for women	◐

STATE POWER

31. Corporal punishment by state	None legally but degree of state complicity in routine torture cannot be ignored	◑
32. Radio and TV broadcasts	Close government supervision. Retired military officers attached to stations	◑
33. Book publishing	Government approval required before any book may be distributed.	◑
34. Number of police and military per 100,000 citizens	Police 140, military 1300 (excluding local militia)	◑
35. % of national income spent on above	9%	◐
36. Weapons normally carried by civil police	Pistols	◐
37. Capital punishment by state	By hanging or shooting. For treason, murder etc.	●

MAXIMUM PUNISHMENTS IN PENAL CODE FOR:
(Freedom-related offences)

38. Non-violent anti-government activities	10 years' prison. No criticism of present or past presidents	◑
39. Possession of banned political literature	10 years' prison	◐
40. Refusing compulsory national service	Heavy prison sentences or labour work depending on motives	◑

(Criminal offences)

41. Unlawful possession of 'hard' drugs	Death penalty for trafficking
42. Trading in pornography	1 years' prison
43. Illegal abortion	1 year when self-induced
44. Bigamy	2 years' prison
45. Rape without other injury	3 years' prison

COMPULSORY DOCUMENTS FOR CITIZENS

46. Legally required at all times	ID card
47. For employment	ID card
48. When applying for passport	Proof of purpose abroad (work, business etc.). ID card, birth certificate
49. Period of validity of passport	1 year. Tourism only for citizens over 50
50. Countries forbidden to holder	All communist countries and South Africa

MALAYSIA

Human rights rating: 54%

Population: 14,350,000
Life expectancy: 69
Infant mortality (0–1 year) per 1000 births: 30

Form of government: parliamentary democracy
Income per capita: US$ 1586

Observations: The Internal Security Act of 1969 enables the government to introduce emergency measures as and when they wish. The severity of such measures varies with the assessment of 'communist threats'.

FREEDOM/RIGHTS		Further comments	
1. Of movement in own country	YES		○
2. To leave own country	yes	Certain controls on ethnic Chinese wishing to visit China	◐
3. From deprivation of nationality	yes	Very rare 'security' cases	◑
4. To seek information and teach ideas	no	Academic restrictions on Marxist and extreme political and religious subjects	◐
5. From serfdom, slavery, forced or child labour	yes	Degree of tolerated child labour	◑
6. Of peaceful political opposition	NO	'State of emergency' outlaws Communist Party. 2 years' preventive detention without trial	●
7. Of peaceful assembly and association	no	Restrictions to reduce periodic tensions between Malays and Chinese	◐
8. Of women to equal rights	no	Islamic and oriental constraints on women but position improving	◐
9. From directed employment or work permits	YES		○
10. Of inter-racial, inter-religious and civil marriage	yes	In practice Islamic law prevails with 60% of population	◑
11. To practise any religion	YES	But Muslim fundamentalists attempting to impose Islamic law countrywide	○
12. From compulsory religion or state ideology in schools	no	Orthodox Islamic schools adhere to strict teaching of religion	◐
13. From political press censorship	no	Communist 'propaganda' forbidden but non-left opposition has relative freedom	◐
14. From police detention without charge	NO	Internal Security Act covers arrests of 'subversives'	●
15. From police searches of home without warrant	NO	Homes of political suspects frequently raided	●
16. From torture or coercion by state	yes	Local abuses only	◑
17. Of assumption of innocence until guilt proved	NO	State of emergency since 1969 permits detention without trial	●
18. Of accused to be promptly brought before judge or court	no	Not when suspect is a 'security' risk	◐
19. Of all courts to total independence	no	Internal Security Act can by-pass normal court procedures but fair trial for non-security offences	◐
20. From civilian trials in secret	NO	Emergency permits secret trials (Communist Party seen as constant threat)	●

21. For independent trade unions	yes	Partly controlled by government pressures on political issues	◐
22. From censorship of mail	no	Surveillance of 'subversive' and 'immoral' mail	◑
23. To publish and educate in ethnic languages	YES		○
24. From deliberate state policies to control artistic works	YES		○
25. From compulsory military service	YES		○
26. To purchase and drink alcohol	YES		○
27. To practise homosexuality between consenting adults	NO	Law applied with some diligence	●
28. To use contraceptive pills and devices	YES	Government support	○
29. Of early abortion	no	Only when mother's life at risk	◑
30. Of divorce (for men and women equally)	yes	Majority abide by Islamic law rather than risk apostasy	○

STATE POWER

31. Corporal punishment by state	Flogging	◑
32. Radio and TV broadcasts	Government-controlled. No discussion of sensitive ethnic topics	◑
33. Book publishing	Careful regard for government guidelines	◑
34. Number of police and military per 100,000 citizens	1000 (including Police Field Force)	◑
35. % of national income spent on above	8%	◑
36. Weapons normally carried by civil police	Revolvers	◑
37. Capital punishment by state	Treason, murder, drug-trafficking, possession of firearms etc.	●

MAXIMUM PUNISHMENTS IN PENAL CODE FOR:
(Freedom-related offences)

38. Non-violent anti-government activities	2 years for actions encouraging social unrest	◑
39. Possession of banned political literature	As 38 (under state of emergency)	◑
40. Refusing compulsory national service	None	○

(Criminal offences)

41. Unlawful possession of 'hard' drugs	2 years but trafficking a capital offence
42. Trading in pornography	6 months' prison
43. Illegal abortion	3 years self-induced, 10 years other parties
44. Bigamy	7 years but does not apply to Muslim majority
45. Rape without other injury	Periods up to life imprisonment

COMPULSORY DOCUMENTS FOR CITIZENS

46. Legally required at all times	ID cards at all times
47. For employment	ID card
48. When applying for passport	ID card and birth certificate
49. Period of validity of passport	5 years
50. Countries forbidden to holder	Israel, South Africa, Albania, China and others

Human rights rating: 96%

Population: 3,200,000
Life expectancy: 73
Infant mortality (0–1 year) per 1000 births: 14

Form of government: parliamentary democracy
Income per capita: US$ 7000

Observations: Satisfactory.

	FREEDOM/RIGHTS		Further comments	
1.	Of movement in own country	YES		○
2.	To leave own country	YES		○
3.	From deprivation of nationality	YES		○
4.	To seek information and teach ideas	YES		○
5.	From serfdom, slavery, forced or child labour	YES		○
6.	Of peaceful political opposition	YES		○
7.	Of peaceful assembly and association	YES		○
8.	Of women to equal rights	YES	First country to grant women the vote (1893)	○
9.	From directed employment or work permits	YES		○
10.	Of inter-racial, inter-religious and civil marriage	YES		○
11.	To practise any religion	YES		○
12.	From compulsory religion or state ideology in schools	YES		○
13.	From political press censorship	YES	But offence to encourage race discrimination	○
14.	From police detention without charge	YES		○
15.	From police searches of home without warrant	YES		○
16.	From torture or coercion by state	YES		○
17.	Of assumption of innocence until guilt proved	YES		○
18.	Of accused to be promptly brought before judge or court	YES		○
19.	Of all courts to total independence	YES		○
20.	From civilian trials in secret	YES		○
21.	For independent trade unions	YES		○
22.	From censorship of mail	YES		○
23.	To publish and educate in ethnic languages	YES		○
24.	From deliberate state policies to control artistic works	YES		○
25.	From compulsory military service	YES		○
26.	To purchase and drink alcohol	YES		○
27.	To practise homosexuality between consenting adults	NO	5 years maximum jail sentence. No charge against boys under 16	●
28.	To use contraceptive pills and devices	YES	Government-supported	○
29.	Of early abortion	yes	Wide medical reasons	◐

| 30. Of divorce (for men and women equally) | **YES** | Liberal laws | ○ |

STATE POWER
31. Corporal punishment by state	None	○
32. Radio and TV broadcasts	No political interference	○
33. Book publishing	Free of state interference	○
34. Number of police and military per 100,000 citizens	156 police, 406 military	◑
35. % of national income spent on above	3%	○
36. Weapons normally carried by civil police	Basically unarmed	○
37. Capital punishment by state	None	○

MAXIMUM PUNISHMENTS IN PENAL CODE FOR:
(Freedom-related offences)
38. Non-violent anti-government activities	None	○
39. Possession of banned political literature	None	○
40. Refusing compulsory national service	None	○

(Criminal offences)
41. Unlawful possession of 'hard' drugs	6 months/$1000, fine
42. Trading in pornography	3 months' prison
43. Illegal abortion	7 years if self-induced. 14 otherwise
44. Bigamy	7 years' prison
45. Rape without other injury	14 years' prison

COMPULSORY DOCUMENTS FOR CITIZENS
46. Legally required at all times	None
47. For employment	None
48. When applying for passport	Birth certificate
49. Period of validity of passport	10 years
50. Countries forbidden to holder	None

Human rights rating: 42%

Population: 78,527,000
Life expectancy: 52
Infant mortality (0–1 year) per 1000 births: 100

Form of government: Islamic military regime
Income per capita: US$ 340

Observations: For most of the period since independence in 1947, Pakistan has been governed by martial law. Together with an increasingly fundamentalist interpretation of Islamic law, it has meant that human rights are incidental to policy. An offence recently recommended for capital punishment is prostitution.

FREEDOM/RIGHTS		Further comments	
1. Of movement in own country	yes	Except for a few opposition politicians	◐
2. To leave own country	yes	Except for a few opposition politicians	◐
3. From deprivation of nationality	yes	Opposition politicians abroad face 14 years' prison on refusing to return for trial	◐
4. To seek information and teach ideas	NO	Universities subject to controls and pro-establishment bias	●
5. From serfdom, slavery, forced or child labour	NO	Bonded and child labour	●
6. Of peaceful political opposition	NO	Suspended under martial law	●
7. Of peaceful assembly and association	NO	Suspended under martial law	●
8. Of women to equal rights	NO	Strict Islamic and state discrimination	●
9. From directed employment or work permits	YES		○
10. Of inter-racial, inter-religious and civil marriage	NO	Severe Islamic law often overrides state law	●
11. To practise any religion	yes	Religions not believing Mohammed to be last prophet are denied certain rights	◐
12. From compulsory religion or state ideology in schools	NO	Usually compulsion applies only to Muslim children	●
13. From political press censorship	NO	Local censors review publications. No criticism of president and martial law	●
14. From police detention without charge	NO	Held under Martial Law Order	●
15. From police searches of home without warrant	yes	Occasional violations	◐
16. From torture or coercion by state	yes	Constitution increasingly violated at local level	◐
17. Of assumption of innocence until guilt proved	yes	Usually respected	◐
18. Of accused to be promptly brought before judge or court	yes	Constitution occasionally violated when 'security' involved	◐
19. Of all courts to total independence	yes	Except for a few 'security' prosecutions	◐
20. From civilian trials in secret	yes	Infrequently under Martial Law Order	◐
21. For independent trade unions	no	Limitations on strikes etc.	◑
22. From censorship of mail	NO	Political dissidents' mail and that from India under constant scrutiny	●
23. To publish and educate in ethnic languages	YES		○
24. From deliberate state policies to control artistic works	yes	New 'Islamization' policies restrict women's opportunities in the arts	◐

25. From compulsory military service	**YES**	Armed forces all volunteers	○
26. To purchase and drink alcohol	**NO**	80 lashes for culprits	●
27. To practise homosexuality between consenting adults	no	Illegal but socially tolerated	◑
28. To use contraceptive pills and devices	**YES**		○
29. Of early abortion	no	Only on real risk to life	◐
30. Of divorce (for men and women equally)	no	Only by complex Islamic law	◑

STATE POWER

31. Corporal punishment by state	Usually flogging	◐
32. Radio and TV broadcasts	Controlled by government. No contrary views permitted	●
33. Book publishing	Anti-president or anti-state publications may be proscribed	◑
34. Number of police and military per 100,000 citizens	630 (including para-military)	◔
35. % of national income spent on above	6% (1979)	◕
36. Weapons normally carried by civil police	Pistols, rifles, sten guns	◑
37. Capital punishment by state	By hanging (approx. 800 annually)	●

MAXIMUM PUNISHMENTS IN PENAL CODE FOR:
(Freedom-related offences)

38. Non-violent anti-government activities	7 years' prison and 10 lashes	●
39. Possession of banned political literature	5 years' prison and 20 lashes	◑
40. Refusing compulsory national service	None	○

(Criminal offences)

41. Unlawful possession of 'hard' drugs	5 years' prison
42. Trading in pornography	5 years' prison
43. Illegal abortion	2 years' prison. Court compassionate in cases of rape victims
44. Bigamy	2 years. But first wife and 'family' court may decide in husband's favour
45. Rape without other injury	7 years but Islamic law may decide on stoning to death

COMPULSORY DOCUMENTS FOR CITIZENS

46. Legally required at all times	ID card
47. For employment	None
48. When applying for passport	ID card
49. Period of validity of passport	5 years
50. Countries forbidden to holder	Israel, South Africa

Human rights rating: 93%

Population: 3,250,000
Life expectancy: 52
Infant mortality (0–1 year) per 1000 births: 130

Form of government: parliamentary democracy
Income per capita: US$ 750

Observations: Satisfactory.

FREEDOM/RIGHTS		Further comments	
1. Of movement in own country	YES		○
2. To leave own country	YES		○
3. From deprivation of nationality	YES		○
4. To seek information and teach ideas	YES		○
5. From serfdom, slavery, forced or child labour	yes	Child labour follows traditional rural and tribal customs	◑
6. Of peaceful political opposition	YES		○
7. Of peaceful assembly and association	YES		○
8. Of women to equal rights	yes	Traditional roles widespread despite enlightened constitution	◑
9. From directed employment or work permits	YES		○
10. Of inter-racial, inter-religious and civil marriage	YES		○
11. To practise any religion	YES		○
12. From compulsory religion or state ideology in schools	YES		○
13. From political press censorship	YES		○
14. From police detention without charge	YES		○
15. From police searches of home without warrant	YES	Court must issue warrant	○
16. From torture or coercion by state	YES		○
17. Of assumption of innocence until guilt proved	YES		○
18. Of accused to be promptly brought before judge or court	yes	Period to be under 90 days	◑
19. Of all courts to total independence	YES		○
20. From civilian trials in secret	YES		○
21. For independent trade unions	YES		○
22. From censorship of mail	YES		○
23. To publish and educate in ethnic languages	YES		○
24. From deliberate state policies to control artistic works	YES		○
25. From compulsory military service	YES		○
26. To purchase and drink alcohol	YES		○
27. To practise homosexuality between consenting adults	yes	Transition to a modern society creates local/tribal anomalies	◑
28. To use contraceptive pills and devices	YES		○
29. Of early abortion	yes	When mother's life at risk but new policy being formulated	◑
30. Of divorce (for men and women equally)	yes	As 27	◑

STATE POWER

31. Corporal punishment by state	None	◯
32. Radio and TV broadcasts	Government-owned but generally unbiased (no television)	◑
33. Book publishing	Embryo industry but free	◯
34. Number of police and military per 100,000 citizens	Total local police force 5000. Total military force 3500 men	◯
35. % of national income spent on above	Small % of Australian government grant	◯
36. Weapons normally carried by civil police	Batons only	◯
37. Capital punishment by state	None. Attempt to reintroduce was defeated in 1980	◯

MAXIMUM PUNISHMENTS IN PENAL CODE FOR:

(Freedom-related offences)

38. Non-violent anti-government activities	3 years' prison for certain forms of incitement	◑
39. Possession of banned political literature	None	◯
40. Refusing compulsory national service	None	◯

(Criminal offences)

41. Unlawful possession of 'hard' drugs	10 years' prison
42. Trading in pornography	2 years' prison
43. Illegal abortion	7 years' prison when self-induced, 14 years by other party
44. Bigamy	5 years' prison but traditional customs persist in certain areas
45. Rape without other injury	Life imprisonment

COMPULSORY DOCUMENTS FOR CITIZENS

46. Legally required at all times	None
47. For employment	None
48. When applying for passport	Birth and marriage certificates
49. Period of validity of passport	5 years
50. Countries forbidden to holder	None

Human rights rating: 52%

Population: 50,100,000
Life expectancy: 63
**Infant mortality (0–1 year) per 1000
  births:** 55

Form of government: parliamentary
  system (nominally)
Income per capita: US$ 800

Observations: Although martial law was lifted in 1981, the president's authority is maintained through his power to issue emergency decrees. This is exercised against guerrilla factions scattered throughout the islands, with predictable violations of human rights.

FREEDOM/RIGHTS		Further comments	
1. Of movement in own country	NO	Armed insurrection in scattered areas	●
2. To leave own country	yes	But former political detainees need special permission	◐
3. From deprivation of nationality	YES		○
4. To seek information and teach ideas	no	Pro-communist or other 'subversive' subjects banned or limited	◐
5. From serfdom, slavery, forced or child labour	yes	Child labour in rural areas. Widespread illegal child prostitution	◐
6. Of peaceful political opposition	no	Charges framed as 'subversion' or 'against public order' but position improving	◐
7. Of peaceful assembly and association	no	Banned in rural insurgency areas and risk of random arrest as terrorists	◐
8. Of women to equal rights	yes	Subject to customs and prejudices of society and regions	◐
9. From directed employment or work permits	YES		○
10. Of inter-racial, inter-religious and civil marriage	YES		○
11. To practise any religion	YES		○
12. From compulsory religion or state ideology in schools	YES		○
13. From political press censorship	no	President and security matters to be reported carefully. Papers banned	◐
14. From police detention without charge	NO	Under emergency laws president may order 'preventive detention'	●
15. From police searches of home without warrant	no	Many instances of illegal entry by police, particularly insurgency areas	◐
16. From torture or coercion by state	NO	Muslim and communist guerrillas tortured under interrogation	●
17. Of assumption of innocence until guilt proved	NO	Not when detained on 'security' or public order charge	●
18. Of accused to be promptly brought before judge or court	no	72 hours legal limit but prisoners often held years without charge	◐
19. Of all courts to total independence	NO	Constitution gives president authority to appoint Supreme Court justices	●
20. From civilian trials in secret	NO	'State of emergency' cases in camera. Wide application	●
21. For independent trade unions	yes	In private sector only. President retains emergency powers	◐
22. From censorship of mail	NO	Although martial law lifted in 1981, all mail subject to security surveillance	●
23. To publish and educate in ethnic languages	YES		○

24. From deliberate state policies to control artistic works	**YES**		○
25. From compulsory military service	yes	Selective conscription	◑
26. To purchase and drink alcohol	**YES**		◐
27. To practise homosexuality between consenting adults	yes	'Corruption of minors' charge may mean 12 years' prison	◑
28. To use contraceptive pills and devices	**YES**	Government support	○
29. Of early abortion	no	Only when mother's life at risk	◖
30. Of divorce (for men and women equally)	**NO**	If divorced abroad, not recognized on return to Philippines	●

STATE POWER

31. Corporal punishment by state — Numerous rebel movements encourage arbitrary violence by state forces   ◖

32. Radio and TV broadcasts — Most stations under National Commission control   ◖

33. Book publishing — Freedom except for extreme left ideas   ◑

34. Number of police and military per 100,000 citizens — 800 (including para-military etc.)   ◐

35. % of national income spent on above — 5%   ◑

36. Weapons normally carried by civil police — .38 revolvers   ◑

37. Capital punishment by state — By firing squad or electrocution for treason, murder, piracy etc. But not above age 70   ●

MAXIMUM PUNISHMENTS IN PENAL CODE FOR:
(Freedom-related offences)

38. Non-violent anti-government activities — Indefinite detention under emergency regulations   ◖

39. Possession of banned political literature — Long detention for possession of Communist Party and other subversive literature   ◖

40. Refusing compulsory national service — 2 years' prison   ◑

(Criminal offences)

41. Unlawful possession of 'hard' drugs — Death penalty

42. Trading in pornography — 2 years' prison

43. Illegal abortion — 20 years' prison

44. Bigamy — 12 years' prison

45. Rape without other injury — Life imprisonment; death for gang rape

COMPULSORY DOCUMENTS FOR CITIZENS

46. Legally required at all times — ID card

47. For employment — ID card

48. When applying for passport — ID card, birth certificate

49. Period of validity of passport — 2 years

50. Countries forbidden to holder — Lebanon

SAUDI ARABIA

Human rights rating: 29%

Population: 10,395,000
Life expectancy: 55
Infant mortality (0–1 year) per 1000 births: 60

Form of government: Islamic kingdom
Income per capita: US$ 11,000

Observations: Human rights are not respected and strict Koranic law prevails. As this is considered to be divinely inspired, and therefore perfect, conflicting ideas must be wrong and cannot be tolerated.

FREEDOM/RIGHTS		Further comments	
1. Of movement in own country	yes	But women must not drive cars or travel alone	◐
2. To leave own country	no	Exit permit required. Women must have male guardian's permission	◑
3. From deprivation of nationality	YES		○
4. To seek information and teach ideas	NO	All ideas hostile to Islam or government forbidden. No public cinemas	●
5. From serfdom, slavery, forced or child labour	yes	But traditional tribal patterns persist with child labour etc.	◐
6. Of peaceful political opposition	NO	No political parties permitted	●
7. Of peaceful assembly and association	NO	Public criticism of state or religion forbidden	●
8. Of women to equal rights	NO	Women's place in society and employment permitted to her must conform to Islamic law	●
9. From directed employment or work permits	NO	Large numbers of foreign workers require strict permit control	●
10. Of inter-racial, inter-religious and civil marriage	NO	Saudi's cannot marry foreigners without government permission	●
11. To practise any religion	NO	Non-Muslims must pray in private. Wearing of crosses forbidden	●
12. From compulsory religion or state ideology in schools	NO	Strict Islamic instruction	●
13. From political press censorship	no	All newspaper editors must be sanctioned by Information minister. No pictures of women permitted.	◑
14. From police detention without charge	NO	Person's arrest only discovered when family make inquiries	●
15. From police searches of home without warrant	yes	Warrants usually available from provincial governor; strict pursuit of alcohol and drug suspects	◐
16. From torture or coercion by state	no	The need to obtain 'confessions' encourages local police abuses	◑
17. Of assumption of innocence until guilt proved	yes	Burden of proof on accuser or prosecutor	◐
18. Of accused to be promptly brought before judge or court	NO	Sharia law above 'human rights' considerations	●
19. Of all courts to total independence	no	Sharia law applies but judges can be overruled by Interior minister	◑
20. From civilian trials in secret	no	Security and 'drug' trials, embezzlement and forgery, often in secret	◑
21. For independent trade unions	NO	Unions illegal but local practices permit worker/employer negotiations	●

22. From censorship of mail	no	Surveillance of large foreign and non-Islamic influx of workers
23. To publish and educate in ethnic languages	YES	
24. From deliberate state policies to control artistic works	NO	Sharia law limits artistic expression to 'inoffensive' subjects
25. From compulsory military service	YES	
26. To purchase and drink alcohol	NO	Flogging for possession, drunkenness etc. 2 years for manufacturing
27. To practise homosexuality between consenting adults	no	Illegal but tolerated if practised discreetly
28. To use contraceptive pills and devices	yes	But restrictions on availability
29. Of early abortion	no	Only when mother's life at risk
30. Of divorce (for men and women equally)	no	Only by complex Islamic law

STATE POWER

31. Corporal punishment by state — Flogging, amputation of hand for theft are Islamic customs

32. Radio and TV broadcasts — Under Ministry of Information except for American oil companies service

33. Book publishing — All 'offensive' (anti-Islamic, political, erotic) books banned

34. Number of police and military per 100,000 citizens — 970 (including National Guard)

35. % of national income spent on above — 20%

36. Weapons normally carried by civil police — Variety of firearms

37. Capital punishment by state — By beheading. Sometimes in public. Also stoning to death for adultery and beheading for renouncing Islam

MAXIMUM PUNISHMENTS IN PENAL CODE FOR:

(Freedom-related offences)

38. Non-violent anti-government activities — Strict Islamic law. Discretionary sentencing by *Kadi* (religious judge) up to death penalty.

39. Possession of banned political literature — As previous answer

40. Refusing compulsory national service — None

(Criminal offences)

41. Unlawful possession of 'hard' drugs — 30 lashes and/or discretionary prison sentence

42. Trading in pornography — As previous answer

43. Illegal abortion — Regarded as murder

44. Bigamy — No crime. Polygamy legal

45. Rape without other injury — Regarded as unlawful intercourse. Stoning to death or state execution

COMPULSORY DOCUMENTS FOR CITIZENS

46. Legally required at all times — None

47. For employment — Labour card. Visa for foreign workers

48. When applying for passport — Birth certificate

49. Period of validity of passport — 5 years

50. Countries forbidden to holder — Israel

Human rights rating: 61%

Population: 2,400,000
Life expectancy: 70
Infant mortality (0–1 year) per 1000 births: 12

Form of government: parliamentary system (nominally)
Income per capita: US$ 3500

Observations: The human rights position is unsatisfactory. The Internal Security Act, Banishment Act, Arms Offences Act and others may be applied in such a way as to give absolute power to the government and to prevent meaningful political opposition.

FREEDOM/RIGHTS		Further comments	
1. Of movement in own country	YES	Change of address to be reported within 14 days	○
2. To leave own country	yes	Rare cases of passport denied for political reasons	◖
3. From deprivation of nationality	yes	A Banishment Act not used since 1959	◖
4. To seek information and teach ideas	yes	But limits on teaching likely to encourage community tensions. Government 'suitability certificates' required by students	◖
5. From serfdom, slavery, forced or child labour	YES		○
6. Of peaceful political opposition	no	Government opponents occasionally detained as security risks	◑
7. Of peaceful assembly and association	no	Gathering of more than 5 people requires police permit	◑
8. Of women to equal rights	yes	Legal equality but discrimination in labour market and socially	○
9. From directed employment or work permits	YES		○
10. Of inter-racial, inter-religious and civil marriage	YES		○
11. To practise any religion	YES		○
12. From compulsory religion or state ideology in schools	YES	Government considering whether to introduce religious teachings to counter current materialism	○
13. From political press censorship	no	3 years' prison for 'seditious tendencies'. Anti-government journalists have been detained	◑
14. From police detention without charge	no	2 years without charge and renewed indefinitely (under Internal Security Act)	◑
15. From police searches of home without warrant	yes	Except with drug suspects or 'security cases'	◖
16. From torture or coercion by state	no	Occasional local assault and beatings when under interrogation	◑
17. Of assumption of innocence until guilt proved	NO		●
18. Of accused to be promptly brought before judge or court	NO	Internal Security Act may deny habeas corpus	●
19. Of all courts to total independence	YES		○
20. From civilian trials in secret	NO	All 'public order' trials may be held in camera	●
21. For independent trade unions	yes	Essential services strikes illegal Unions affiliated to ruling party	◖
22. From censorship of mail	YES		○

23. To publish and educate in ethnic languages	YES		○
24. From deliberate state policies to control artistic works	YES		○
25. From compulsory military service	NO	2–3 years' military service	●
26. To purchase and drink alcohol	YES		○
27. To practise homosexuality between consenting adults	no	Illegal but areas where tolerated	◑
28. To use contraceptive pills and devices	YES		○
29. Of early abortion	YES	By medical practitioner with mother's consent	○
30. Of divorce (for men and women equally)	YES		○

STATE POWER

31. Corporal punishment by state	Caning. 24-stroke maximum	◑
32. Radio and TV broadcasts	Functions within strict government guidelines	◑
33. Book publishing	Circumspection on political themes	◑
34. Number of police and military per 100,000 citizens	5400 (including Home Guard and paramilitary)	●
35. % of national income spent on above	13%	◑
36. Weapons normally carried by civil police	Pistols	◑
37. Capital punishment by state	Many. Including gang robbery, abetting suicides of under-18s. By hanging and not always reported	●

MAXIMUM PUNISHMENTS IN PENAL CODE FOR:
(Freedom-related offences)

38. Non-violent anti-government activities	3 years for 'seditious tendencies' (creating hatred or contempt of government)	◑
39. Possession of banned political literature	1–2 years' prison	◑
40. Refusing compulsory national service	2 years' 'labour' force or prison	○

(Criminal offences)

41. Unlawful possession of 'hard' drugs	6 months in rehabilitation centre and 2 years supervision. Death penalty for trafficking.
42. Trading in pornography	6 months
43. Illegal abortion	10 years' prison if by non-medical person
44. Bigamy	10 years' prison
45. Rape without other injury	Life imprisonment

COMPULSORY DOCUMENTS FOR CITIZENS

46. Legally required at all times	ID card
47. For employment	ID card
48. When applying for passport	ID card
49. Period of validity of passport	5–10 years
50. Countries forbidden to holder	Kampuchea, Laos, N. Korea, Vietnam. Limitations on China, South Africa

Human rights rating: 75%

Population: 15,200,000
Life expectancy: 68
Infant mortality (0–1 year) per 1000 births: 43

Form of government: multi-party democracy
Income per capita: US$ 250

Observations: Violence between Sinhalese and Tamils is regarded as a justification for the Prevention of Terror Act (1979). Periodic states of emergency also infringe human rights. The country recently ratified the UN Covenant.

FREEDOM/RIGHTS		Further comments
1. Of movement in own country	YES	
2. To leave own country	YES	
3. From deprivation of nationality	YES	
4. To seek information and teach ideas	YES	
5. From serfdom, slavery, forced or child labour	yes	Certain child labour abuses at local level
6. Of peaceful political opposition	yes	Minority race groups have suffered intermittent repression
7. Of peaceful assembly and association	yes	Police permits needed for rallies
8. Of women to equal rights	YES	Universal suffrage from 1931 but certain ethnic groups have own customs
9. From directed employment or work permits	YES	
10. Of inter-racial, inter-religious and civil marriage	YES	
11. To practise any religion	YES	Buddhism has preferred status
12. From compulsory religion or state ideology in schools	no	Numerous religions with doctrinal schools
13. From political press censorship	no	State of emergency bannings may be contested in Supreme Court
14. From police detention without charge	NO	Up to 18 months' detention under anti-terrorist law
15. From police searches of home without warrant	no	But under Dangerous Drugs Act and Anti-Terrorist Law no warrant required
16. From torture or coercion by state	yes	Abuses during periodic inter-racial disturbances
17. Of assumption of innocence until guilt proved	no	Long periods of detention invalidate constitution
18. Of accused to be promptly brought before judge or court	yes	Within 24 hours but can be remanded for 3 months or longer
19. Of all courts to total independence	YES	Trial by jury customary
20. From civilian trials in secret	yes	Exceptions under Anti-Terrorist Law
21. For independent trade unions	yes	Strikes in essential services may be banned. Dismissal for disobedience
22. From censorship of mail	yes	Rare violations of constitution
23. To publish and educate in ethnic languages	YES	
24. From deliberate state policies to control artistic works	YES	
25. From compulsory military service	YES	

26. To purchase and drink alcohol	**YES**		○
27. To practise homosexuality between consenting adults	no	Illegal but prosecutions unlikely	◑
28. To use contraceptive pills and devices	**YES**		○
29. Of early abortion	no	Restricted to saving mother's life	◑
30. Of divorce (for men and women equally)	**YES**		○

STATE POWER

31. Corporal punishment by state	Caning of juveniles	○
32. Radio and TV broadcasts	Government control limits criticism and free discussion.	○
33. Book publishing	Rare instances of government interference and pressures	◑
34. Number of police and military per 100,000 citizens	320	○
35. % of national income spent on above	3%	○
36. Weapons normally carried by civil police	Normally unarmed	○
37. Capital punishment by state	By hanging. Clemency now customary	◑

MAXIMUM PUNISHMENTS IN PENAL CODE FOR:
(Freedom-related offences)

38. Non-violent anti-government activities	'Creating disaffection' against head of state, government etc., 'promoting ill-will' between different classes may mean 2 years' prison under penal code or 20 years under Emergency Regulations	◑
39. Possession of banned political literature	As 38	◑
40. Refusing compulsory national service	None	○

(Criminal offences)

41. Unlawful possession of 'hard' drugs	20 years' prison
42. Trading in pornography	Discretion of court
43. Illegal abortion	7 years for 'intentional miscarriage' with mother's consent, 12 years without
44. Bigamy	7 years' prison
45. Rape without other injury	20 years' prison

COMPULSORY DOCUMENTS FOR CITIZENS

46. Legally required at all times	ID card
47. For employment	ID card
48. When applying for passport	ID card and birth certificate
49. Period of validity of passport	5 years
50. Countries forbidden to holder	None

Human rights rating: 34%

Population: 8,979,000
Life expectancy: 65
Infant mortality (0–1 year) per 1000
   births: 81

Form of government: one-party state
Income per capita: US$ 1200

Observations: Severe curtailment of human rights despite having ratified the UN Covenant. The conflict with Israel has added 'wartime' controls to harsh policies.

FREEDOM/RIGHTS		Further comments	
1. Of movement in own country	yes	Except in security and war zones	◐
2. To leave own country	yes	Exit visa required. Bond may be required to guarantee applicant's return	◐
3. From deprivation of nationality	no	May be deprived on absence abroad	◑
4. To seek, receive and impart information and teach ideas	NO	Teaching must accept Ba'ath Party control and respect for president	◕
5. From serfdom, slavery, forced or child labour	yes	Regional child labour	◐
6. Of peaceful political opposition	NO	'State of emergency' since 1965. Only token opposition permitted	●
7. Of peaceful assembly and association	NO	Only pro-government assemblies and associations	●
8. Of women to equal rights	no	Despite constitution, tradition and Islam ensure continued social inferiority	◑
9. From directed employment or work permits	YES		○
10. Of inter-racial, inter-religious and civil marriage	YES	Only for non-Muslim minority	○
11. To practise any religion	yes	Except for Seventh Day Adventists	◐
12. From compulsory religion or state ideology in schools	no	Under Sharia law compulsory instruction in Muslim schools	◑
13. From political press censorship	no	Editorial guidance from government. Self-censorship practised	◑
14. From police detention without charge	NO	Indefinite detention for major political opponents	●
15. From police searches of home without warrant	NO	Homes of political dissidents raided frequently	●
16. From torture or coercion by state	NO	Torture a feature of police interrogation. No government restraints on practice (particularly of political opponents)	●
17. Of assumption of innocence until guilt proved	NO	Summary executions follow political protests. 150 unarmed men reported shot in Hama by military in 1980 (other reports give a figure of 'thousands')	●
18. Of accused to be promptly brought before judge or court	NO	No time limit. Estimate of 5000 detainees	●
19. Of all courts to total independence	no	For non-political cases only. Military have authority to take over cases	◑
20. From civilian trials in secret	NO	Political offences tried by military in camera	●
21. For independent trade unions	NO	Strikes illegal. Labour organizations under ruling Ba'ath Party	●
22. From censorship of mail	NO	All mail subject to surveillance	●

23. To publish and educate in ethnic languages	**YES**		○
24. From deliberate state policies to control artistic works	yes	Strict prohibitions on erotica and illustrations of genitalia.	◑
25. From compulsory military service	**NO**	30 months	●
26. To purchase and drink alcohol	**YES**	Except during feast of Ramadan	●
27. To practise homosexuality between consenting adults	**NO**	Maximum 3 months' prison	●
28. To use contraceptive pills and devices	**YES**		○
29. Of early abortion	yes	Medical/juridical reasons	◑
30. Of divorce (for men and women equally)	yes	Only for non-Muslim minority	◑

STATE POWER

31. Corporal punishment by state	Despite constitution, no restraints on official use of torture (a form of corporal punishment)	◑
32. Radio and TV broadcasts	Official voice of the government	●
33. Book publishing	Books including any criticism of Arab cause against Israel banned	◐
34. Number of police and military per 100,000 citizens	3100	●
35. % of national income spent on above	26%	●
36. Weapons normally carried by civil police	Sidearms	◑
37. Capital punishment by state	By hanging (sometimes in public) and shooting. Treason, murder, robbery, arson, verbal attacks on party. Also, by assassination, of opponents abroad	●

MAXIMUM PUNISHMENTS IN PENAL CODE FOR:
(Freedom-related offences)

38. Non-violent anti-government activities	Death penalty (and for membership of Muslim Brotherhood)	●
39. Possession of banned political literature	Death penalty if motives considered to endanger the state	●
40. Refusing compulsory national service	Regarded as deserter. 5 years' prison. If abroad, passport withdrawn etc.	◐

(Criminal offences)

41. Unlawful possession of 'hard' drugs	Life imprisonment for trafficking
42. Trading in pornography	3 years' prison
43. Illegal abortion	Self-induced 1–3 years' prison but usually unpunished. Doctors reported to Medical Association
44. Bigamy	Polygamy for Muslims. Medical, financial and family background certificates seen as safeguards
45. Rape without other injury	Death penalty

COMPULSORY DOCUMENTS FOR CITIZENS

46. Legally required at all times	ID cards from age 15
47. For employment	ID card and extract of civil status
48. When applying for passport	ID card, tax and military clearance
49. Period of validity of passport	2–6 years
50. Countries forbidden to holder	Israel, South Africa (primarily)

Human rights rating: 53%

Population: 17,878,000
Life expectancy: 72
Infant mortality (0–1 year) per 1000 births: 24

Form of government: one-party state
Income per capita: US$ 2500

Observations: The Statute for the Punishment of Sedition (1949) is part of a general state of siege which gives the government absolute powers. Human rights are not always recognized and Taiwan is not a member state of the United Nations, being technically part of China.

FREEDOM/RIGHTS		Further comments	
1. Of movement in own country	YES	Except to military areas	
2. To leave own country	yes	Boys over 13 must remain until military service at 18 is completed	
3. From deprivation of nationality	yes	But non-acceptance of Chinese who have lived in communist territories during previous 5 years	
4. To seek, receive and impart information and teach ideas	no	No ideas that question the political legitimacy of authorities or nationalism	
5. From serfdom, slavery, forced or child labour	yes	Extensive child labour	
6. Of peaceful political opposition	NO	Martial law since 1949. Unlawful to disagree with Taiwan's claim to represent all China	
7. Of peaceful assembly and association	no	Questioning regime's legality seen as sedition. Otherwise political rallies occur	
8. Of women to equal rights	yes	Position of women improving with industrialization but not for divorce	
9. From directed employment or work permits	YES		
10. Of inter-racial, inter-religious and civil marriage	YES		
11. To practise any religion	yes	Increasing tension with government. More controls on religious activities	
12. From compulsory religion or state ideology in schools	YES		
13. From political press censorship	NO	Censorship under publications law. 453 issues affected during 1981. Licence may be suspended for one year	
14. From police detention without charge	no	3 months' 'investigation'	
15. From police searches of home without warrant	yes	Occasional abuses	
16. From torture or coercion by state	no	Beatings, denial of sleep etc.	
17. Of assumption of innocence until guilt proved	yes		
18. Of accused to be promptly brought before judge or court	yes		
19. Of all courts to total independence	no	Ultimate jurisdiction given to military courts but position improving	
20. From civilian trials in secret	no	Cases often taken over by military if secrecy considered necessary	
21. For independent trade unions	no	Unions undeveloped. Strikes prohibited under martial law	

22. From censorship of mail	yes	Surveillance of political dissidents	◑
23. To publish and educate in ethnic languages	yes	Languages usually have common written characters but Mandarin is official dialect	◑
24. From deliberate state policies to control artistic works	**YES**		○
25. From compulsory military service	**NO**	2 years	●
26. To purchase and drink alcohol	**YES**		○
27. To practise homosexuality between consenting adults	**NO**	Death penalty maximum sentence but discretion of court permitted and practised	●
28. To use contraceptive pills and devices	**YES**		○
29. Of early abortion	yes	Law recently relaxed. Broad social and medical reasons	◐
30. Of divorce (men and women equally)	yes	Law favours men. Particularly over inheritance	◐

STATE POWER

31. Corporal punishment by state	Official canings discontinued	○
32. Radio and TV broadcasts	Subject to government control and censorship	◑
33. Book publishing	Banning of politically or morally undesirable books. Copyright piracy permitted	◑
34. Number of police and military per 100,000 citizens	3000 (not including Reserves equal to 6% of population)	●
35. % of national income spent on above	9%	◑
36. Weapons normally carried by civil police	Pistols	◑
37. Capital punishment by state	By firing squad for nearly 50 crimes including armed robbery, disrupting the money market or water supplies, corruption etc.	●

MAXIMUM PUNISHMENTS IN PENAL CODE FOR:
(Freedom-related offences)

38. Non-violent anti-government activities	Life sentence for participating in human rights rally (Kaohsiung Incident, 1979)	◑
39. Possession of banned political literature	14 years' prison	◑
40. Refusing compulsory national service	1 year's prison to be followed by repeat call-up	◑

(Criminal offences)

41. Unlawful possession of 'hard' drugs	6 months' prison and/or fine
42. Trading in pornography	Fine and confiscation
43. Illegal abortion	6 months' prison and/or fine when self-induced
44. Bigamy	5 years' prison
45. Rape without other injury	5–7 years' prison

COMPULSORY DOCUMENTS FOR CITIZENS

46. Legally required at all times	ID card
47. For employment	None
48. When applying for passport	ID card, birth certificate
49. Period of validity of passport	Average 3 years
50. Countries forbidden to holder	People's Republic of China

Human rights rating: 64%

Population: 46,280,000
Life expectancy: 62
Infant mortality (0–1 year) per 1000 births: 68

Form of government: constitutional monarchy
Income per capita: US$ 650

Observations: Harsh measures are taken against people under the Anti-Communist Activities Act (1979) but otherwise human rights are generally respected.

FREEDOM/RIGHTS		Further comments	
1. Of movement in own country	yes	Except in active insurgent areas	◐
2. To leave own country	YES		◐
3. From deprivation of nationality	YES	Only rarely for treason	◐
4. To seek information and teach ideas	yes	Pro-communist teachings proscribed	◐
5. From serfdom, slavery, forced or child labour	no	Child labour estimated to be 3–5 million. Ages 11–15 years	◑
6. Of peaceful political opposition	no	No public sympathies with communism, no insulting monarchy etc.	◑
7. Of peaceful assembly and association	yes	Restrictions seldom applied except when pro-communist	◐
8. Of women to equal rights	yes	Equal legal status widely disregarded though well-represented in professions	◐
9. From directed employment or work permits	YES		○
10. Of inter-racial, inter-religious and civil marriage	YES		○
11. To practise any religion	YES		○
12. From compulsory religion or state ideology in schools	YES		○
13. From political press censorship	yes	Anti-communist law occasionally applied. Government may and does close newspapers	◐
14. From police detention without charge	no	Arbitrary arrests declining but still a factor	◑
15. From police searches of home without warrant	yes	Except when on communist pursuit operations	◐
16. From torture or coercion by state	yes	Local abuses frequently reported	◐
17. Of assumption of innocence until guilt proved	yes	But denied to pro-communist suspects	◐
18. Of accused to be promptly brought before judge or court	no	Up to 210 days' delay if communist suspect. 480 days if handed to military	◑
19. Of all courts to total independence	yes	Military courts empowered to take over certain cases	◐
20. From civilian trials in secret	no	Some 'public order' trials in camera	◑
21. For independent trade unions	yes	But only 2% of workers unionized. Prohibitions on certain activities	◑
22. From censorship of mail	YES		○
23. To publish and educate in ethnic languages	YES		○

24.	From deliberate state policies to control artistic works	**YES**		○
25.	From compulsory military service	**NO**	2 years' military service	●
26.	To purchase and drink alcohol	**YES**		◔
27.	To practise homosexuality between consenting adults	yes	Official policy of 'benign' tolerance	◑
28.	To use contraceptive pills and devices	**YES**	Government support	○
29.	Of early abortion	yes	Medical and juridical reasons	◑
30.	Of divorce (for men and women equally)	**YES**		○

STATE POWER

31.	Corporal punishment by state	Prison punishments include flogging	◑
32.	Radio and TV broadcasts	State control and direction	●
33.	Book publishing	Books often banned on security grounds (96 in 1980)	◐
34.	Number of police and military per 100,000 citizens	720 (approx.)	◑
35.	% of national income spent on above	6%	◑
36.	Weapons normally carried by civil police	Revolvers	◑
37.	Capital punishment by state	For murder and treason. By machine-gun	●

MAXIMUM PUNISHMENTS IN PENAL CODE FOR:
(Freedom-related offences)

38.	Non-violent anti-government activities	Indefinite detention for those considered 'security' risks	◐
39.	Possession of banned political literature	Indefinite detention if suspected of communist affiliation	◐
40.	Refusing compulsory national service	Service enforced. Labour, detention camp etc.	◐

(Criminal offences)

41.	Unlawful possession of 'hard' drugs	Up to death penalty
42.	Trading in pornography	6 months and/or heavy fine
43.	Illegal abortion	3 years if by mother. 5 years by other parties
44.	Bigamy	Loose arrangements common, usually to woman's disadvantage
45.	Rape without other injury	10 years' prison

COMPULSORY DOCUMENTS FOR CITIZENS

46.	Legally required at all times	ID card
47.	For employment	ID card
48.	When applying for passport	Birth certificate, guarantor, police clearance
49.	Period of validity of passport	5 years
50.	Countries forbidden to holder	None

Human rights rating: 29%

Population: 60,000,000
Life expectancy: 62
Infant mortality (0–1 year) per 1000 births: 60

Form of government: one-party communist state
Income per capita: US$ 200

Observations: Unsatisfactory. The need to 're-educate' part of the population to the ideology of a national communist government, and to eradicate 'bourgeois' behaviour, has meant the subordination of human rights to state policies.

FREEDOM/RIGHTS		Further comments	
1. Of movement in own country	no	Indirect controls through food rationing and work permits. Buddhist monks must stay near pagoda	◑
2. To leave own country	no	Limited emigration. Frequent policy changes affecting ethnic Chinese	◑
3. From deprivation of nationality	YES		○
4. To seek information and teach ideas	NO	All education conforms to government's ideology. Curricula very selective	◕
5. From serfdom, slavery, forced or child labour	no	Re-education camps are centres of forced labour	◑
6. Of peaceful political opposition	NO	Over 100,000 in re-education camps following unification of country	●
7. Of peaceful assembly and association	NO	Only in support of Communist Party	●
8. Of women to equal rights	YES	But regional attitudes of female subservience not totally eradicated	○
9. From directed employment or work permits	NO	All work by directed labour or within the national programme	●
10. Of inter-racial, inter-religious and civil marriage	YES		○
11. To practise any religion	yes	But not if openly counter-revolutionary. Sermons subject to government approval	◑
12. From compulsory religion or state ideology in schools	NO	Marxist-Leninism part of curriculum	●
13. From political press censorship	NO	All papers must promote 'revolutionary culture'	●
14. From police detention without charge	NO	Detention may last years for suspected 'reactionaries'	●
15. From police searches of home without warrant	NO	Suspected counter-revolutionaries picked up without warrants	●
16. From torture or coercion by state	yes	But re-education camps may practise unauthorized beatings	◑
17. Of assumption of innocence until guilt proved	NO	Fact of arrest often constitutes assumption of guilt	●
18. Of accused to be promptly brought before judge or court	NO	Many accused promptly sent to re-education camps	●
19. Of all courts to total independence	NO	Communist Party ultimate authority	●
20. From civilian trials in secret	NO	Public trials frequently denied	●
21. For independent trade unions	NO	Communist Party has total control	●
22. From censorship of mail	NO	Strict surveillance, particularly with mail from abroad	●

23. To publish and educate in ethnic languages	yes	But suspicion of southern minorities a legacy of recent war	◖
24. From deliberate state policies to control artistic works	NO	Support for artists and writers depends on adherence to 'revolutionary culture'	●
25. From compulsory military service	NO	2 years' military service	●
26. To purchase and drink alcohol	YES		○
27. To practise homosexuality between consenting adults	no	Illegal but no official action	◐
28. To use contraceptive pills and devices	YES		○
29. Of early abortion	YES		○
30. Of divorce (for men and women equally)	YES		○

STATE POWER

31. Corporal punishment by state	Illegal but beatings in re-education camps	◖
32. Radio and TV broadcasts	State control total and propagandist	●
33. Book publishing	Strict control by Ministry of Culture	●
34. Number of police and military per 100,000 citizens	4000 (including Armed Militia)	●
35. % of national income spent on above	20% estimated	◑
36. Weapons normally carried by civil police	Variety of firearms	●
37. Capital punishment by state	By shooting. Purge following recent war has given way to greatly reduced number of executions	●

MAXIMUM PUNISHMENTS IN PENAL CODE FOR:
(Freedom-related offences)

38. Non-violent anti-government activities	Re-education camp for long periods. Execution for some unrepentant counter-revolutionaries	●
39. Possession of banned political literature	As 38	●
40. Refusing compulsory national service	Re-education. 2 years or more	◑

(Criminal offences)

41. Unlawful possession of 'hard' drugs	Trafficking can be capital offence
42. Trading in pornography	Not applicable in present-day society
43. Illegal abortion	Abortion encouraged
44. Bigamy	Social priorities make bigamy a minor offence
45. Rape without other injury	Heavy indeterminate sentences, often by 'people's tribunals'

COMPULSORY DOCUMENTS FOR CITIZENS

46. Legally required at all times	ID card
47. For employment	Comprehensive dossiers on all directed labour
48. When applying for passport	ID card. Strict police clearance
49. Period of validity of passport	One-trip visa
50. Countries forbidden to holder	Those with no diplomatic relations (numerous)

Human rights rating: BAD

Population: 15,551,358
Life expectancy: 41 (1978)
Infant mortality (0–1 year) per 1000 births: 237 (1978)

Form of government: one-party communist state
Income per capita: figures not available

Observations: The presence of a Soviet army of occupation numbering 90,000, and advisers supervising all Ministries, ensure that the Soviet Union will control events and the human rights situation until they are withdrawn. Every effort is being made to indoctrinate schoolchildren and students with pro-Soviet and Marxist ideas.

Summary

In present circumstances it would be impossible to complete the Guide's questionnaire. Following the Soviety military intervention at the end of 1979 and the ensuing civil war, summary executions and disappearances, the destruction of villages, and the use of torture by both combatants are common occurrences. Normal life outside the main towns remains at the mercy of military action and large areas of the countryside are controlled by anti-government forces.

In urban areas controlled by the puppet regime, political dissent is widespread but expressed only at great risk to life or freedom. The press and broadcasting are government-run though attempts are being made to placate the Muslim population by showing more tolerance towards Islam. This tolerance does not extend to young men of military age who are forcibly inducted into an army which frequently deserts to the anti-government forces.

The number of political detainees in one prison alone, Pol-e-Charkhi in Kabul, is approximately 600. The court system is being refashioned by Soviet advisers and political cases are decided by the secret police.

Travel within the country is severely restricted for both political and military reasons and exit permits are limited though not beyond those rich enough to bribe officials. But between 10% and 15% have left the country without such permits – to become refugees in Pakistan and other neighbouring states.

Human rights rating: POOR

Population: 33,500,000
Life expectancy: 55
**Infant mortality (0–1 year) per 1000
   births:** 100

Form of government: one-party system
Income per capita: US$ 180

Observations: This country is presented in summary form because of the unreliability of information and the failure of official sources to reply to inquiries.

Summary

The present socialist government came to power after a military coup in 1962. Opponents who were jailed at the time have been progressively released over the years. In 1980, 15,000 opponents and convicted criminals were given freedom. Inquiries from human rights organizations have been ignored and an authoritarian one-party regime with strong military backing is indifferent to international opinion.

Burma is among the countries that have signed fewest of the human rights agreements. Death sentences and torture are practised or are lawful and the anti-subversion legislation permits indefinite detention. The system of People's Courts has been devised as a compromise between current socialist principles and Buddhist ethics but lay judges are chosen by the ruling party. In political trials this may influence verdicts. The denial of political opposition is accompanied by severe censorship and controls in all areas of broadcasting, publishing and the press.

Visits by foreigners are strictly controlled and usually of limited duration, a tourist visa being for 7 days and hotel accommodation compulsory.

Human rights rating: BAD

Population: 37,447,000
Life expectancy: 54
Infant mortality (0–1 year) per 1000 births: figures not available

Form of government: fundamentalist Islamic
Income per capita: figures not available

Observations: The country is presented in summary form because of the unreliability of information and the refusal of official sources to reply to inquiries.

Summary

In present circumstances it would be impossible to complete the Guide's questionnaire. Almost any action, statement or offence could be grounds for summary execution. People who had adopted a modern Western style of life have found it prudent to revert to traditional habits. This opposition to progress is manifested in two quotations from Ayatollah Khomeini: 'Universities have created all our miseries,' and 'Universities do more damage than cluster bombs.'

Since the overthrow of the monarchy, it can be said, therefore, that the country has been seized by social, religious and ideological turmoil. A major war with Iraq and rebellions by Kurds and other minority peoples have reinforced clerical rule, encouraging further excesses in the name of the 'Great Islamic Revolution'. These are not only carried out by the religious courts but by groups of undisciplined followers, fanatics and the para-military. Thousands of executions have taken place for anti-state 'plots', drug-smuggling, sexual offences and for 'fourth drinking offences'.

Belonging to certain religions (i.e. Baha'i, Jewish etc.) has also incurred the death penalty and torture is justified on religious grounds. Freedom of speech is not tolerated, opposition newspapers banned, movements within the country and permits to leave tightly controlled, and women must conform to Koranic law. The *chador* (all-concealing veil) became mandatory for women in 1981.

In the present state of the country, human rights have no meaning. Executions have been known to exceed a hundred a day. In 1981, seeking to justify the execution of children who supported the opposition, a judge, Ayatollah Gilani, reportedly said: '. . . on the basis of Islam, a nine-year-old girl is considered mature. So there is no difference for us between a nine-year-old girl and a forty-year-old man, and it does not prohibit us from issuing any kind of sentence' (*The Guardian*, London, 24 June 1981).

Iran has ratified the UN Covenant.

JORDAN

Human rights rating: POOR

Population: 2,153,273
Life expectancy: 61
Infant mortality (0–1 year) per 1000 births: 70

Form of government: nominated by King
Income per capita: US$ 1875

Observations: Jordan has ratified the UN Covenant. Martial law has been in force since 1967.

Summary

Jordan is one of the few countries in which a monarch has retained absolute power. A prime minister and cabinet are appointed and exercise executive functions over the economy and domestic matters. The country's geographical position as a neighbour of Israel and the significant number of Palestinian refugees absorbed into its society are reasons for the continued state of martial law.

This permits detention without trial, cases to be tried by both military and civil courts, and the sentences to be increased or modified by the prime minister. Radio and television are subject to similar controls and newspapers are banned when they incur the disapproval of the authorities.

The Communist Party is prohibited and, as an Islamic community, Sharia law extends over much of family and personal life. Polygamy is therefore permitted, as is divorce for the male by the unilateral repudiation of his wife. In her case, however, divorce must be granted by a religious court. A woman's role, in general, still follows Muslim traditions.

The severity of martial law fluctuates with the tensions of the area and recurring crises, and with threats to the monarchy. In recent years the death penalty has been exercised sparingly, by hanging, and it has been pronounced 'in absentia' on West Bank Arabs who sell land to Israelis.

Human rights rating: BAD

Population: 9,000,000 (approx.)
Life expectancy: figures not available
Infant mortality (0–1 year) per 1000
   births: figures not available

Form of government: one-party system
Income per capita: figures not available

Observations: This country is presented in summary form because of the unreliability of information and the failure of official sources to reply to inquiries.

Summary

The country has been virtually occupied since 1979 by 200,000 Vietnamese troops. The local Khmer administration, which is intended to legitimize the occupation, has been mainly concerned with reconstructing the country after the devastation of war and of the Pol Pot period. In the circumstances, human rights are considered unrealistic in face of the urgent need to provide the elementary requirements of life and to maintain the disciplines regarded as indispensable for this.

Press and radio are therefore totally controlled, homes may be searched without warrants, unions are government-organized and overt political opposition is a capital offence. Indefinite detentions and long 're-education' sentences are common features, as are retroactive punishments. There is increasing equality for women provided they support the authorities but the educational system is conditioning the young to regard the occupying forces as liberators.

Small areas of the country are still under the control of the previous oppressive regime of Pol Pot, which claims to have adopted more humanitarian policies, and the occupying Vietnamese are seeking to wipe out these last strongholds.

Human rights rating: POOR

Population: 1,500,000
Life expectancy: 70
Infant mortality (0–1 year) per 1000
  births: 38

Form of government: emirate with
  nominal parliamentary system
Income per capita: US$ 18,000

Observations: The emergence of Kuwait as a major oil producer has, in a short period, changed its society from that of a poor and undeveloped country to a regional centre for finance, commerce and communications. Human rights questions are therefore subordinate to the new economic climate.

Summary

In 1961 the country became independent, having been a British protectorate. The traditional ruling family then drew up a written constitution for Kuwait and this includes a bill of rights and free elections for the local parliament. Nevertheless, the Amir has power to dissolve the assembly and to govern directly, and a 'war powers' act in the event of a national emergency would supplement his authority.

The social transformation caused by the recent oil wealth has meant that over 50% of the population are non-Kuwaitis and their political activities are therefore limited. Only about 5% of the total population are eligible to vote in the periodic national elections.

Compared with neighbouring countries, the censorship regulations are relaxed, though criticism of the ruling family, violations of what is defined as 'public morality' or 'contrary to the national interests' are grounds for the suspension of newspapers.

Capital punishment by hanging is practised and flogging in prisons of recalcitrant inmates is permitted. Secret or oppressive trials are rare, though normal legal procedures are not always followed. The Amir has powers to set aside sentences of both civil and military courts.

Although an Islamic country, women enjoy many rights and participate in academic life. They may also drive cars and appear unveiled in public.

Human rights rating: BAD

Population: 3,650,000
Life expectancy: 43
Infant mortality (0–1 year) per 1000 births: 130

Form of government: one-party communist state
Income per capita: figures not available

Observations: This country is presented in summary form because of the unreliability of information and the failure of official sources to reply to inquiries.

Summary

Since the current government came to power in 1975, when the old constitution was suspended, the major breach of human rights has been in its efforts to re-educate followers and 'bourgeois' elements of the *ancien regime*. At present between 10,000 and 15,000 are in re-education camps, being promoted by stages towards ultimate freedom when 'correct thinking' has been achieved. To these detainees should be added prostitutes, social 'idlers', drug addicts and homosexuals. No trial precedes such detention.

The Lao press and other media are government-controlled, as are all forms of economic activity. Internal travel requires official permission and external travel is restricted to officials and approved individuals.

In general there is religious tolerance with the government attempting to gain the support of Buddhist clergy, the national religion, for its policies.

Insurgent movements still operate, making security a high priority for the government. In this it has the active support of the Vietnamese.

Human rights rating: POOR

Population: 14,500,000
Life expectancy: 43
**Infant mortality (0–1 year) per 1000
    births:** 133

Form of government: absolute
    monarch
Income per capita: US$ 130

Observations: This country is presented in summary form because of the unreliability of information and the failure of official sources to reply to inquiries.

Summary

The King is the absolute ruler though in 1981, after 22 years, the people were allowed an election which offered them a choice between a multi-party parliament and the traditional *panchayet* system, an assembly that may be dissolved by the monarch at any time. The electors chose their traditional way of life and political parties were then banned.

A Public Security Act affects all human rights. Those arrested, for example, may be held for six months before being charged. Judges are appointed by the executive and are expected to follow official policy, and newspapers guilty of 'upsetting relations among the people' are suspended.

As a Hindu kingdom it is illegal for Buddhism to try to gain converts and there are minor restrictions on other religions. Women participate to a limited extent in local politics and official policy is to redress the old inequalities between the sexes.

District officers have authority under emergency powers to summarily execute 'lawless individuals' if they are arrested in regions regarded as rebellious. Less serious cases are imprisoned for up to three years for 'sedition'. In 1945 the death penalty was abolished but reintroduced in 1962 for treason, violence against the royal family and 'outraging' the chastity of a Queen or Princess.

YEMEN ARAB REPUBLIC

Human rights rating: BAD

Population: 6,200,000
Life expectancy: 41
Infant mortality (0–1 year) per 1000 births: 170

Form of government: executive president
Income per capita: US$ 650

Observations: The country is a conglomeration of tribes, fiefs and religions, and the mountainous terrain and lack of roads limit the authority of the central government. The assassinations of two recent presidents have not helped the establishment of a unified state.

Summary

The president also commands the armed forces, which are frequently in action against dissident tribes, attempted coups and in border skirmishes. As a devout Muslim country, Koranic law is the basis of the legal system and although not recently practised, such punishments as stoning for adultery and the amputation of limbs could be inflicted on the guilty.

The national security force is given wide independence and detentions and unpublicized arrests are common. There are legal safeguards for 'non-security' cases, and police and court treatment is usually milder. The courts divide between the Islamic, the commercial and that of 'special security'.

With regard to political expression, anything that seriously challenges the government is banned or suppressed. Trade unions and strikes are illegal, the press, radio and TV are government-controlled and religious proselytizing is a crime. Local sheiks and other traditional leaders often represent the authorities in their areas.

There is freedom to travel within the country but there is always the danger of finding oneself in parts outside the protection of government forces. There is military conscription (where practicable) but payment of $445 enables the individual to emigrate to find work abroad. Some political opponents choose voluntary exile, which is frequently permitted.

Human rights rating: BAD

Population: 2,200,000
Life expectancy: 45
Infant mortality (0–1 year) per 1000
  births: figures not available

Form of government: one-party
Marxist state
Income per capita: US$ 525

Observations: This country is presented in summary form because of the unreliability of information and the failure of official sources to reply to inquiries.

Summary

In South Yemen (the People's Democratic Republic of Yemen) all political power is exercised by the Yemen Socialist Party, the only party allowed to function. Freedom of speech, press, and public assembly do not exist and a widespread informant network limits surreptitious attempts at self-expression. Exit permits are not easily acquired, although large numbers of Yemenis work abroad, particularly in the oil states, and remittances sent home form an important part of the Yemen economy.

Although the constitution forbids torture, there have been reports of its practice. Thousands of political prisoners are being held in detention without charge or trial and conditions and treatment are harsh. Disappearances are common.

Poverty is widespread, with many basic foods in short supply and rationed. There is some movement towards union with North Yemen (the Yemen Arab Republic) but a history of border clashes and assassinations leaves both sides deeply suspicious of one another.

Since independence in 1967 the government's attempts to eliminate traditional tribal armed forces and subject them to central control has led to much social and economic dislocation, including the exodus of between 300,000 and 500,000 people, 15–20% of the population.

Most human rights respected

Many human rights denied

Most human rights denied

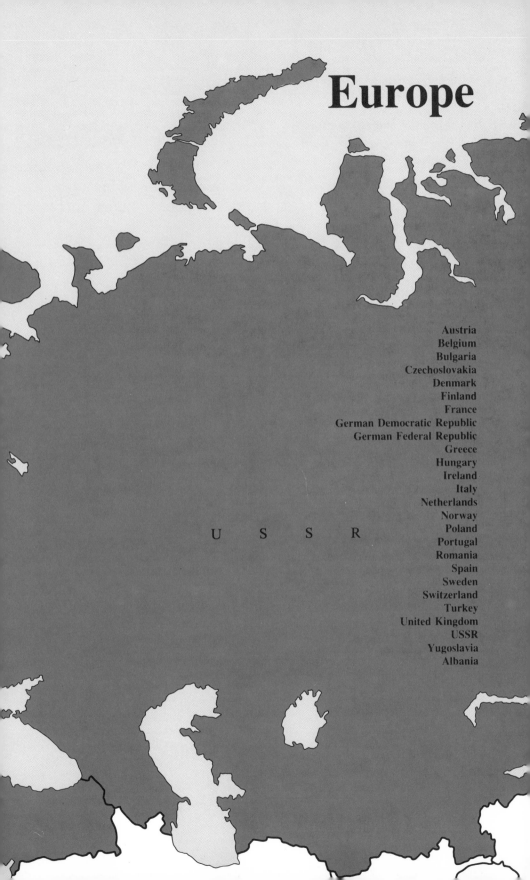

Europe

Austria
Belgium
Bulgaria
Czechoslovakia
Denmark
Finland
France
German Democratic Republic
German Federal Republic
Greece
Hungary
Ireland
Italy
Netherlands
Norway
Poland
Portugal
Romania
Spain
Sweden
Switzerland
Turkey
United Kingdom
USSR
Yugoslavia
Albania

U S S R

Human rights rating: 92%

Population: 7,549,440
Life expectancy: 72
Infant mortality (0–1 year) per 1000 births: 14

Form of government: democratic republic
Income per capita: US$ 10,255

Observations: Satisfactory.

FREEDOM/RIGHTS		Further comments	
1. Of movement in own country	YES		◯
2. To leave own country	YES		◯
3. From deprivation of nationality	YES		◯
4. To seek information and teach ideas	YES		◯
5. From serfdom, slavery, forced or child labour	YES		◯
6. Of peaceful political opposition	YES		◯
7. Of peaceful assembly and association	YES		◯
8. Of women to equal rights	YES	Special government appointee to monitor women's rights	◯
9. From directed employment or work permits	YES		◯
10. Of inter-racial, inter-religious and civil marriage	YES		◯
11. To practise any religion	YES		◯
12. From compulsory religion or state ideology in schools	YES	Letter from parent will exempt child	◯
13. From political press censorship	YES		◯
14. From police detention without charge	yes	This must be related to long investigation before trial	◖
15. From police searches of home without warrant	YES	Exception when in 'hot pursuit'	◯
16. From torture or coercion by state	YES		◯
17. Of assumption of innocence until guilt proved	YES		◯
18. Of accused to be promptly brought before judge or court	no	Pre-investigative detention may last 6–12 months	◑
19. Of all courts to total independence	YES		◯
20. From civilian trials in secret	YES	In certain cases accused may wish trial in camera	◯
21. For independent trade unions	YES	Cooperative arrangements between unions, industry and government	◯
22. From censorship of mail	YES		◯
23. To publish and educate in ethnic languages	yes	Certain small minorities in dispute over their 'rights'	◖
24. From deliberate state policies to control artistic works	YES		◯
25. From compulsory military service	no	9 months' military service. Objectors can choose civic alternative	◑
26. To purchase and drink alcohol	YES	From 19 years old	◯
27. To practise homosexuality between consenting adults	YES	From 19 years old	◯
28. To use contraceptive pills and devices	YES	Government support	◯

29. Of early abortion	**YES**	
30. Of divorce (for men and women equally)	**YES**	

STATE POWER
31. Corporal punishment by state — None
32. Radio and TV broadcasts — State-owned but no direct political interference
33. Book publishing — Freedom from controls
34. Number of police and military per 100,000 citizens — 800
35. % of national income spent on above — 1.5%
36. Weapons normally carried by civil police — Pistols
37. Capital punishment by state — Abolished in 1950

MAXIMUM PUNISHMENTS IN PENAL CODE FOR:
(Freedom-related offences)
38. Non-violent anti-government activities — None
39. Possession of banned political literature — None
40. Refusing compulsory national service — 5 years' prison but committees usually treat objectors leniently

(Criminal offences)
41. Unlawful possession of 'hard' drugs — 6 months. 10 years for trafficking
42. Trading in pornography — 1 year or a fine
43. Illegal abortion — 1 year if self-induced, 3 years for non-medical or profit-seeking medical
44. Bigamy — 3 years' prison
45. Rape without other injury — 10 years' prison

COMPULSORY DOCUMENTS FOR CITIZENS
46. Legally required at all times — None
47. For employment — None
48. When applying for passport — Birth certificate and citizenship of Austria papers
49. Period of validity of passport — 5 years
50. Countries forbidden to holder — None

Human rights rating: 92%

Population: 9,900,000
Life expectancy: 72
Infant mortality (0–1 year) per 1000 births: 12

Form of government: parliamentary monarchy
Income per capita: US$ 10,890

Observations: Satisfactory.

FREEDOM/RIGHTS		Further comments
1. Of movement in own country	YES	
2. To leave own country	YES	
3. From deprivation of nationality	YES	
4. To seek information and teach ideas	YES	
5. From serfdom, slavery, forced or child labour	YES	
6. Of peaceful political opposition	YES	
7. Of peaceful assembly and association	YES	Police permission required for marches
8. Of women to equal rights	YES	
9. From directed employment or work permits	YES	
10. Of inter-racial, inter-religious and civil marriage	YES	
11. To practise any religion	YES	
12. From compulsory religion or state ideology in schools	YES	
13. From political press censorship	YES	
14. From police detention without charge	YES	
15. From police searches of home without warrant	YES	
16. From torture or coercion by state	YES	
17. Of assumption of innocence until guilt proved	YES	
18. Of accused to be promptly brought before judge or court	YES	Within 24 hours or released
19. Of all courts to total independence	YES	
20. From civilian trials in secret	YES	Trials of minors occasionally in camera
21. For independent trade unions	YES	
22. From censorship of mail	YES	
23. To publish and educate in ethnic languages	YES	
24. From deliberate state policies to control artistic works	YES	
25. From compulsory military service	no	8–10 months' conscription
26. To purchase and drink alcohol	YES	
27. To practise homosexuality between consenting adults	YES	Legal from age 18
28. To use contraceptive pills and devices	YES	
29. Of early abortion	no	Only when mother's life at risk
30. Of divorce (for men and women equally)	YES	

STATE POWER

31. Corporal punishment by state	None	○
32. Radio and TV broadcasts	State-owned but not direct control	○
33. Book publishing	Free except for prohibitions on 'public order' issues (pornography etc.)	○
34. Number of police and military per 100,000 citizens	141 police, 909 military	◐
35. % of national income spent on above	4%	○
36. Weapons normally carried by civil police	9mm automatic pistols	◐
37. Capital punishment by state	Penalty retained but last public execution in 1918	◑

MAXIMUM PUNISHMENTS IN PENAL CODE FOR:
(Freedom-related offences)

38. Non-violent anti-government activities	6 months' prison	◑
39. Possession of banned political literature	None	○
40. Refusing compulsory national service	3 months' to 5 years' prison	◑

(Criminal offences)

41. Unlawful possession of 'hard' drugs	5 years' prison
42. Trading in pornography	6 months' prison
43. Illegal abortion	2 years' prison
44. Bigamy	A fine at discretion of court
45. Rape without other injury	15 years' prison

COMPULSORY DOCUMENTS FOR CITIZENS

46. Legally required at all times	ID cards issued by City halls
47. For employment	Nothing
48. When applying for passport	ID card, Certificate of Nationality
49. Period of validity of passport	5 years
50. Countries forbidden to holder	None

Human rights rating: 37%

Population: 8,900,000
Life expectancy: 73
Infant mortality (0–1 year) per 1000 births: 22

Form of government: communist people's republic
Income per capita: US$ 2750

Observations: Severe curtailment of human rights despite having signed and ratified the UN Covenant.

FREEDOM/RIGHTS		Further comments	
1. Of movement in own country	NO	Internal passport obligatory. Police to be informed of destination	●
2. To leave own country	NO	Exit permits refused when journey not 'in interests of the state'	●
3. From deprivation of nationality	YES		○
4. To seek information and teach ideas	NO	All teaching to conform with state and party policies	●
5. From serfdom, slavery, forced or child labour	YES		○
6. Of peaceful political opposition	NO	No opposition permitted	●
7. Of peaceful assembly and association	NO	Only in support of state policies or 'socialist morality'	●
8. Of women to equal rights	yes	50% of students are female but traditional role continues in many areas	◑
9. From directed employment or work permits	NO	Labour-controlled and directed	●
10. Of inter-racial, inter-religious and civil marriage	YES		○
11. To practise any religion	yes	Provided no political involvement. Periodic harassment of Muslims	◑
12. From compulsory religion or state ideology in schools	NO	Marxist-Leninism a compulsory subject	●
13. From political press censorship	NO	Strict control. All editors are party members	●
14. From police detention without charge	no	10-day limit not honoured when suspects are political or social dissidents	◑
15. From police searches of home without warrant	no	Police do not produce warrants in cases considered 'urgent'	◑
16. From torture or coercion by state	no	Beatings, sleep deprivation. Psychological pressures etc.	◑
17. Of assumption of innocence until guilt proved	no	Political and security cases treated more harshly than criminal cases	◑
18. Of accused to be promptly brought before judge or court	no	Preliminary investigations can be lengthy	◑
19. Of all courts to total independence	no	Intimidation and 'court-crowding' in political cases	◑
20. From civilian trials in secret	NO	When trial concerns state secrets or 'socialist morality'. Recent hijacking case also in camera	●
21. For independent trade unions	NO	No freedom to strike or negotiate	●
22. From censorship of mail	no	Frequent screening of foreign mail etc.	◑
23. To publish and educate in ethnic languages	no	Forced assimilation of Muslims etc. Policy of 'Bulgarianization'	◑

24. From deliberate state policies to control artistic works	NO	Art and literature subject to censorship and market restrictions	◐
25. From compulsory military service	NO	2–3 years' military service	●
26. To purchase and drink alcohol	YES		○
27. To practise homosexuality between consenting adults	NO	Illegal. 'Bourgeois perversion', 3–5 years' imprisonment	●
28. To use contraceptive pills and devices	YES		○
29. Of early abortion	YES	By authorized practitioners	○
30. Of divorce (for men and women equally)	YES		○

STATE POWER

31. Corporal punishment by state	None	○
32. Radio and TV broadcasts	State-owned and controlled	●
33. Book publishing	State-owned and controlled	●
34. Number of police and military per 100,000 citizens	800 (including Reserves but not People's Militia)	◐
35. % of national income spent on above	7%	◑
36. Weapons normally carried by civil police	Variety of firearms. Police duties shared with security forces and militia	◑
37. Capital punishment by state	For treason, murder, economic crimes, 'weakening the state' etc.	●

MAXIMUM PUNISHMENTS IN PENAL CODE FOR:
(Freedom-related offences)

38. Non-violent anti-government activities	12 years for being member of 'anti-state' organization	◑
39. Possession of banned political literature	5 years' prison if material for propaganda purposes	◑
40. Refusing compulsory national service	Varying heavy sentences, 5 years' prison maximum	◑

(Criminal offences)

41. Unlawful possession of 'hard' drugs	3 years' prison and 300 leva fine
42. Trading in pornography	500 leva fine and confiscation
43. Illegal abortion	5 years maximum if by unauthorized parties
44. Bigamy	3 years' prison
45. Rape without other injury	8 years' prison

COMPULSORY DOCUMENTS FOR CITIZENS

46. Legally required at all times	ID card
47. For employment	ID card
48. When applying for passport	ID card, police clearance etc.
49. Period of validity of passport	Varying periods related to purpose. Usually one-trip passports
50. Countries forbidden to holder	All countries except those for which passport issued

Human rights rating: 36%

Population: 15,234,000
Life expectancy: 71
Infant mortality (0–1 year) per 1000 births: 18

Form of government: one-party communist state
Income per capita: US$ 5510

Observations: Severe curtailment of human rights despite having signed and ratified the UN Covenant.

FREEDOM/RIGHTS		Further comments	
1. Of movement in own country	yes	Except in proscribed border areas	◗
2. To leave own country	NO	Exit permits refused when not 'in interests of state'	●
3. From deprivation of nationality	NO	Particularly dissident intellectuals already abroad	●
4. To seek, receive and impart information and teach ideas	NO	No teachings hostile to party or state. No anti-Soviet ideas	●
5. From serfdom, slavery, forced or child labour	yes	Labour camps for dissidents must be seen as forced labour	◗
6. Of peaceful political opposition	NO	Illegal. Human rights groups suffer constant house searches, arrests etc.	●
7. Of peaceful assembly and association	NO	Only in support of state or party. Charter 77 supporters subject to harassment and arrest	●
8. Of women to equal rights	YES		◯
9. From directed employment or work permits	NO		◐
10. Of inter-racial, inter-religious and civil marriage	YES		◯
11. To practise any religion	no	Prison for religious activists if distributing tracts. Churches under surveillance and clergy paid by state	◑
12. From compulsory religion or state ideology in schools	NO	Marxist-Leninism a compulsory subject	●
13. From political press censorship	NO	State and party control. Nothing to be published against 'socialist principles'	●
14. From police detention without charge	NO	48-hour limit but indefinite detention for suspected subversives	●
15. From police searches of home without warrant	NO	Widespread disregard of law. Harshest against those with 'Western' contacts	●
16. From torture or coercion by state	no	Beatings and psychological pressures during interrogation	◑
17. Of assumption of innocence until guilt proved	no	Not when in conflict with state or party. No habeas corpus	◑
18. Of accused to be promptly brought before judge or court	NO	At discretion of police. Accused may be denied lawyer in pre-trial period	●
19. Of all courts to total independence	no	Judges can be removed by higher authority	◑
20. From civilian trials in secret	no	Politically sensitive cases in camera and calculated 'crowding of court'	◑
21. For independent trade unions	NO	Controlled by party. Strikes illegal	●
22. From censorship of mail	no	Foreign and dissidents' mail subject to random checking	◖
23. To publish and educate in ethnic languages	no	Prohibitions on Ruthenian, Romany languages etc.	◑

24. From deliberate state policies to control artistic works	yes	Content and form should conform to preconceived party ideas
25. From compulsory military service	**NO**	Army 2 years, air force 3 years
26. To purchase and drink alcohol	**YES**	
27. To practise homosexuality between consenting adults	**YES**	From 18 years old
28. To use contraceptive pills and devices	**YES**	State encouragement
29. Of early abortion	yes	Broad medical and social reasons
30. Of divorce (men and women equally)	**YES**	

STATE POWER

31. Corporal punishment by state	Legally none but state-condoned torture during interrogation
32. Radio and TV broadcasts	State and party-controlled
33. Book publishing	State and party-controlled
34. Number of police and military per 100,000 citizens	1600 (approx.)
35. % of national income spent on above	6%
36. Weapons normally carried by civil police	Sidearms
37. Capital punishment by state	For treason, murder, anti-state activities, stealing from the dead etc.

MAXIMUM PUNISHMENTS IN PENAL CODE FOR:
(Freedom-related offences)

38. Non-violent anti-government activities	10 years for wide categories under 'agitation' and 'subversion'
39. Possession of banned political literature	As 38. Charges may also come under 'illicit trading' (attempted sale of books)
40. Refusing compulsory national service	3 years' prison

(Criminal offences)

41. Unlawful possession of 'hard' drugs	2 years' prison. 8 years for major 'gang' trafficking
42. Trading in pornography	2 years (endangering morality)
43. Illegal abortion	No punishment for self-induced but 5 years' prison for accomplices
44. Bigamy	2 years' prison
45. Rape without other injury	8 years' prison

COMPULSORY DOCUMENTS FOR CITIZENS

46. Legally required at all times	ID card
47. For employment	ID card, police clearance etc.
48. When applying for passport	As 47. A decision for police
49. Period of validity of passport	Usually one-trip visas of short duration
50. Countries forbidden to holder	All except those for which external visa issued

Human rights rating: 96%

Population: 5,113,000
Life expectancy: 74
Infant mortality (0–1 year) per 1000 births: 9

Form of government: democratic monarchy
Income per capita: US$ 12,761

Observations: Satisfactory.

FREEDOM/RIGHTS		Further comments	
1. Of movement in own country	YES		○
2. To leave own country	YES		○
3. From deprivation of nationality	YES		○
4. To seek information and teach ideas	YES		○
5. From serfdom, slavery, forced or child labour	YES		○
6. Of peaceful political opposition	YES		○
7. Of peaceful assembly and association	YES		○
8. Of women to equal rights	YES		○
9. From directed employment or work permits	YES		○
10. Of inter-racial, inter-religious and civil marriage	YES		○
11. To practise any religion	YES		○
12. From compulsory religion or state ideology in schools	YES		○
13. From political press censorship	YES		○
14. From police detention without charge	YES		○
15. From police searches of home without warrant	YES		○
16. From torture or coercion by state	YES		○
17. Of assumption of innocence until guilt proved	YES		○
18. Of accused to be promptly brought before judge or court	YES	Within 24 hours. Judge may detain for further 3 days	○
19. Of all courts to total independence	YES		○
20. From civilian trials in secret	YES		○
21. For independent trade unions	YES		○
22. From censorship of mail	YES		○
23. To publish and educate in ethnic languages	YES		○
24. From deliberate state policies to control artistic works	YES		○
25. From compulsory military service	no	9 months. Chosen by ballot	◐
26. To purchase and drink alcohol	YES		○
27. To practise homosexuality between consenting adults	YES		○
28. To use contraceptive pills and devices	YES		○
29. Of early abortion	YES	Usually within 12 weeks	○
30. Of divorce (for men and women equally)	YES		○

STATE POWER

31. Corporal punishment by state	None	○
32. Radio and TV broadcasts	No state pressures on broadcasting system	○
33. Book publishing	No unreasonable interference	○
34. Number of police and military per 100,000 citizens	196 police, 627 military	◑
35. % of national income spent on above	3%	○
36. Weapons normally carried by civil police	7.65mm pistols	◑
37. Capital punishment by state	None	○

MAXIMUM PUNISHMENTS IN PENAL CODE FOR:

(*Freedom-related offences*)

38. Non-violent anti-government activities	None	○
39. Possession of banned political literature	None	○
40. Refusing compulsory national service	2 years' prison	◑

(*Criminal offences*)

41. Unlawful possession of 'hard' drugs	2 years' prison
42. Trading in pornography	A fine if sold to children
43. Illegal abortion	4 years' prison if by non-medical person
44. Bigamy	6 years' prison
45. Rape without other injury	4 years. 10 when with violence

COMPULSORY DOCUMENTS FOR CITIZENS

46. Legally required at all times	ID card
47. For employment	Nothing
48. When applying for passport	Birth certificate
49. Period of validity of passport	10 years
50. Countries forbidden to holder	None

FINLAND

Human rights rating: 96%

Population: 4,800,000
Life expectancy: 72
Infant mortality (0–1 year) per 1000 births: 9

Form of government: parliamentary democracy
Income per capita: US$ 10,500

Observations: Satisfactory but there is some criticism that the need to placate its neighbour the Soviet Union on certain matters is a breach of its sovereignty (only European democracy not a full member of Council of Europe).

FREEDOM/RIGHTS		Further comments	
1. Of movement in own country	YES		◯
2. To leave own country	YES		◯
3. From deprivation of nationality	YES		◯
4. To seek information and teach ideas	YES		◯
5. From serfdom, slavery, forced or child labour	YES		◯
6. Of peaceful political opposition	YES		◯
7. Of peaceful assembly and association	YES	6 hours' notice to be given to local authorities	◯
8. Of women to equal rights	YES	Women granted vote in 1906. Equality Council created in 1972	◯
9. From directed employment or work permits	YES		◯
10. Of inter-racial, inter-religious and civil marriage	YES		◯
11. To practise any religion	YES		◯
12. From compulsory religion or state ideology in schools	YES		◯
13. From political press censorship	YES	Self-censorship to placate USSR	◯
14. From police detention without charge	YES	False arrest entitles accused to damages	◯
15. From police searches of home without warrant	YES	When issued, crime must be serious enough for 6-month sentence	◯
16. From torture or coercion by state	YES		◯
17. Of assumption of innocence until guilt proved	YES		◯
18. Of accused to be promptly brought before judge or court	yes	Within 10 days of arrest	◑
19. Of all courts to total independence	YES		◯
20. From civilian trials in secret	YES	Juvenile, matrimonial, guardianship cases sometimes held in camera	◯
21. For independent trade unions	YES		◯
22. From censorship of mail	YES		◯
23. To publish and educate in ethnic languages	YES		◯
24. From deliberate state policies to control artistic works	YES		◯
25. From compulsory military service	no	8–11 months' military service	◑
26. To purchase and drink alcohol	YES	Beer at 18, spirits at 21	◯
27. To practise homosexuality between consenting adults	YES		◯
28. To use contraceptive pills and devices	YES	State support	◯

| 29. Of early abortion | **YES** | |
| 30. Of divorce (for men and women equally) | **YES** | |

STATE POWER

31. Corporal punishment by state	None	
32. Radio and TV broadcasts	State control	
33. Book publishing	No controls. Every individual may publish	
34. Number of police and military per 100,000 citizens	1000 (not including Reservists)	
35. % of national income spent on above	2%	
36. Weapons normally carried by civil police	Usually unarmed	
37. Capital punishment by state	Abolished for all crimes 1972	

MAXIMUM PUNISHMENTS IN PENAL CODE FOR:
(Freedom-related offences)

38. Non-violent anti-government activities	None	
39. Possession of banned political literature	None	
40. Refusing compulsory national service	9 months' prison	

(Criminal offences)

41. Unlawful possession of 'hard' drugs	2 years' prison. 10 for trafficking
42. Trading in pornography	6 months' prison
43. Illegal abortion	4 years' prison by woman. 8 years' if without woman's consent
44. Bigamy	4 years' prison
45. Rape without other injury	10 years' prison

COMPULSORY DOCUMENTS FOR CITIZENS

46. Legally required at all times	None
47. For employment	Only tax document
48. When applying for passport	Citizen's registration certificate
49. Period of validity of passport	5 years
50. Countries forbidden to holder	None

FRANCE

Human rights rating: 88%

Population: 53,800,000
Life expectancy: 74
Infant mortality (0–1 year) per 1000 births: 11

Form of government: democratic republic
Income per capita: US$ 11,500

Observations: Satisfactory.

FREEDOM/RIGHTS		Further comments
1. Of movement in own country	YES	
2. To leave own country	YES	
3. From deprivation of nationality	YES	
4. To seek information and teach ideas	YES	
5. From serfdom, slavery, forced or child labour	YES	
6. Of peaceful political opposition	YES	
7. Of peaceful assembly and association	YES	
8. Of women to equal rights	YES	Minor violations in pay and socially
9. From directed employment or work permits	YES	
10. Of inter-racial, inter-religious and civil marriage	YES	
11. To practise any religion	YES	
12. From compulsory religion or state ideology in schools	YES	
13. From political press censorship	YES	
14. From police detention without charge	yes	Narcotics 4 days, security cases 6 days but occasional excesses
15. From police searches of home without warrant	YES	
16. From torture or coercion by state	YES	
17. Of assumption of innocence until guilt proved	yes	But 'security' cases may be investigated for indefinite period
18. Of accused to be promptly brought before judge or court	yes	Pretrial confinement for certain felonies 4 months or longer but usually 24–48 hours
19. Of all courts to total independence	YES	
20. From civilian trials in secret	YES	
21. For independent trade unions	YES	
22. From censorship of mail	YES	
23. To publish and educate in ethnic languages	YES	
24. From deliberate state policies to control artistic works	YES	
25. From compulsory military service	NO	12 months' military conscription
26. To purchase and drink alcohol	YES	
27. To practise homosexuality between consenting adults	YES	From age 18
28. To use contraceptive pills and devices	YES	
29. Of early abortion	YES	
30. Of divorce (for men and women equally)	YES	

STATE POWER

31. Corporal punishment by state	None	○
32. Radio and TV broadcasts	No state interference but many government appointees exert influence	◑
33. Book publishing	No state intrusion though rights reserved in penal code	◑
34. Number of police and military per 100,000 citizens	335 police and gendarmerie, 950 military	◐
35. % of national income spent on above	5.5%	◑
36. Weapons normally carried by civil police	.38 or .45 pistols	◑
37. Capital punishment by state	Recently abolished	○

MAXIMUM PUNISHMENTS IN PENAL CODE FOR:

(Freedom-related offences)

38. Non-violent anti-government activities	5 years' prison for non-treasonable acts affecting country's 'essential economic interests'	◑
39. Possession of banned political literature	None in practice though foreign propaganda prejudicial to state is constitutionally an offence	○
40. Refusing compulsory national service	2 years' prison (usually Jehovah's Witnesses)	◑

(Criminal offences)

41. Unlawful possession of 'hard' drugs	10 years' prison. Trafficking 20 years
42. Trading in pornography	2 years' prison
43. Illegal abortion	2 years' prison if self-induced. Other persons 3 years
44. Bigamy	3 years' prison
45. Rape without other injury	20 years' prison

COMPULSORY DOCUMENTS FOR CITIZENS

46. Legally required at all times	ID card
47. For employment	Social security papers
48. When applying for passport	Recent copy of birth certificate, ID card, military clearance
49. Period of validity of passport	5 years
50. Countries forbidden to holder	None

Human rights rating: 35%

Population: 16,744,692
Life expectancy: 72
Infant mortality (0–1 year) per 1000 births: 13

Form of government: communist system
Income per capita: US$ 6430

Observations: Severe curtailment of human rights despite having signed and ratified the UN Covenant

FREEDOM/RIGHTS		Further comments	
1. Of movement in own country	yes	Except for certain frontier areas	◖
2. To leave own country	NO	Frontier guards shoot to kill escapees to W. Germany	●
3. From deprivation of nationality	NO	Many citizens abroad stripped of nationality	●
4. To seek, receive and impart information and teach ideas	NO	All intellectual inquiry controlled by party	●
5. From serfdom, slavery, forced or child labour	yes	But camps for dissidents may be seen as forced labour	◖
6. Of peaceful political opposition	NO	4000–5000 political prisoners. State frees prisoners to W. Germany for a price per head	●
7. Of peaceful assembly and association	NO	No group assemblies unless officially controlled	●
8. Of women to equal rights	YES		◔
9. From directed employment or work permits	NO	Directed labour	●
10. Of inter-racial, inter-religious and civil marriage	YES		○
11. To practise any religion	yes	But under constant government scrutiny for criticizing system	◖
12. From compulsory religion or state ideology in schools	NO	Marxist-Leninist instruction	●
13. From political press censorship	NO	Total control by state and party	●
14. From police detention without charge	NO	Indefinite detention	●
15. From police searches of home without warrant	NO	Permission can be sought by police retroactively	●
16. From torture or coercion by state	no	Political opponents face harsh physical and psychological interrogation procedures	◑
17. Of assumption of innocence until guilt proved	NO	No habeas corpus	●
18. Of accused to be promptly brought before judge or court	NO	The 3-month limit can be disregarded	●
19. Of all courts to total independence	NO	Council of State ultimately controls all trials and judges	●
20. From civilian trials in secret	no	Judge can order closed trial. Almost all political trials in camera	◑
21. For independent trade unions	NO	Party-controlled. No strikes permitted	●
22. From censorship of mail	NO	Government can legally open all mail	●
23. To publish and educate in ethnic languages	YES	Sorbs minority culture encouraged	○
24. From deliberate state policies to control artistic works	no	State disapproval of 'bourgeois art' limits markets and opportunities	◑

25. From compulsory military service	NO	18–24 months	●
26. To purchase and drink alcohol	YES		○
27. To practise homosexuality between consenting adults	YES	In private and not with minors or close relatives	○
28. To use contraceptive pills and devices	YES		○
29. Of early abortion	YES		○
30. Of divorce (for men and women equally)	YES		○

STATE POWER

31. Corporal punishment by state — Not lawfully but excesses by officers tolerated by superiors ◑

32. Radio and TV broadcasts — Totally state-controlled and owned ●

33. Book publishing — Totally state-controlled and owned ●

34. Number of police and military per 100,000 citizens — 1500 (approx.) not including Reservists ◕

35. % of national income spent on above — 9% ◔

36. Weapons normally carried by civil police — Variety of firearms ◑

37. Capital punishment by state — By shooting. For murder, political actions against state and 'for opposing human rights'. Not recently used but many border-guard killings of escapees ●

MAXIMUM PUNISHMENTS IN PENAL CODE FOR:
(Freedom-related offences)

38. Non-violent anti-government activities — 12 years' prison for anti-state propaganda, illegal emigration etc. ◑

39. Possession of banned political literature — 5 years' prison for possession or distribution of pamphlets ◑

40. Refusing compulsory national service — Heavy sentences but exemption or civic service for certain religious objectors ◑

(Criminal offences)

41. Unlawful possession of 'hard' drugs — 2 years' prison

42. Trading in pornography — 2 years' prison

43. Illegal abortion — 3 years' prison

44. Bigamy — 2 years but necessary marriage documentation makes offence unlikely

45. Rape without other injury — 5 years' prison

COMPULSORY DOCUMENTS FOR CITIZENS

46. Legally required at all times — ID card

47. For employment — ID card ('not to be employed is an offence')

48. When applying for passport — Birth certificate, police clearance, ID card etc.

49. Period of validity of passport — Various periods but usually one-trip passports for ordinary citizens

50. Countries forbidden to holder — All countries except those for which passport issued

Human rights rating: 91%

Population: 61,600,000
Life expectancy: 72
Infant mortality (0–1 year) per 1000 births: 14

Form of government: parliamentary federal republic
Income per capita: US$ 12,500

Observations: Satisfactory.

FREEDOM/RIGHTS		Further comments	
1. Of movement in own country	YES		○
2. To leave own country	YES		○
3. From deprivation of nationality	YES		○
4. To seek information and teach ideas	YES		○
5. From serfdom, slavery, forced or child labour	YES		○
6. Of peaceful political opposition	YES	Active supporters of imprisoned terrorists may be prosecuted	○
7. Of peaceful assembly and association	yes	Police permits required. Only withheld when violence threatened	◑
8. Of women to equal rights	YES	Anomalies such as no women in military service	○
9. From directed employment or work permits	YES	Immigrant labour treated separately	○
10. Of inter-racial, inter-religious and civil marriage	YES		○
11. To practise any religion	YES		○
12. From compulsory religion or state ideology in schools	YES		○
13. From political press censorship	YES		○
14. From police detention without charge	YES		○
15. From police searches of home without warrant	YES		○
16. From torture or coercion by state	YES		○
17. Of assumption of innocence until guilt proved	YES		○
18. Of accused to be promptly brought before judge or court	YES	Within 24 hours, but many cases of prolonged pre-trial custody	○
19. Of all courts to total independence	YES		○
20. From civilian trials in secret	YES		○
21. For independent trade unions	YES		○
22. From censorship of mail	YES		○
23. To publish and educate in ethnic languages	YES		○
24. From deliberate state policies to control artistic works	YES		○
25. From compulsory military service	NO	15 months' military service (civic service as alternative)	●
26. To purchase and drink alcohol	YES	Over 18 years old. Wine and beer at 16	○
27. To practise homosexuality between consenting adults	YES		○
28. To use contraceptive pills and devices	YES		○

29. Of early abortion	yes	Broad medical and social reasons
30. Of divorce (for men and women equally)	**YES**	

STATE POWER

31. Corporal punishment by state — None
32. Radio and TV broadcasts — No federal interference. No advertising
33. Book publishing — No direct controls
34. Number of police and military per 100,000 citizens — 1000 (combined federal and state forces)
35. % of national income spent on above — 4%
36. Weapons normally carried by civil police — 7.65mm pistols
37. Capital punishment by state — None

MAXIMUM PUNISHMENTS IN PENAL CODE FOR:

(Freedom-related offences)

38. Non-violent anti-government activities — None
39. Possession of banned political literature — 3 years' prison. Certain categories of fascist and neo-Nazi works
40. Refusing compulsory national service — Up to 5 years if refusal accompanied by self-injury to avoid service

(Criminal offences)

41. Unlawful possession of 'hard' drugs — 3 years' prison. 10 for traffickers
42. Trading in pornography — 1 year's prison
43. Illegal abortion — 3 years' prison
44. Bigamy — 3 years' prison
45. Rape without other injury — Life imprisonment

COMPULSORY DOCUMENTS FOR CITIZENS

46. Legally required at all times — None, but ID cards issued at age 16
47. For employment — Tax and insurance papers only
48. When applying for passport — Birth certificate and evidence of being locally registered
49. Period of validity of passport — 10 years
50. Countries forbidden to holder — None

Human rights rating: 80%

Population: 9,500,000
Life expectancy: 73
Infant mortality (0–1 year) per 1000
  births: 20

Form of government: parliamentary
democracy
Income per capita: US$ 4250

Observations: A few irregularities affect an otherwise satisfactory human rights situation.

FREEDOM/RIGHTS		Further comments	
1. Of movement in own country	YES		○
2. To leave own country	YES		○
3. From deprivation of nationality	YES		○
4. To seek information and teach ideas	YES		○
5. From serfdom, slavery, forced or child labour	YES		○
6. Of peaceful political opposition	YES		◑
7. Of peaceful assembly and association	yes	But police may act if social or economic life is considered threatened	
8. Of women to equal rights	yes	Constitution's equal rights widely disregarded in male-oriented society	◖
9. From directed employment or work permits	YES		○
10. Of inter-racial, inter-religious and civil marriage	no	Religious marriages only but parliament about to introduce civil marriage	◑
11. To practise any religion	YES		○
12. From compulsory religion or state ideology in schools	yes	But strict adherence by Greek Orthodox schools	◑
13. From political press censorship	yes	But seizure permitted for insulting president or offending religious beliefs	◖
14. From police detention without charge	YES	Within 24 hours. Release in 3 days if not charged	○
15. From police searches of home without warrant	YES	Issued by District Attorney	○
16. From torture or coercion by state	YES	Degree of leniency towards local police abuses	○
17. Of assumption of innocence until guilt proved	YES		○
18. Of accused to be promptly brought before judge or court	YES	As 14	○
19. Of all courts to total independence	YES		◑
20. From civilian trials in secret	yes	But 'public order' cases may be in camera. Also juvenile offences	
21. For independent trade unions	YES		○
22. From censorship of mail	YES		○
23. To publish and educate in ethnic languages	YES		○
24. From deliberate state policies to control artistic works	YES		○
25. From compulsory military service	NO	22–26 months' military service but reduction in prospect	●
26. To purchase and drink alcohol	YES		○

27. To practise homosexuality between consenting adults	**YES**	Over 17 years old. But strict laws on prostitution	○
28. To use contraceptive pills and devices	yes	No government support	◑
29. Of early abortion	yes	Medical/juridical grounds only	◑
30. Of divorce (for men and women equally)	**YES**		○

STATE POWER

31. Corporal punishment by state	None	○
32. Radio and TV broadcasts	Exclusively state-run but objectivity guaranteed and practised	◑
33. Book publishing	Free but no offensive literature against president or any religion	◑
34. Number of police and military per 100,000 citizens	2400	◐
35. % of national income spent on above	6%	○
36. Weapons normally carried by civil police	Revolvers and batons	◑
37. Capital punishment by state	Treason and certain murder cases. No executions since 1972. Abolition imminent	◑

MAXIMUM PUNISHMENTS IN PENAL CODE FOR:
(Freedom-related offences)

38. Non-violent anti-government activities	3 years' prison if considered 'subversive'	◑
39. Possession of banned political literature	No ban but rare 'subversive' charges may mean 3 years' prison	◑
40. Refusing compulsory national service	Usually non-military service up to 4 years. Jehovah's Witnesses up to 4½ years' prison	◐

(Criminal offences)

41. Unlawful possession of 'hard' drugs	2–20 years. Maximum for trafficking
42. Trading in pornography	3 years' prison
43. Illegal abortion	5 years' prison
44. Bigamy	5 years' prison
45. Rape without other injury	20 years' prison

COMPULSORY DOCUMENTS FOR CITIZENS

46. Legally required at all times	ID card
47. For employment	Perhaps military service 'clearance'
48. When applying for passport	Birth certificate, military clearance for certain groups
49. Period of validity of passport	5 years
50. Countries forbidden to holder	None

Human rights rating: 54%

Population: 10,700,000
Life expectancy: 71
Infant mortality (0–1 year) per 1000 births: 24

Form of government: one-party state
Income per capita: US$ 4000

Observations: Curtailment of many human rights despite having signed and ratified the UN Covenant.

FREEDOM/RIGHTS		Further comments	
1. Of movement in own country	YES		◐
2. To leave own country	yes	More liberal policies now prevail on tourism and emigration	◐
3. From deprivation of nationality	yes	Rare cases of dissidents being 'expelled'	◑
4. To seek information and teach ideas	no	Technique of limited freedom is called 'self-censorship' rather than suppression	◑
5. From serfdom, slavery, forced or child labour	YES		○
6. Of peaceful political opposition	NO	New penal code (1979) prosecutes for a wide range of inciting statements	●
7. Of peaceful assembly and association	NO	As 6. Approx. 200 charges each year. No anti-Soviet meetings	●
8. Of women to equal rights	yes	Certain areas where equality, despite constitution, is denied	◑
9. From directed employment or work permits	NO		●
10. Of inter-racial, inter-religious and civil marriage	YES	Anomaly of 'no intermarriage with gipsies'	○
11. To practise any religion	YES	19 religions recognized by state	○
12. From compulsory religion or state ideology in schools	NO	Marxist-Leninism a compulsory subject	●
13. From political press censorship	no	Government-owned. 'Self-censorship' includes no anti-Soviet writings	◑
14. From police detention without charge	yes	Within 72 hours but extreme cases up to 3 months	◑
15. From police searches of home without warrant	yes	Except for significant security cases	◑
16. From torture or coercion by state	no	Occasional abuses. Particularly use of psychological methods	◑
17. Of assumption of innocence until guilt proved	yes	Position improving except with anti-Soviet suspects	◑
18. Of accused to be promptly brought before judge or court	yes	As 17	◑
19. Of all courts to total independence	yes	Except for rare cases when party factors are paramount	◑
20. From civilian trials in secret	yes	But security cases in camera	◑
21. For independent trade unions	NO	Communist Party controlled	●
22. From censorship of mail	no	All mail from abroad subject to scrutiny	◑
23. To publish and educate in ethnic languages	YES		○
24. From deliberate state policies to control artistic works	yes	State policy much less rigorous than in USSR	◑

25. From compulsory military service	**NO**	18 months' military service	●
26. To purchase and drink alcohol	**YES**		○
27. To practise homosexuality between consenting adults	no	Law not seriously enforced	◐
28. To use contraceptive pills and devices	**YES**	State support	○
29. Of early abortion	**YES**		○
30. Of divorce (for men and women equally)	**YES**		○

STATE POWER

31. Corporal punishment by state	None	○
32. Radio and TV broadcasts	Total state control	●
33. Book publishing	Small number of private publishers operating with discretion	◐
34. Number of police and military per 100,000 citizens	1800	◐
35. % of national income spent on above	4%	○
36. Weapons normally carried by civil police	Sidearms	◐
37. Capital punishment by state	Anti-state crimes, murder, hijacking etc. By hanging	●

MAXIMUM PUNISHMENTS IN PENAL CODE FOR:
(Freedom-related offences)

38. Non-violent anti-government activities	'Weakening' the state. 8 years' prison for initiators, 5 for others (anti-state rumours etc.)	◐
39. Possession of banned political literature	5–15 years' prison if classed as 'agitation'	◐
40. Refusing compulsory national service	5 years' prison	◐

(Criminal offences)

41. Unlawful possession of 'hard' drugs	5 years' prison
42. Trading in pornography	1 years' prison
43. Illegal abortion	3 years if by non-medical person
44. Bigamy	3 years' prison
45. Rape without other injury	8 years' prison. 10 years for gang rape

COMPULSORY DOCUMENTS FOR CITIZENS

46. Legally required at all times	ID booklet
47. For employment	Labour and ID booklet
48. When applying for passport	ID booklet
49. Period of validity of passport	5 years
50. Countries forbidden to holder	Those not having diplomatic relations with Hungary

Human rights rating: 86%

Population: 3,250,000
Life expectancy: 72
Infant mortality (0–1 year) per 1000 births: 12.5

Form of government: democratic republic
Income per capita: US$ 5000

Observations: Apart from a few restrictions in line with Roman Catholic beliefs, the national religion, the human rights position is satisfactory.

FREEDOM/RIGHTS		Further comments	
1. Of movement in own country	YES		○
2. To leave own country	YES		○
3. From deprivation of nationality	YES		○
4. To seek information and teach ideas	YES		○
5. From serfdom, slavery, forced or child labour	yes	Some child labour on farms	◑
6. Of peaceful political opposition	YES	Except for organizations advocating violence	○
7. Of peaceful assembly and association	YES		○
8. Of women to equal rights	yes	Legal equality not reflected in equal pay and certain traditions. Legal marriage at 16	◑
9. From directed employment or work permits	YES		○
10. Of inter-racial, inter-religious and civil marriage	YES		○
11. To practise any religion	YES		○
12. From compulsory religion or state ideology in schools	yes	Wide degree of traditional compulsion but not by law	◑
13. From political press censorship	yes	Constitution gives power to control statements that endanger public order and state authority. Rarely used	◑
14. From police detention without charge	YES	2-day maximum before charge	○
15. From police searches of home without warrant	YES		○
16. From torture or coercion by state	YES		○
17. Of assumption of innocence until guilt proved	YES		○
18. Of accused to be promptly brought before judge or court	YES		○
19. Of all courts to total independence	YES		○
20. From civilian trials in secret	YES		○
21. For independent trade unions	YES		○
22. From censorship of mail	YES		○
23. To publish and educate in ethnic languages	YES		○
24. From deliberate state policies to control artistic works	YES		○
25. From compulsory military service	YES		○
26. To purchase and drink alcohol	YES		○
27. To practise homosexuality between consenting adults	NO		●

28. To use contraceptive pills and devices	no	Usually only on doctor's prescription	◑
29. Of early abortion	no	Only when mother's life at risk	◑
30. Of divorce (for men and women equally)	NO		●

STATE POWER

31. Corporal punishment by state	None	○
32. Radio and TV broadcasts	No state interference apart from anti-terrorist precautions	○
33. Book publishing	Restrictions very severe on 'pornography'	◑
34. Number of police and military per 100,000 citizens	Police 218, Military 1000 (over 50% army Reservists)	◑
35. % of national income spent on above	2%	○
36. Weapons normally carried by civil police	Not normally armed	○
37. Capital punishment by state	By hanging for murder of police or prison warders but government considering abolition	◑

MAXIMUM PUNISHMENTS IN PENAL CODE FOR:
(Freedom-related offences)

38. Non-violent anti-government activities	None	○
39. Possession of banned political literature	None	○
40. Refusing compulsory national service	None	○

(Criminal offences)

41. Unlawful possession of 'hard' drugs	£1500 fine and/or 7 years' prison
42. Trading in pornography	£100 fine and/or 6 months' prison
43. Illegal abortion	Life imprisonment
44. Bigamy	7 years' prison
45. Rape without other injury	Life imprisonment

COMPULSORY DOCUMENTS FOR CITIZENS

46. Legally required at all times	None
47. For employment	None
48. When applying for passport	Birth certificate
49. Period of validity of passport	5–10 years
50. Countries forbidden to holder	None

ITALY

Human rights rating: 88%

Population: 57,500,000
Life expectancy: 73
Infant mortality (0–1 year) per 1000 births: 15

Form of government: constitutional democracy
Income per capita: US$ 6914

Observations: Satisfactory.

	FREEDOM/RIGHTS		Further comments	
1.	Of movement in own country	YES	Mafia suspects may be restricted	○
2.	To leave own country	YES		○
3.	From deprivation of nationality	YES		○
4.	To seek information and teach ideas	YES		○
5.	From serfdom, slavery, forced or child labour	yes	Illegal child labour particularly in south	◑
6.	Of peaceful political opposition	yes	Restrictions on neo-fascists	◐
7.	Of peaceful assembly and association	yes	Police to be notified and may refuse	◑
8.	Of women to equal rights	YES	Social prejudices declining. Women given vote in 1945	○
9.	From directed employment or work permits	YES		○
10.	Of inter-racial, inter-religious and civil marriage	YES		○
11.	To practise any religion	YES		◑
12.	From compulsory religion or state ideology in schools	no	Strict compulsion in many Catholic schools	◐
13.	From political press censorship	YES		◑
14.	From police detention without charge	yes	Exception is up to 10½ years in terrorist cases	◑
15.	From police searches of home without warrant	YES	But anti-terrorism law of 1980 has introduced search warrants by telephone	○
16.	From torture or coercion by state	YES		○
17.	Of assumption of innocence until guilt proved	YES		○
18.	Of accused to be promptly brought before judge or court	YES	Within 48 hours but terrorist cases in special category	○
19.	Of all courts to total independence	YES		○
20.	From civilian trials in secret	YES		○
21.	For independent trade unions	YES		○
22.	From censorship of mail	yes	Current terrorism gives authorities wide discretion	◑
23.	To publish and educate in ethnic languages	YES	French- and German-speaking minorities in north protected	○
24.	From deliberate state policies to control artistic works	YES		○
25.	From compulsory military service	NO	12–18 months	●
26.	To purchase and drink alcohol	YES		◑
27.	To practise homosexuality between consenting adults	YES		○
28.	To use contraceptive pills and devices	YES	But Catholic influences still pervasive in certain rural areas	○
29.	Of early abortion	YES	But strong Catholic opposition can influence local attitudes	○

30. Of divorce (for men and women | **YES** | ⭘
    equally)

STATE POWER
31. Corporal punishment by state   None
32. Radio and TV broadcasts   Channels divided between three major
    political parties. No government
    control
33. Book publishing   Rare seizures on grounds of
    defamation of political or Church
    leaders or institutions
34. Number of police and military per 100,000   Police 147, military 631
    citizens
35. % of national income spent on above   3.5%
36. Weapons normally carried by civil police   Small pistols
37. Capital punishment by state   Abolished in 1944

MAXIMUM PUNISHMENTS IN PENAL CODE FOR:
(Freedom-related offences)
38. Non-violent anti-government activities   None
39. Possession of banned political literature   None
40. Refusing compulsory national service   2 years' prison after trial by Military
    Tribunal

(Criminal offences)
41. Unlawful possession of 'hard' drugs   2–6 years. Trafficking 4–18. (1975 law)
42. Trading in pornography   3 years' prison
43. Illegal abortion   2–5 years with mother's consent. 7–12
    without consent
44. Bigamy   Up to 5 years' prison
45. Rape without other injury   10 years' prison

COMPULSORY DOCUMENTS FOR CITIZENS
46. Legally required at all times   ID card
47. For employment   Tax code
48. When applying for passport   Birth certificate. Character certificate
    from municipality
49. Period of validity of passport   5 years
50. Countries forbidden to holder   None

NETHERLANDS

Human rights rating: 94%

Population: 14,179,000
Life expectancy: 74
**Infant mortality (0–1 year) per 1000
 births:** 8

Form of government: democratic
 parliamentary monarchy
Income per capita: US$ 10,175

Observations: Satisfactory.

	FREEDOM/RIGHTS		Further comments	
1.	Of movement in own country	YES		○
2.	To leave own country	YES	Unless court case pending	○
3.	From deprivation of nationality	YES		○
4.	To seek, receive and impart information and teach ideas	YES		○
5.	From serfdom, slavery, forced or child labour	YES		○
6.	Of peaceful political opposition	YES		○
7.	Of peaceful assembly and association	YES	Public meetings occasionally require police permission	○
8.	Of women to equal rights	YES		○
9.	From directed employment or work permits	YES		○
10.	Of inter-racial, inter-religious and civil marriage	YES		○
11.	To practise any religion	YES		○
12.	From compulsory religion or state ideology in schools	YES		○
13.	From political press censorship	YES		○
14.	From police detention without charge	YES	Usually no more than 6 hours without charge	○
15.	From police searches of home without warrant	YES		○
16.	From torture or coercion by state	YES		○
17.	Of assumption of innocence until guilt proved	YES		○
18.	Of accused to be promptly brought before judge or court	YES		○
19.	Of all courts to total independence	YES		○
20.	From civilian trials in secret	YES		○
21.	For independent trade unions	YES		○
22.	From censorship of mail	YES		○
23.	To publish and educate in ethnic languages	YES		○
24.	From deliberate state policies to control artistic works	YES		○
25.	From compulsory military service	NO	14–17 months' military service	●
26.	To purchase and drink alcohol	YES	From age 18. Beer from 16	○
27.	To practise homosexuality between consenting adults	YES		○
28.	To use contraceptive pills and devices	YES	Parent's consent for under-16s (law freely disregarded)	○
29.	Of early abortion	yes	Medical and juridical reasons (law freely disregarded)	◑
30.	Of divorce (for men and women equally)	YES		○

STATE POWER
31. Corporal punishment by state   None

32. Radio and TV broadcasts   No government interference.
                                                   Autonomous programmes

33. Book publishing   No state controls

34. Number of police and military per 100,000   936
    citizens

35. % of national income spent on above   4%

36. Weapons normally carried by civil police   7.65mm pistols

37. Capital punishment by state   None

MAXIMUM PUNISHMENTS IN PENAL CODE FOR:
(Freedom-related offences)

38. Non-violent anti-government activities   None. But infringing rights of others
                                                   may be an offence

39. Possession of banned political literature   None

40. Refusing compulsory national service   2 years' prison under military law

(Criminal offences)

41. Unlawful possession of 'hard' drugs   4 years. 12 years for trafficking

42. Trading in pornography   2 months' prison for unsolicited
                                                   offerings etc.

43. Illegal abortion   4 years' prison

44. Bigamy   6 years' prison

45. Rape without other injury   12 years' prison

COMPULSORY DOCUMENTS FOR CITIZENS

46. Legally required at all times   None

47. For employment   None

48. When applying for passport   Birth certificate and proof of
                                                   nationality

49. Period of validity of passport   5 years

50. Countries forbidden to holder   None

Human rights rating: 95%

Population: 4,100,000
Life expectancy: 75
Infant mortality (0–1 year) per 1000 births: 9

Form of government: parliamentary monarchy
Income per capita: US$ 11,800

Observations: Satisfactory.

	FREEDOM/RIGHTS		Further comments	
1.	Of movement in own country	YES		○
2.	To leave own country	YES		○
3.	From deprivation of nationality	YES		○
4.	To seek information and teach ideas	YES		○
5.	From serfdom, slavery, forced or child labour	YES		○
6.	Of peaceful political opposition	YES		○
7.	Of peaceful assembly and association	YES		○
8.	Of women to equal rights	YES		○
9.	From directed employment or work permits	YES		○
10.	Of inter-racial, inter-religious and civil marriage	YES		○
11.	To practise any religion	YES		○
12.	From compulsory religion or state ideology in schools	YES		○
13.	From political press censorship	YES		○
14.	From police detention without charge	YES	Charge to be brought within 24 hours	○
15.	From police searches of home without warrant	YES	Except when police are in 'hot pursuit'	○
16.	From torture or coercion by state	YES		○
17.	Of assumption of innocence until guilt proved	YES		○
18.	Of accused to be promptly brought before judge or court	YES		○
19.	Of all courts to total independence	YES		○
20.	From civilian trials in secret	YES		○
21.	For independent trade unions	YES		○
22.	From censorship of mail	YES		○
23.	To publish and educate in ethnic languages	YES		○
24.	From deliberate state policies to control artistic works	YES		○
25.	From compulsory military service	NO	14–17 months' military service	●
26.	To purchase and drink alcohol	YES	From age 18. Beer from age 16	○
27.	To practise homosexuality between consenting adults	YES	Legal at 16 years	○
28.	To use contraceptive pills and devices	YES		○
29.	Of early abortion	YES		○
30.	Of divorce (for men and women equally)	YES		○

STATE POWER

31. Corporal punishment by state	None
32. Radio and TV broadcasts	No political or state bias. No commercials
33. Book publishing	No controls
34. Number of police and military per 100,000 citizens	1000 (excluding Home Guard and Reservists)
35. % of national income spent on above	7%
36. Weapons normally carried by civil police	Batons
37. Capital punishment by state	None

MAXIMUM PUNISHMENTS IN PENAL CODE FOR:

(Freedom-related offences)

38. Non-violent anti-government activities	None
39. Possession of banned political literature	Limited restrictions on 'neo-Nazi' literature
40. Refusing compulsory national service	2 years' prison

(Criminal offences)

41. Unlawful possession of 'hard' drugs	2 years' prison
42. Trading in pornography	2 years' prison
43. Illegal abortion	6 years if by non-medical person
44. Bigamy	6 years' prison
45. Rape without other injury	10 years' prison

COMPULSORY DOCUMENTS FOR CITIZENS

46. Legally required at all times	ID card
47. For employment	None
48. When applying for passport	ID card/birth certificate
49. Period of validity of passport	10 years
50. Countries forbidden to holder	None

Human rights rating: 36%

Population: 38,000,000
Life expectancy: 71
Infant mortality (0–1 year) per 1000 births: 21

Form of government: one-party state under martial law
Income per capita: US$ 3500

Observations: Since the close of 1981 Poland has in reality been under continuous martial law. Decrees and restrictions are subject to frequent changes, most of which infringe the human rights obligations of the UN Covenant, which has been ratified by the country.

FREEDOM/RIGHTS		Further comments	
1. Of movement in own country	yes	But subject to changes in martial law	◖
2. To leave own country	NO	Exit permits refused when not 'in interests of state'	●
3. From deprivation of nationality	NO	Device of a one-way passport issued to dissidents and others	●
4. To seek, receive and impart information and teach ideas	NO	Martial law restrictions. No anti-Soviet teaching etc.	●
5. From serfdom, slavery, forced or child labour	YES		○
6. Of peaceful political opposition	NO	No opposition permitted. Recent liberalization reversed under martial law	●
7. Of peaceful assembly and association	NO	Forbidden under martial law decree	●
8. Of women to equal rights	YES		○
9. From directed employment or work permits	NO	Special courts may sentence to 3 months in labour camps those not employed in approved occupations	●
10. Of inter-racial, inter-religious and civil marriage	YES		○
11. To practise any religion	YES		○
12. From compulsory religion or state ideology in schools	NO	Compulsory Marxist-Leninism comes under lessons in 'ethics'	●
13. From political press censorship	NO	Censorship absolute under martial law	●
14. From police detention without charge	NO	Permitted under present martial law. Previously 48 hours	●
15. From police searches of home without warrant	NO	Previous infrequent breaches of law more numerous under martial law	●
16. From torture or coercion by state	yes	But local abuses and psychological pressures	◖
17. Of assumption of innocence until guilt proved	NO	Normal habeas corpus guarantees suspended	●
18. Of accused to be promptly brought before judge or court	NO	Constitutional rights and normal procedures subject to martial law changes	●
19. Of all courts to total independence	NO	Arbitrary state powers under martial law	●
20. From civilian trials in secret	NO	As 19	●
21. For independent trade unions	NO	Martial law controls despite government claim of 'understanding' with unions	●
22. From censorship of mail	NO	Constant surveillance	●
23. To publish and educate in ethnic languages	YES		○

24. From deliberate state policies to control artistic works — no — Direct and indirect pressures to conform to ideological or state policies ◑

25. From compulsory military service — NO — 2 years' conscription ●
26. To purchase and drink alcohol — YES ○
27. To practise homosexuality between consenting adults — YES — 1–10 years' prison if with minor ○

28. To use contraceptive pills and devices — YES ○

29. Of early abortion — yes — Broad social and medical reasons ◑
30. Of divorce (for men and women equally) — YES — But majority follow Roman Catholic teachings on divorce ○

STATE POWER
31. Corporal punishment by state — Not permitted but abuses at local level ◑
32. Radio and TV broadcasts — Total state control ●
33. Book publishing — Total state control ●
34. Number of police and military per 100,000 citizens — 1300 (approx.) including conscripts but not military reserves ◑
35. % of national income spent on above — 5% ◑
36. Weapons normally carried by civil police — Pistols and range of military equipment ◑
37. Capital punishment by state — By hanging. For treason, murder, anti-state activities etc. ●

MAXIMUM PUNISHMENTS IN PENAL CODE FOR:
(Freedom-related offences)
38. Non-violent anti-government activities — 25 years' prison for serious offence against 'state interests' ◑

39. Possession of banned political literature — 5 years' prison if work insults 'Polish nation or supreme organs' ◑

40. Refusing compulsory national service — 6 months' to 5 years' prison ◑

(Criminal offences)
41. Unlawful possession of 'hard' drugs — 5 years' prison
42. Trading in pornography — 2 years' prison
43. Illegal abortion — 3 years when with mother's consent
44. Bigamy — 5 years' prison
45. Rape without other injury — 10 years' prison

COMPULSORY DOCUMENTS FOR CITIZENS
46. Legally required at all times — ID card
47. For employment — ID card
48. When applying for passport — ID card, security clearance etc.
49. Period of validity of passport — Related to purpose of travel. Usually one-trip passport

50. Countries forbidden to holder — All except those for which passport issued

Human rights rating: 87%

Population: 10,067,000
Life expectancy: 71
Infant mortality (0–1 year) per 1000 births: 39

Form of government: multi-party democracy
Income per capita: US$ 2375

Observations: Satisfactory.

FREEDOM/RIGHTS		Further comments	
1. Of movement in own country	YES		○
2. To leave own country	YES		○
3. From deprivation of nationality	YES		○
4. To seek, receive and impart information and teach ideas	YES		○
5. From serfdom, slavery, forced or child labour	yes	Degree of unlawful child labour	◑
6. Of peaceful political opposition	yes	But infrequent imprisonment for insulting civil or military bodies	◑
7. Of peaceful assembly and association	YES		○
8. Of women to equal rights	yes	But traditional attitudes in pay and social areas still favour men	◑
9. From directed employment or work permits	YES		○
10. Of inter-racial, inter-religious and civil marriage	YES		○
11. To practise any religion	YES		○
12. From compulsory religion or state ideology in schools	YES		○
13. From political press censorship	yes	Rare cases of journalists prosecuted for 'insulting' president etc. Maximum 8 years' prison	◑
14. From police detention without charge	YES	48-hour limit	○
15. From police searches of home without warrant	YES		○
16. From torture or coercion by state	YES		○
17. Of assumption of innocence until guilt proved	YES		○
18. Of accused to be promptly brought before judge or court	yes	Overburdened system means lengthy delays	◑
19. Of all courts to total independence	YES		○
20. From civilian trials in secret	YES		○
21. For independent trade unions	YES		○
22. From censorship of mail	YES		○
23. To publish and educate in ethnic languages	YES		○
24. From deliberate state policies to control artistic works	YES		○
25. From compulsory military service	NO	16–24 months' military service from age 18	●
26. To purchase and drink alcohol	YES		○
27. To practise homosexuality between consenting adults	YES	Legal over 18 years	○
28. To use contraceptive pills and devices	YES	But Catholic family planning centres advise only rhythm method	○

29. Of early abortion	no	Only when mother's life at risk
30. Of divorce (for men and women equally)	**YES**	

STATE POWER

31. Corporal punishment by state — None
32. Radio and TV broadcasts — Part government-owned but no significant interference
33. Book publishing — No significant interference
34. Number of police and military per 100,000 citizens — 140 police, 700 military (including National Guard etc.)
35. % of national income spent on above — 4%
36. Weapons normally carried by civil police — .38 revolvers
37. Capital punishment by state — Abolished 1867 (first European country)

MAXIMUM PUNISHMENTS IN PENAL CODE FOR:
(Freedom-related offences)
38. Non-violent anti-government activities — Anti-Fascist Law 1978. 8 years' prison for violations. No prosecutions to date
39. Possession of banned political literature — As 38
40. Refusing compulsory national service — Considered to be desertion. 2–3 years' 'internment'

(Criminal offences)
41. Unlawful possession of 'hard' drugs — 8–12 years' prison
42. Trading in pornography — 6 months' prison and/or fine
43. Illegal abortion — 8 years' prison
44. Bigamy — 8 years' prison
45. Rape without other injury — 12 years' prison

COMPULSORY DOCUMENTS FOR CITIZENS
46. Legally required at all times — ID card
47. For employment — ID card
48. When applying for passport — ID card, certificate of good conduct, sometimes birth certificate
49. Period of validity of passport — 5 years
50. Countries forbidden to holder — None

Human rights rating: 32%

Population: 22,310,000
Life expectancy: 70
Infant mortality (0–1 year) per 1000 births: 31

Form of government: Communist Party state
Income per capita: US$ 2000

Observations: Severe curtailment of human rights despite having signed and ratified the UN Covenant.

FREEDOM/RIGHTS		Further comments	
1. Of movement in own country	yes	But permit required for change of residence	◑
2. To leave own country	NO	'A passport is a privilege not a right'	●
3. From deprivation of nationality	NO	Device of a one-way passport issued to dissidents and others	◐
4. To seek information and teach ideas	NO	Restrictions on university curricula. Courses monitored by party and state	●
5. From serfdom, slavery, forced or child labour	no	Labour camps. Unpaid work in forced domicile ('corrective labour')	◑
6. Of peaceful political opposition	NO	15 years' prison for propaganda 'to change the socialist order'	●
7. Of peaceful assembly and association	no	Only when purpose is approved by government	◑
8. Of women to equal rights	YES		○
9. From directed employment or work permits	NO		●
10. Of inter-racial, inter-religious and civil marriage	YES		○
11. To practise any religion	yes	14 recognized religions may practice. Others not in public. Official harassment	◑
12. From compulsory religion or state ideology in schools	NO	Marxist-Leninism compulsory	●
13. From political press censorship	NO	Editors all party members. Must conform. Constant monitoring	●
14. From police detention without charge	NO	Government power total and unquestioned	●
15. From police searches of home without warrant	NO	Religious and political dissidents subject to sudden searches	●
16. From torture or coercion by state	NO	Kept in darkness, beatings, psychiatric abuses etc.	●
17. Of assumption of innocence until guilt proved	NO	Vague charges of 'parasitism'. Also used when religious proselytizing suspected	●
18. Of accused to be promptly brought before judge or court	no	Religious and political dissidents held for lengthy interrogation	◑
19. Of all courts to total independence	NO	Judges members of party. Trials usually of brief duration	●
20. From civilian trials in secret	NO	Government exercises arbitrary powers	●
21. For independent trade unions	NO	Previous attempt (in 1979) resulted in imprisonment or exile of leaders	●
22. From censorship of mail	no	Dissidents and suspects and mail from abroad under scrutiny	◑

#			
23.	To publish and educate in ethnic languages	no	Intensification of Romanization process against 2 m. Hungarians and others
24.	From deliberate state policies to control artistic works	NO	'Art should serve the people'
25.	From compulsory military service	NO	16–24 months' conscription
26.	To purchase and drink alcohol	YES	
27.	To practise homosexuality between consenting adults	NO	Prosecutions common. 5 years' prison. Used as false offence when state wishes to imprison
28.	To use contraceptive pills and devices	YES	Strong religious opposition still evident
29.	Of early abortion	YES	By authorized medical practitioners only
30.	Of divorce (for men and women equally)	YES	

STATE POWER

#		
31.	Corporal punishment by state	Legally none but condoned state torture cannot be ignored
32.	Radio and TV broadcasts	State-operated and owned
33.	Book publishing	State-operated and owned
34.	Number of police and military per 100,000 citizens	1800 (not including Patriotic Guard)
35.	% of national income spent on above	4%
36.	Weapons normally carried by civil police	Pistols
37.	Capital punishment by state	By firing squad. Murder, theft of public property, treason etc.

MAXIMUM PUNISHMENTS IN PENAL CODE FOR:
(Freedom-related offences)

#		
38.	Non-violent anti-government activities	Discretionary death sentence for 'hostility to socialism' but usually lengthy prison sentence
39.	Possession of banned political literature	Long period of detention or re-education in labour camp
40.	Refusing compulsory national service	4 years' prison for religious objectors

(Criminal offences)

#		
41.	Unlawful possession of 'hard' drugs	5 years' prison
42.	Trading in pornography	2 years' prison
43.	Illegal abortion	3 years' prison. Possession of abortion instruments – 1 year
44.	Bigamy	5 years' prison
45.	Rape without other injury	7 years' prison

COMPULSORY DOCUMENTS FOR CITIZENS

#		
46.	Legally required at all times	ID document
47.	For employment	ID document
48.	When applying for passport	ID document, police clearance etc.
49.	Period of validity of passport	Different categories from 5-year to one-trip passports
50.	Countries forbidden to holder	Exit visa stipulates countries to be visited

Human rights rating: 78%

Population: 37,500,000
Life expectancy: 73
Infant mortality (0–1 year) per 1000 births: 13

Form of government: democratic monarchy
Income per capita: US$ 5578

Observations: The human rights situation, although moderately satisfactory, is affected by government action to combat regional terrorism.

FREEDOM/RIGHTS		Further comments
1. Of movement in own country	YES	
2. To leave own country	YES	
3. From deprivation of nationality	YES	
4. To seek, receive and impart information and teach ideas	YES	No pro-terrorist sympathies to be expressed
5. From serfdom, slavery, forced or child labour	yes	Casual child labour in rural areas
6. Of peaceful political opposition	YES	
7. Of peaceful assembly and association	YES	
8. Of women to equal rights	yes	Legal rights not enforced in economic and social areas
9. From directed employment or work permits	YES	
10. Of inter-racial, inter-religious and civil marriage	YES	
11. To practise any religion	YES	
12. From compulsory religion or state ideology in schools	yes	Strict Catholic disciplines in many schools
13. From political press censorship	yes	Cases of prison for insulting the King, the military etc. or not condemning armed subversion
14. From police detention without charge	yes	Anti-terrorist law permits 10-day interrogation period. Otherwise 4 days
15. From police searches of home without warrant	yes	Except for terrorist suspects, usually in Basque region
16. From torture or coercion by state	no	Suspected terrorists subject to unlawful beatings etc. during interrogation
17. Of assumption of innocence until guilt proved	yes	Except for terrorist suspects
18. Of accused to be promptly brought before judge or court	YES	Civilians no longer tried by military (1981 law)
19. Of all courts to total independence	YES	
20. From civilian trials in secret	YES	
21. For independent trade unions	YES	
22. From censorship of mail	yes	Anti-terrorist surveillance
23. To publish and educate in ethnic languages	YES	
24. From deliberate state policies to control artistic works	YES	
25. From compulsory military service	NO	15 months' military service at age 20
26. To purchase and drink alcohol	YES	From age 16

27. To practise homosexuality between consenting adults	**YES**		○
28. To use contraceptive pills and devices	yes	Strict controls on manufacture and sale. Church opposition	◐
29. Of early abortion	no	Only when mother's life at risk but new government promises liberalization	◑
30. Of divorce (men and women equally)	**YES**		○

STATE POWER

31. Corporal punishment by state	None	○
32. Radio and TV broadcasts	State-controlled and private stations. Degree of state 'guidance'	◑
33. Book publishing	Offence to be disrespectful towards monarchy, Church, military, judiciary	◐
34. Number of police and military per 100,000 citizens	Police 250, military 900	◑
35. % of national income spent on above	3.5%	○
36. Weapons normally carried by civil police	9mm or .38 revolvers	◐
37. Capital punishment by state	Abolished 1978 except for offences by military personnel	○

MAXIMUM PUNISHMENTS IN PENAL CODE FOR:
(Freedom-related offences)

38. Non-violent anti-government activities	12 years' prison	◑
39. Possession of banned political literature	30 years for promoting seditious literature favouring terrorists	◑
40. Refusing compulsory national service	Under 25 years old 1 year's prison. Over age 25 3-year sentence	◑

(Criminal offences)

41. Unlawful possession of 'hard' drugs	12 years' prison
42. Trading in pornography	Fine of US$ 2000 (approx.)
43. Illegal abortion	6 years with mother's consent, 12 years without
44. Bigamy	6 years' prison
45. Rape without other injury	20 years' prison

COMPULSORY DOCUMENTS FOR CITIZENS

46. Legally required at all times	ID card
47. For employment	National Insurance
48. When applying for passport	Birth certificate
49. Period of validity of passport	5 years
50. Countries forbidden to holder	None

Human rights rating: 94%

Population: 8,273,000
Life expectancy: 75
Infant mortality (0–1 year) per 1000 births: 7

Form of government: parliamentary monarchy
Income per capita: US$ 11,920

Observations: Satisfactory.

FREEDOM/RIGHTS		Further comments
1. Of movement in own country	YES	
2. To leave own country	YES	
3. From deprivation of nationality	YES	
4. To seek information and teach ideas	YES	
5. From serfdom, slavery, forced or child labour	YES	
6. Of peaceful political opposition	YES	
7. Of peaceful assembly and association	YES	
8. Of women to equal rights	YES	
9. From directed employment or work permits	YES	
10. Of inter-racial, inter-religious and civil marriage	YES	
11. To practise any religion	YES	
12. From compulsory religion or state ideology in schools	YES	
13. From political press censorship	YES	
14. From police detention without charge	YES	Suspects may be held for maximum of 12 hours
15. From police searches of home without warrant	yes	Entry permitted when 'delay entails risks'
16. From torture or coercion by state	YES	
17. Of assumption of innocence until guilt proved	YES	
18. Of accused to be promptly brought before judge or court	YES	In most serious cases court may extend investigative period. Legal violations unlikely
19. Of all courts to total independence	YES	
20. From civilian trials in secret	YES	
21. For independent trade unions	YES	
22. From censorship of mail	YES	
23. To publish and educate in ethnic languages	YES	Discrimination against or contempt of ethnic groups can mean 2 years' prison
24. From deliberate state policies to control artistic works	YES	
25. From compulsory military service	NO	Military service up to 15 months
26. To purchase and drink alcohol	YES	
27. To practise homosexuality between consenting adults	YES	Legal age over 15
28. To use contraceptive pills and devices	YES	
29. Of early abortion	YES	
30. Of divorce (for men and women equally)	YES	

STATE POWER
31. Corporal punishment by state	None
32. Radio and TV broadcasts	No political or state bias. No commercials
33. Book publishing	No state controls
34. Number of police and military per 100,000 citizens	170 police, 800 military (including conscripts)
35. % of national income spent on above	4.5%
36. Weapons normally carried by civil police	Pistols and batons
37. Capital punishment by state	None

MAXIMUM PUNISHMENTS IN PENAL CODE FOR:
(Freedom-related offences)
38. Non-violent anti-government activities	None. Incitement of servicemen to disobedience by serviceman 1 year's prison
39. Possession of banned political literature	None
40. Refusing compulsory national service	2 years' prison

(Criminal offences)
41. Unlawful possession of 'hard' drugs	10 years' prison
42. Trading in pornography	6 months' prison
43. Illegal abortion	On request but 6 months for non-medical practitioners
44. Bigamy	2 years' prison
45. Rape without other injury	10 years' prison

COMPULSORY DOCUMENTS FOR CITIZENS
46. Legally required at all times	Non-compulsory ID card for practical convenience
47. For employment	Tax details to be produced
48. When applying for passport	Civil registration number and parish register details
49. Period of validity of passport	10 years
50. Countries forbidden to holder	None

Human rights rating: 92%

Population: 6,279,000
Life expectancy: 74
Infant mortality (0–1 year) per 1000 births: 9

Form of government: democratic federation
Income per capita: US$ 16,500

Observations: Satisfactory.

FREEDOM/RIGHTS		Further comments
1. Of movement in own country	YES	
2. To leave own country	YES	
3. From deprivation of nationality	yes	Except on espionage conviction
4. To seek information and teach ideas	YES	
5. From serfdom, slavery, forced or child labour	YES	
6. Of peaceful political opposition	YES	
7. Of peaceful assembly and association	YES	
8. Of women to equal rights	yes	Federal franchise granted in 1971. 3 small cantons still deny women votes in local elections
9. From directed employment or work permits	YES	
10. Of inter-racial, inter-religious and civil marriage	YES	
11. To practise any religion	YES	
12. From compulsory religion or state ideology in schools	YES	
13. From political press censorship	YES	
14. From police detention without charge	YES	
15. From police searches of home without warrant	YES	Except when in 'hot pursuit'
16. From torture or coercion by state	YES	
17. Of assumption of innocence until guilt proved	YES	
18. Of accused to be promptly brought before judge or court	YES	Within 24 hours but cantonal procedures to be respected
19. Of all courts to total independence	YES	
20. From civilian trials in secret	YES	
21. For independent trade unions	YES	
22. From censorship of mail	YES	
23. To publish and educate in ethnic languages	YES	
24. From deliberate state policies to control artistic works	YES	
25. From compulsory military service	no	17-week recruit training course
26. To purchase and drink alcohol	YES	
27. To practise homosexuality between consenting adults	YES	
28. To use contraceptive pills and devices	yes	Certain controls on pill prescriptions
29. Of early abortion	yes	Broad medical/social grounds
30. Of divorce (for men and women equally)	yes	Women subject to isolated disadvantages

STATE POWER

31. Corporal punishment by state	None	O
32. Radio and TV broadcasts	No political controls or bias. Private stations licensed by Federal Council	O
33. Book publishing	Free from state interference	O
34. Number of police and military per 100,000 citizens	450 in peacetime	O
35. % of national income spent on above	3%	O
36. Weapons normally carried by civil police	7.65mm Walther pistols	◑
37. Capital punishment by state	None	O

MAXIMUM PUNISHMENTS IN PENAL CODE FOR:
(Freedom-related offences)

38. Non-violent anti-government activities	None	O
39. Possession of banned political literature	None	O
40. Refusing compulsory national service	3 years' prison. Conscientious objectors 6 months	◑

(Criminal offences)

41. Unlawful possession of 'hard' drugs	1 year. Traffickers up to 20 years
42. Trading in pornography	3 years' prison
43. Illegal abortion	By mother 3 years. By other party 5 years
44. Bigamy	5 years' prison
45. Rape without other injury	20 years' prison

COMPULSORY DOCUMENTS FOR CITIZENS

46. Legally required at all times	None
47. For employment	None but certificate showing clean criminal record may be requested
48. When applying for passport	Proof of citizenship
49. Period of validity of passport	5 years. Renewable for 15 years
50. Countries forbidden to holder	None

TURKEY

Human rights rating: 43%

Population: 44,700,000
Life expectancy: 62
Infant mortality (0–1 year) per 1000 births: 118

Form of government: military council/ executive president
Income per capita: US$ 1450

Observations: The country is under temporary martial law, which may be extended. The human rights position has worsened and must be regarded as most unsatisfactory. 30,000 political prisoners (approx.)

FREEDOM/RIGHTS		Further comments	
1. Of movement in own country	yes	Except to sensitive 'security' areas	◐
2. To leave own country	no	Passports denied to those whose exit would be detrimental to security	◑
3. From deprivation of nationality	NO	Citizens abroad lose nationality on refusing to return when ordered by government	●
4. To seek information and teach ideas	NO	Government seeking to 'depoliticize' universities. Teachers dismissed	●
5. From serfdom, slavery, forced or child labour	yes	Child labour common in rural areas	◐
6. Of peaceful political opposition	NO	Suspended 1980. Military council promises elections in 1983 for civilian government	●
7. Of peaceful assembly and association	NO	Not if politically motivated	●
8. Of women to equal rights	no	Constitutional rights not reflected in society. 40% illiterate. No women in present cabinet	◑
9. From directed employment or work permits	YES		○
10. Of inter-racial, inter-religious and civil marriage	YES		○
11. To practise any religion	YES		○
12. From compulsory religion or state ideology in schools	YES		○
13. From political press censorship	NO	Martial law commanders control all contents. Journalists imprisoned, no editorials on political subjects	●
14. From police detention without charge	no	45 days maximum but under martial law may be extended	◑
15. From police searches of home without warrant	NO	Searches permitted under martial law 'emergency'	●
16. From torture or coercion by state	NO	Numerous torture cases and deaths while in police custody	●
17. Of assumption of innocence until guilt proved	no	45 days' detention on arbitrary precautionary arrests	◑
18. Of accused to be promptly brought before judge or court	no	Within 45 days but overworked courts create long delays	◑
19. Of all courts to total independence	no	Accused terrorists tried by martial law courts. Judges Board selected by Head of State	◑
20. From civilian trials in secret	no	Martial Law Act may transfer cases to military courts sitting in camera	◑
21. For independent trade unions	NO	Under Martial Law Act some union leaders imprisoned after 1980 military takeover. Strikes may be prohibited	●

22. From censorship of mail	NO		●
23. To publish and educate in ethnic languages	YES		○
24. From deliberate state policies to control artistic works	YES		○
25. From compulsory military service	NO	20 months' military conscription	●
26. To purchase and drink alcohol	YES		○
27. To practise homosexuality between consenting adults	yes	Socially tolerated	◐
28. To use contraceptive pills and devices	YES		○
29. Of early abortion	no	Risk to mother's life only	◑
30. Of divorce (for men and women equally)	YES	Secular society despite Islam being majority religion	○

STATE POWER

31. Corporal punishment by state	None legally but extent of torture indicates government approval	◐
32. Radio and TV broadcasts	Government-controlled	●
33. Book publishing	Martial law control. Book banning	●
34. Number of police and military per 100,000 citizens	1700	◐
35. % of national income spent on above	6%	◑
36. Weapons normally carried by civil police	Pistols	◑
37. Capital punishment by state	By hanging. For murder, treason, anti-state activities etc.	●

MAXIMUM PUNISHMENTS IN PENAL CODE FOR:
(Freedom-related offences)

38. Non-violent anti-government activities	Death penalty	●
39. Possession of banned political literature	6 years' prison but much more if anti-state intentions proved	◑
40. Refusing compulsory national service	5 years' prison	◑

(Criminal offences)

41. Unlawful possession of 'hard' drugs	10 years' minimum
42. Trading in pornography	1 month's prison
43. Illegal abortion	4 years' prison when self-induced, 2–6 years for accomplices
44. Bigamy	5 years' prison (3 years for women committing adultery)
45. Rape without other injury	7 years' prison

COMPULSORY DOCUMENTS FOR CITIZENS

46. Legally required at all times	ID card
47. For employment	ID card
48. When applying for passport	ID card, military service exemption and clearance by public prosecutor
49. Period of validity of passport	1 year tourist, 3 years migrant workers
50. Countries forbidden to holder	None

Human rights rating: 95%

Population: 55,850,000
Life expectancy: 73
Infant mortality (0–1 year) per 1000
    births: 13

Form of government: parliamentary
monarchy
Income per capita: US$ 7500

Observations: Satisfactory despite the major problem of Northern Ireland. Proposed new Criminal Procedure bill will increase police powers.

FREEDOM/RIGHTS		Further comments	
1. Of movement in own country	YES	Home Secretary under Prevention of Terrorism Act may confine suspects (which can affect families) to either N. Ireland or Great Britain	○
2. To leave own country	YES		○
3. From deprivation of nationality	YES		○
4. To seek information and teach ideas	YES		○
5. From serfdom, slavery, forced or child labour	YES	Minor instances of child labour, especially among immigrant groups	○
6. Of peaceful political opposition	YES		○
7. Of peaceful assembly and association	yes	Exceptions when authorities fear inter-factional violence	◑
8. Of women to equal rights	YES	Minor violations in areas of pay and pensions etc.	○
9. From directed employment or work permits	YES		○
10. Of inter-racial, inter-religious and civil marriage	YES		○
11. To practise any religion	YES		○
12. From compulsory religion or state ideology in schools	YES		○
13. From political press censorship	YES		○
14. From police detention without charge	YES		○
15. From police searches of home without warrant	YES	Proposed new Criminal Procedure bill may extend police search powers	○
16. From torture or coercion by state	yes	Local security forces abuses against suspected N. Ireland terrorists and police harassment of non-whites	◑
17. Of assumption of innocence until guilt proved	yes	Exceptions in Northern Ireland. Police abuse of emergency powers has led to unlawful detention	◑
18. Of accused to be promptly brought before judge or court	YES	Under Prevention of Terrorism Act, may be held for 48 hours. Special ministerial powers to extend to 7 days (rare)	○
19. Of all courts to total independence	YES	Following Diplock Report (1972), single judge trials for terrorist suspects but right maintained to appeal to Court of Criminal Appeal	○
20. From civilian trials in secret	YES		○
21. For independent trade unions	YES		○
22. From censorship of mail	YES		○
23. To publish and educate in ethnic languages	YES		○

24. From deliberate state policies to control artistic works	**YES**		◯
25. From compulsory military service	**YES**		◯
26. To purchase and drink alcohol	**YES**		◯
27. To practise homosexuality between consenting adults	**YES**	From age 21	◯
28. To use contraceptive pills and devices	**YES**		◯
29. Of early abortion	yes	Broad medical and social reasons	◑
30. Of divorce (for men and women equally)	**YES**		◯

STATE POWER
31. Corporal punishment by state	None	◯
32. Radio and TV broadcasts	No direct political interference except in 'state of emergency'	◯
33. Book publishing	Total independence for publishers	◯
34. Number of police and military per 100,000 citizens	220 police and 500 military	◑
35. % of national income spent on above	7%	◑
36. Weapons normally carried by civil police	Truncheons (exceptions in N. Ireland)	◯
37. Capital punishment by state	None. Treason still capital offence. Last hanging 1964	◯

MAXIMUM PUNISHMENTS IN PENAL CODE FOR:
(Freedom-related offences)
38. Non-violent anti-government activities	None	◯
39. Possession of banned political literature	None	◯
40. Refusing compulsory national service	None	◯

(Criminal offences)
41. Unlawful possession of 'hard' drugs	7 years' prison
42. Trading in pornography	3 years' prison
43. Illegal abortion	5 years' prison
44. Bigamy	7 years' prison
45. Rape without other injury	Life imprisonment

COMPULSORY DOCUMENTS FOR CITIZENS
46. Legally required at all times	None
47. For employment	Insurance card
48. When applying for passport	Birth certificate or similar and identity to be certified
49. Period of validity of passport	10 years
50. Countries forbidden to holder	None

Human rights rating: 27%

Population: 263,206,000
Life expectancy: 70.4
Infant mortality (0–1 year) per 1000 births: 20

Form of government: one-party communist state
Income per capita: US$ 4110

Observations: Severe curtailment of human rights despite having ratified the UN Covenant.

FREEDOM/RIGHTS		Further comments	
1. Of movement in own country	NO	Advance notice for internal permit needed	●
2. To leave own country	NO	Illegal attempts can invoke death penalty if treason alleged	●
3. From deprivation of nationality	NO	Frequently practised	●
4. To seek, receive and impart information and teach ideas	NO	Rigid state controls	●
5. From serfdom, slavery, forced or child labour	no	Estimated 3,000,000 in forced labour camps	◐
6. Of peaceful political opposition	NO	None permitted	●
7. Of peaceful assembly and association	NO	Permitted only to further party version of 'the interests of the people'	●
8. Of women to equal rights	YES	Though fewer women in senior political and social roles	○
9. From directed employment or work permits	NO	Rigid state controls. Graduates assigned to jobs for 2-year minimum	●
10. Of inter-racial, inter-religious and civil marriage	YES		○
11. To practise any religion	yes	But subject to harassment, denial of social advantages, discrimination	◐
12. From compulsory religion or state ideology in schools	NO	Marxist-Leninism a compulsory subject	●
13. From political press censorship	NO	All editors are party members	●
14. From police detention without charge	NO	Pre-trial detention up to 9 months without consulting lawyer	●
15. From police searches of home without warrant	NO	Constitutional guarantees ignored by state	●
16. From torture or coercion by state	no	Usually psychological (threats against family etc.)	◐
17. Of assumption of innocence until guilt proved	no	Legal rights ignored when accused in conflict with party	◐
18. Of accused to be promptly brought before judge or court	NO	At discretion of state	●
19. Of all courts to total independence	NO	All lawyers state employees. 60% party members	●
20. From civilian trials in secret	NO	Also device of excluding public by filling courts with state servants	●
21. For independent trade unions	NO	Unions are government agents and denied right to strike	●
22. From censorship of mail	NO	Particularly of known dissidents and contacts with outside world	●
23. To publish and educate in ethnic languages	yes	But certain harassment and limitations on Hebrew, Ukrainian etc.	◐
24. From deliberate state policies to control artistic works	NO	Works in modern styles may meet state condemnation and be denied markets and public attention	●

25. From compulsory military service	NO	Military service up to 3 years	●
26. To purchase and drink alcohol	YES		○
27. To practise homosexuality between consenting adults	NO	Condemned as bourgeois perversion	●
28. To use contraceptive pills and devices	YES		○
29. Of early abortion	YES		○
30. Of divorce (for men and women equally)	YES	1 in 3 recent marriages end in divorce	○

STATE POWER

31. Corporal punishment by state	State-condoned abuses of constitution and psychological terrors	◑
32. Radio and TV broadcasts	Total control by state and party	●
33. Book publishing	Pre-release censorship and total state control	●
34. Number of police and military per 100,000 citizens	Estimated 2000	◐
35. % of national income spent on above	Estimated 14–15%	●
36. Weapons normally carried by civil police	Pistols and range of military weapons	●
37. Capital punishment by state	By shooting for 18 different offences such as murder, group rape, economic offences etc.	●

MAXIMUM PUNISHMENTS IN PENAL CODE FOR:
(Freedom-related offences)

38. Non-violent anti-government activities	7 years' prison for 'slandering' state	●
39. Possession of banned political literature	7 years' deprivation of liberty and up to 5 years internal exile	◐
40. Refusing compulsory national service	7 years' prison	●

(Criminal offences)

41. Unlawful possession of 'hard' drugs	2 years. 10 years for trafficking
42. Trading in pornography	3 years' prison
43. Illegal abortion	2 years when outside medical supervision
44. Bigamy	Small fine for false statement
45. Rape without other injury	7 years. Group rape – death penalty

COMPULSORY DOCUMENTS FOR CITIZENS

46. Legally required at all times	ID documents. Also for internal travel and registration at new destination
47. For employment	ID documents. Further restrictions on members of collective farms
48. When applying for passport	ID documents, police clearance etc.
49. Period of validity of passport	One trip only. External passports difficult to obtain except when on state business.
50. Countries forbidden to holder	Travel restricted to permitted journey

Human rights rating: 55%

Population: 22,500,000
Life expectancy: 70
Infant mortality (0–1 year) per 1000 births: 33

Form of government: one-party socialist state
Income per capita: US$ 3500

Observations: The penal code of Serbia, the most populated of the republics, has been used. Others vary slightly. Yugoslavia has ratified the UN Covenant but this is violated in many ways.

FREEDOM/RIGHTS		Further comments	
1. Of movement in own country	YES		○
2. To leave own country	yes	Small number of dissidents refused passports on political grounds	◑
3. From deprivation of nationality	YES		○
4. To seek, receive and impart information and teach ideas	NO	The need to preserve country as a close unity of nationalities affects open inquiry and teaching	●
5. From serfdom, slavery, forced or child labour	YES		○
6. Of peaceful political opposition	no	Heavy sentences for 'hostile propaganda' against state	◑
7. Of peaceful assembly and association	no	Nationalist groups in the different republics considered a threat. Particularly Albanians in Kosovo region	◑
8. Of women to equal rights	YES		○
9. From directed employment or work permits	no	Labour card required	◑
10. Of inter-racial, inter-religious and civil marriage	YES		○
11. To practise any religion	YES	Subject to staying out of politics	○
12. From compulsory religion or state ideology in schools	NO	Marxist-Leninism a compulsory subject	●
13. From political press censorship	no	Position improving. More press comment on contentious issues.	◑
14. From police detention without charge	no	3 days by law but violations frequent	◑
15. From police searches of home without warrant	no	Usually limited to political suspects and opponents	◑
16. From torture or coercion by state	yes	Local abuses include psychological intimidation	◑
17. Of assumption of innocence until guilt proved	yes	Defence lawyers may be appointed if accused refuses legal aid	◑
18. Of accused to be promptly brought before judge or court	yes	Within 24 hours but national security cases treated differently	◑
19. Of all courts to total independence	NO	Political trials occasionally conducted by state security police	●
20. From civilian trials in secret	NO	Also use of device to exclude public by requiring 'official' court passes	●
21. For independent trade unions	no	Syndicates must follow national and provincial policies	◑
22. From censorship of mail	no	Despite constitution mail subject to surveillance	◑
23. To publish and educate in ethnic languages	YES	Country a federation of equal but distinctive nationalities	○

24. From deliberate state policies to control artistic works	YES		○
25. From compulsory military service	NO	15 months at age 18	●
26. To purchase and drink alcohol	YES		○
27. To practise homosexuality between consenting adults	yes	Wide toleration in practice. Slight variations between the separate republics	◐
28. To use contraceptive pills and devices	YES	State support	○
29. Of early abortion	YES		○
30. Of divorce (for men and women equally)	YES		○

STATE POWER

31. Corporal punishment by state	None	○
32. Radio and TV broadcasts	State-operated and controlled	●
33. Book publishing	Freedom within understood political guidelines	◐
34. Number of police and military per 100,000 citizens	4400 (including reserves but not Civil Defence and Partisans)	●
35. % of national income spent on above	7%	◐
36. Weapons normally carried by police	Sidearms	◐
37. Capital punishment by state	Death sentences mostly devolved to courts of the six republics and two regions. For serious anti-state activities, murder etc. By firing squad	●

MAXIMUM PUNISHMENTS IN PENAL CODE FOR:
(Freedom-related offences)

38. Non-violent anti-government activities	'Hostile propaganda' 10 years' prison	◐
39. Possession of banned political literature	Confiscation but as 38 for grave cases – 10 years' prison	◐
40. Refusing compulsory national service	5 years' prison. 10 years if conscript travels abroad to escape service	◐

(Criminal offences)

41. Unlawful possession of 'hard' drugs	10 years' prison
42. Trading in pornography	1 year's prison
43. Illegal abortion	3 years with mother's consent
44. Bigamy	3 months to 3 years' prison
45. Rape without other injury	1–10 years' prison. 15 for gang rape

COMPULSORY DOCUMENTS FOR CITIZENS

46. Legally required at all times	ID card
47. For employment	Labour card
48. When applying for passport	ID card, birth certificate
49. Period of validity of passport	5–10 years
50. Countries forbidden to holder	None

ALBANIA

7

Human rights rating: BAD

Population: 2,670,000
Life expectancy: 69
Infant mortality (0–1 year) per 1000 births: 87

Form of government: one-party communist state
Income per capita: US$ 950

Observations: This country is presented in summary form because of the unreliability of information and the failure of official sources to reply to inquiries. Albania has not ratified the UN Covenant on civil and political rights and the constitution of the country implies that they 'weaken the socialist state'.

Summary

The government Albanian Workers' Party maintains a strict rule over the population and there is little evidence of adherence to international human rights standards. 'Anti-state activities' and opposition to the national policy of suppressing religion and its teachings can receive long prison sentences and, in the worst cases, summary execution. Movement within the country is controlled and those fleeing it and choosing to remain in exile face the death penalty if they return.

Torture is reportedly a common police practice but since the country, although European, has maintained a policy of strict isolationism, corroborative evidence is limited. Political opponents make up the majority of prison inmates and are subject to harsh treatment.

All press and broadcasting media are in the hands of the government and no opposing views are permitted. The only perceptible progress in human rights relates to women; the improvement in their status now means that they enjoy equality in the fields of compulsory labour and military service.

Thirty-four crimes are punishable by the death penalty, most being political or military offences.